Real-Worl

The Survival Guide for Responding to a System Outage and Maximizing Uptime

Nat Welch

Packt>

BIRMINGHAM - MUMBAI

Real-World SRE

Acquisition Editors: Ben Renow-Clarke, Suresh Jain

Project Editor: Veronica Pais

Technical Editor: Nidhisha Shetty

Proofreader: Safis Editing

Indexer: Rekha Nair

Graphics: Sandip Tadge

Production Coordinator: Sandip Tadge

First published: December 2018

Production reference: 3271218

Published by Packt Publishing Ltd.
Livery Place
35 Livery Street
Birmingham B3 2PB, UK.
ISBN 978-1-78862-888-4
www.packtpub.com

Mapt

Why subscribe?

PacktPub.com

Contributors

About the author

Nat Welch is a software developer based in the US. Since 2005 he has been building websites and keeping them running. He has always had a deep love of infrastructure and building to support the creative efforts of others. In 2012, Nat became a Site Reliability Engineer at Google and fell in love with the specialty. Since then, he has worked at companies of all sizes trying to promote reliability and help developers build reliable systems.

I would like to thank a lot of people for helping me make this book. First off is everyone at Packt Publishing, especially Radhika Atitkar and Veronica Pais. Without them, there is no way I would have ever thought I could write a book, let alone finish one. Also shout-out to all of the wonderful editors, including Pavlos Ratis who helped me shape this book into something great.

Second is everyone at Hillary for America. I value your work more highly than you know. I would especially like to mention Stephanie Hannon and Rohen Peterson for giving me the opportunity to work with HFA. While there, I learned a ton working with a team of operators that have also become amazing friends: Michael Fisher, timball, Amy Hails, Will McCutcheon, and Dylan Ayrey. Also shoutout to Ben Hagen, Ernest W. Durbin III, and Rob Witoff.

Two communities kept me motivated throughout the writing of this book, the Recurse Center and Simple Casual. Everyone in both communities are incredibly supportive, and without your support I would have given up long ago.

Thanks to the love of my life and light of my days, Melissa Cantrell, who put up with my constant hiding in the corner with headphones on to write. The exchange of a croissant delivery for love and affection and never-ending support is not a fair trade, so thank you.

I would not be here without all of the SREs at Google, especially Bill Thiede, Ben Lazarus, stratus, Sumeet Pannu, mglb, wac, and Chris Jones. Thank you for everything you taught me from code reviews, to wheels of misfortunes, basic CIDR math, IRC etiquette, and international handoffs. To the Punchd team: stay reckless. I never would have joined SRE without your constant hustle.

Thank you to Stephanie Harris for her illustrations and help with graphics in this book.

Finally, much love to my family. You went through so much while I was trying to write this book. Your courage, while losing so much, reminds me that no matter the obstacle, I need to keep pushing forward. Mom, Dad, and Travis, we will rebuild. I love you so much.

About the reviewer

Pavlos Ratis is a Site Reliability Engineer at HolidayCheck, where he works on automation software and infrastructure reliability. Over time, he worked on a wide range of projects, from writing software to automate, and managing multi-server cloud-based infrastructure to developing web applications.

Packt is Searching for Authors Like You

If you're interested in becoming an author for Packt, please visit authors. packtpub.com and apply today. We have worked with thousands of developers and tech professionals, just like you, to help them share their insight with the global tech community. You can make a general application, apply for a specific hot topic that we are recruiting an author for, or submit your own idea.

Table of Contents

Preface

At some point, every software developer experiences a catastrophic website failure—customers tweet that they can't access your website for hours; while you are sleeping, no customers can buy the t-shirts you sell, or on your biggest sales day of the year, all of the servers collapse under the load.

Who this book is for

Real-World SRE is aimed at software developers and software operators who want to improve the reliability of their company's software. The book will introduce you to a basic framework for working toward greater reliability and give you an insight into the **Site Reliability Engineering** (**SRE**) profession. For those engineers and developers who have already experienced a major outage, this is the book you wish you'd had. For those developers and engineers lucky enough not to have experienced an outage, buy this book now!

What this book covers

Chapter 1, *Introduction*, explores the relatively new SRE field and outlines the practical framework of the book.

Chapter 2, *Monitoring*, talks about the tools and methodologies used when monitoring. After this chapter, a good experiment for you would be to set up monitoring on services, even if they are just fake services written for testing, and see if you can see how they change over time.

Chapter 3, *Incident Response*, explains how to respond to outages, and preparing your team for the worst. We also focus on setting up on-call rotations best practices around working together as a team and on building processes to make incidents as low stress as possible.

Chapter 4, *Postmortems*, takes you through the act of writing a postmortem and promoting reviews for yourself, your team, and your organization. We talk about data to collect, along with communication and how to track future work.

Chapter 5, *Testing and Releasing*, reviews common practices around testing and releasing.

Chapter 6, *Capacity Planning*, goes over some of the basics of finance and talks about how to build a plan for your infrastructure growth over time.

Chapter 7, *Building Tools*, discusses how to write software in a role focused on responsiveness. We also explore how to find new projects to work on, how to define those projects, and how to plan them. We then talk about execution and the long-term maintenance of software and how to be reflective on the work you have done.

Chapter 8, *User Experience*, gives an overview of the basics of user experience and user testing. We also talk about security and performance budgets.

Chapter 9, *Networking Foundations*, helps you to dive into the basics of networking.

Chapter 10, *Linux and Cloud Foundations*, covers the basics of Linux and common cloud services.

To get the most out of this book

- All Go code in this book is assuming Go version 1.10. You can get the latest version from https://golang.org/dl/.
- All Ruby code in this book assumes Ruby 2.5, which can be acquired from https://www.ruby-lang.org/en/downloads/releases/.

Download the example code files

You can download the example code files for this book from your account at http://www.packtpub.com. If you purchased this book elsewhere, you can visit http://www.packtpub.com/support and register to have the files emailed directly to you.

You can download the code files by following these steps:

1. Log in or register at http://www.packtpub.com.

2. Select the **SUPPORT** tab.

3. Click on **Code Downloads & Errata**.

4. Enter the name of the book in the **Search** box and follow the on-screen instructions.

Once the file is downloaded, please make sure that you unzip or extract the folder using the latest version of:

- WinRAR / 7-Zip for Windows
- Zipeg / iZip / UnRarX for Mac
- 7-Zip / PeaZip for Linux

The code bundle for the book is also hosted on GitHub at `https://github.com/PacktPublishing/Real-World-SRE`. We also have other code bundles from our rich catalog of books and videos available at `https://github.com/PacktPublishing/`. Check them out!

Download the color images

We also provide a PDF file that has color images of the screenshots/diagrams used in this book. You can download it here: `https://www.packtpub.com/sites/default/files/downloads/RealWorldSRE_ColorImages.pdf`.

Conventions used

There are a number of text conventions used throughout this book.

`CodeInText`: indicates code words in text, database table names, folder names, filenames, file extensions, pathnames, dummy URLs, user input, and Twitter handles. For example: "This creates an instance of the `StatsD` class to talk to a StatsD server that is running on port `9125` on the local machine."

A block of code is set as follows:

```
    "hello world"
  end
end
```

When we wish to draw your attention to a particular part of a code block, the relevant lines or items are set in bold:

```
    "hello world"
  end
end
```

Any command-line input or output is written as follows:

```
$ curl google.com
```

Bold: indicates a new term, an important word, or words that you see on the screen, for example, in menus or dialog boxes also appear in the text like this. For example: "A **Service Level Indicator** (**SLI**) is a possible most important metric for the business."

> Warnings or important notes appear like this.

> Tips and tricks appear like this.

Get in touch

Feedback from our readers is always welcome.

General feedback: email feedback@packtpub.com, and mention the book's title in the subject of your message. If you have questions about any aspect of this book, please email us at questions@packtpub.com.

Errata: although we have taken every care to ensure the accuracy of our content, mistakes do happen. If you have found a mistake in this book, we would be grateful if you would report this to us. Please visit http://www.packtpub.com/submit-errata, selecting your book, clicking on the Errata Submission Form link, and entering the details.

Piracy: If you come across any illegal copies of our works in any form on the Internet, we would be grateful if you would provide us with the location address or website name. Please contact us at copyright@packtpub.com with a link to the material.

If you are interested in becoming an author: if there is a topic that you have expertise in and you are interested in either writing or contributing to a book, please visit http://authors.packtpub.com.

Reviews

Please leave a review. Once you have read and used this book, why not leave a review on the site that you purchased it from? Potential readers can then see and use your unbiased opinion to make purchase decisions, we at Packt can understand what you think about our products, and our authors can see your feedback on their book. Thank you!

For more information about Packt, please visit packtpub.com.

1

INTRODUCTION

As the internet has grown, people have become used to having access to content all of the time, from a variety of devices. This means that the reputation of a brand has slowly become connected with the responsiveness and reliability of its products. People choose Google for searching because it always returns relevant and useful results quickly. People share content on Twitter because their message will be seen in real time by their followers. Netflix's great content selection is useless if it cannot deliver consistently on a variety of network speeds. As this reliability has become more important to businesses, a specialization focused on software reliability has emerged: **Site Reliability Engineering** (**SRE**). This chapter will introduce you to the field and also describe what you will learn from this book, helping you to write software to navigate the ever-changing internet landscape.

Before we explain what the field and role of SRE pertains to, let us start with a thought experiment. Imagine that it's early in the morning and you wake up to a screenshot of a blank web page in a text message from a friend with the caption: "I can't load your website."

If your personal website is indeed down, maybe you will message back with an, "I'll check it after breakfast," or an, "Oh yeah, been meaning to look into that." If it is your company's website, or maybe the page hosting your resume that you just sent to 15 possible employers, then a stream of expletives and indecipherable emojis will probably erupt from your mouth and in your text message back. This is because, for many businesses, websites have become the main source of incoming business. For some companies, like Facebook, Amazon, or iFixit, their entire business is a website. For other businesses, like restaurants or advertising agencies, a website acts as a way for people interested in the organization to learn more. It is often part of the marketing flow that helps companies to grow.

It is probably impossible to completely remove the adrenaline spike that comes from discovering a website is down if you are responsible for fixing it. However, we can work to set up a framework to limit how often things break. We can create a world where responding to outages is easy, and transition from, "Oh god, everything is on fire, what do I do?!" to "Oh hey, a page isn't loading, so let's check out what's having a rough day."

This chapter is our introduction to the book and the field of SRE. We will cover the following topics in the next few pages:

- Exploring a brief history of the people who work on information systems

- Defining what SRE is

- Describing what is in the book and providing a rough framework for SRE.

A brief history

SRE is a relatively new field, but it is a slightly different take on many existing ideas. In 1958, the term IT was coined in the Harvard Business Review, and eventually became the descriptor for the maintenance of technology used for collecting, storing, and distributing data and information. At that time, computers were transitioning toward having integrated circuits, but they were still the size of a room and were maintained and programmed by a team of people. As computers shrank, that team started focusing on multiple computers. Over time, some people started to specialize in programming those computers, and others focused on keeping them running. "Dumb terminals" would connect to a single computer, which was maintained by a team while programmers and users used the terminals.

Eventually, these maintainers started taking care of both the machines that individuals used, as well as large arrays of machines that provided services. Users would use a word processor on their local machine, and then upload files to a remote machine. Those who maintained the remote machines became known as system engineers, system administrators, and system operators.

As computers became smaller and more commodified, programmers began spending more time interacting with infrastructure, and configuring their software and infrastructure to work together well. On the other end, system admins were writing more and more complex code to maintain infrastructure. The closer these teams became, the more they began working together. In smaller teams, often, people would start focusing on both code for infrastructure and business code. In larger organizations, teams were created that focused on tools for managing infrastructure in reliable ways, so that product teams could quickly and easily manage the infrastructure they needed. These joint teams were often described as SRE or DevOps (developer and operations) teams.

Benjamin Treynor Sloss of Google, often referred to as just Treynor, says in Google's Site Reliability Engineering book, "SRE is what happens when you ask a software engineer to design an operations team." He is often credited with the creation of the idea that operations work is now just a specialization of software engineering. Given Google's success with reliability, the idea has caught on at many companies.

SRE is still a burgeoning field and, like DevOps, is often used to describe roles that include a wide diversity of work. Some companies give the title of SRE to a position, but it is much closer to a traditional system admin role. You can use this book's framework to evaluate a job before you apply for it, however, the goal of this book is to introduce you to the SRE mindset and help you to apply it to an organization, regardless of your past experience in the tech world.

What is SRE?

SRE is an exciting field. As mentioned earlier, it has evolved from a long line of roles and, as it is a relatively new field, its definition is steadily changing. SRE is an extension and evolution of many past concepts and, as such, concepts relevant to SRE apply to many roles, including but not exclusive to, backend engineering, DevOps, systems engineering, systems administration, operations, and so on. Depending on the company, these roles can involve very similar or very different responsibilities. The point is that, no matter what your job title is, you can apply SRE principles to your role.

In an attempt to define the field, we can learn a lot from its full name, Site Reliability Engineering:

♦ **Site**: As in *website*

♦ **Reliability**: Defined as, "The quality of being trustworthy or of performing consistently well." (*Oxford Living Dictionary*, *2017*, `https://en.oxforddictionaries.com/definition/reliability`)

♦ **Engineering**: Defined as, "The action of working artfully to bring something about." (*Oxford Living*

Dictionary, 2017, `https://en.oxforddictionaries.com/definition/engineering`)

♦ **Site Reliability Engineering: How Google Runs Production Systems**; *B. Beyer, C.D. Jones, J. Petoff, N. Murphy, 2016,* by *O'Reilly Media* (`https://landing.google.com/sre/sre-book/toc/index.html`)

Merging these three definitions, we get something like, "The field focused on working artfully to bring about a website that performs consistently well." While this definition could use some brushing up, it suits our needs for now. If you work, or know people who work, in the web development or software engineering world and you ask them what SRE means, then they may ask you, "Isn't that like *X*?" To someone from that background, *X* might be "DevOps," "ops," "platform engineering," "infrastructure engineering," "24/7 engineering," "a sysadmin," and so on.

This variation of answers presents the first problem we will see throughout this book: every organization is different. SRE's primary goal is making a website perform consistently according to our previous definition, which is difficult because it is dependent on the organization, the business around that organization, and the website's (or product's) requirements. One of the primary goals of this book is to present a framework that you can apply even if you do not belong to an organization with any of the aforementioned roles. The framework should be effective if you work for yourself, and it should also work if you are employed by some gigantic international multi-headed Hydra organization, and anything in between.

I worked as an SRE in 2016 for Hillary for America. It was the lead organization (but definitely not the only one) working to help to elect Hillary Clinton as President of the United States of America. We were not successful, and while this example immediately dates this book, I found it to have the most concrete separation of concerns between the parts of a website that I have ever worked on. The organization was hyper-focused on one goal (electing Hillary Clinton as president), so it had a very explicit list of goals that made my job a lot easier.

There were many separate parts of the campaign that the technology team worked on, including a mobile application, different websites, data pipelines, and large databases. To keep this simple though, and to explain what I mean by a separation of concerns, let me use three separate websites that we built and maintained as an example:

♦ The home page for Hillary Clinton's campaign: `https://www.hillaryclinton.com/`

♦ The donate page for her campaign: `https://www.hillaryclinton.com/donate/`

♦ The voter registration page for her campaign: `https://www.hillaryclinton.com/iwillvote/`

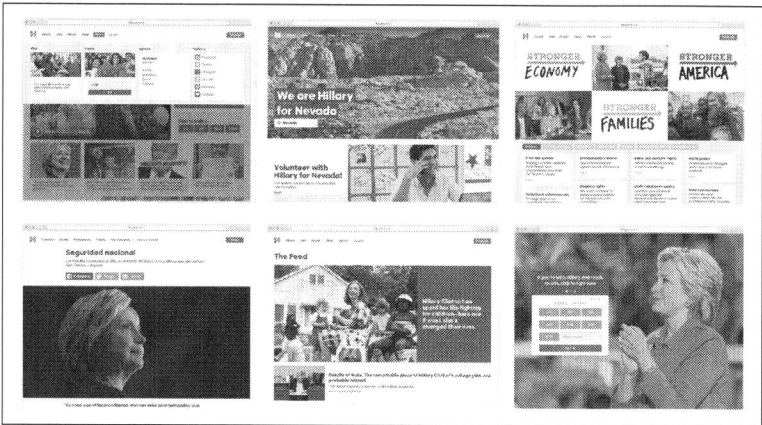

Figure 1: Screenshots of different parts of hillaryclinton.com, courtesy of the Hillary for America design team. From left to right: the header on the home page, a page about Nevada, a page about Hillary's policies, Hillary's home page in Spanish, the campaign blog, and the donate page.

The home page was a general landing page. It needed to be available during the hours that people in North America were awake (as our target audience was mostly based in the United States), but very few people visited the home page unless driven there.

The main reason you would go to `https://www.hillaryclinton.com/` was if you were sent there, not because it was part of your daily browsing like you would visit Twitter or Reddit. Surrogates speaking at rallies, on the radio, or on television supporting Hillary Clinton would often say things like, "Go to hillaryclinton.com now to sign up," or "hillaryclinton.com has more details on her policies on this topic." A five-minute outage here and there was OK, because of this semipredictable traffic spike, but like many media organizations, there were no guarantees of when a large spike of traffic would occur.

The donate page always needed to be up. According to our product team and senior leadership, the donate page's availability was priority number one. If people could not give money, then the campaign might not be able to pay people's salaries or get the candidate to her speaking engagements. The donation site was not the only way that the campaign made money, but it was a significant source of income.

The voter registration page only needed to be fully available when there was an election coming soon. This was because the page let people say they were going to vote for Hillary Clinton and find their nearest polling location. While the donate page needed to be available for the majority of the campaign (May 2015 through to November 2016), the voter registration page only really needed to be available during the lead up to the primary election (September through to November of 2016). If we had built the voter registration page earlier in the election, it also would have been needed in the days leading up to the primaries, but then only for states that were voting on those days. Primary elections are a precursor to the general election and happen from February to June, with different states voting on different days.

The key here is that different websites and features have different requirements and a different definition of being reliable. Nothing will ever be perfect, nor is 100% uptime achievable on the internet, because things are always breaking. So, all we can do is figure out what sort of failures we might have and optimize our product to be resilient in a way that is useful for us. SRE isn't just the analysis of systems; it is also the architecting and building of systems so that they meet the requirements of the product.

> Software on the internet can never be fully reliable for two reasons. The first reason is that the internet is a distributed system and, often, parts fail, which will affect your service's availability. The second reason is that humans write software, and that software will often have bugs, which will also cause outages.

Often, the job of someone working in SRE is to take in reliability requirements for software, and its infrastructure, and then figure out how to make the infrastructure meet those requirements. Steps toward this often require figuring out if existing infrastructure is meeting those needs, collaborating with teams (or people writing software that will run on the infrastructure), evaluating external tools, or just designing and writing what you need yourself.

As I mentioned at the beginning of the chapter, an SRE role can be very diverse. The requirements of an SRE position at a Fortune 500 company can be very different to those of a 20-person video game company. The role could be different at a bank in the USA from a role at a bank on the other side of the world. This is because the organization is different. For smaller organizations, someone working as an SRE may handle everything in the organization related to infrastructure and reliability. On the other hand, larger organizations may have multiple teams of SREs working with many diverse teams of developers. The role between two different banks could be different because of each bank's needs.

A local bank may only need someone to improve the reliability of tools for people who work for the bank, while a much larger bank in London may need someone who can make sure their bank's systems can make trades at very high speeds with the London Stock Exchange or support millions of individual customers. This book will provide a structure for anyone interested in becoming an SRE. The goal is to empower you, no matter your background or current situation. It will not be a panacea but will provide a knowledge base and a framework for making sites more reliable and moving your career forwards.

What is in the book?

I worked as an SRE at Google for four years, and that is where I started specializing, moving away from being a full stack engineer, and instead considering myself an SRE. Google had lots of internal education courses, and when I left, I found it difficult to continue my education. I also quickly discovered that SRE at Google is a very different beast than SRE at much smaller organizations. I decided to write this book for people interested in starting with SRE or applying it to organizations that are much smaller than Google.

To do this, the book is broken up into two parts. The first eight chapters walk through the hierarchy of reliability. This hierarchy was originally designed by Mikey Dickerson of the United States Digital Service (and– surprise, surprise –Google). The hierarchy says that as you are trying to add reliability to a system, you need to walk through each level before you get to the next one.

The following diagram shows a slightly modified version of Mikey's original pyramid. I have updated it to include the all-encompassing aspect of communication:

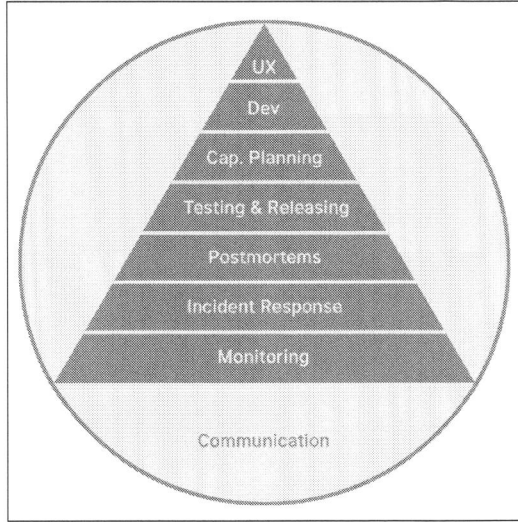

Figure 2: This seven-layer pyramid is encircled with communication. Each layer builds upon and needs the previous layer. It is surrounded by communication because each layer needs communication to succeed.

Let us walk through the layers as a preview of what you can expect in each chapter.

♦ *Chapter 2, Monitoring*: The first level is monitoring, which makes sure that you have insight into a system, tracking health, availability, and what is happening internally in the system. Monitoring is not just tools though, because it also requires communication. Monitoring is a very contentious part of SRE and operations because, depending on implementation, it can either be very useful or very pointless. Figuring out what to monitor, how to monitor it, where to store the monitoring data, who can access historical monitoring data, and how to look at data often takes time. Many people in your engineering organization will have opinions on these points based on past experiences.

Some engineers will have had bad experiences and will not think monitoring is worth the investment, whereas others will have religious zealotry toward certain tools, and some will just ignore you. This chapter will help you to navigate all of these competing opinions and find and create the implementation that is best for your project and team.

♦ *Chapter 3, Incident Response*: The next level is incident response. If something is broken, how do you alert people and respond? While tools help with this, as they define the rules by which to alert humans, most of incident response is about defining policy and setting up training so humans know what to do when they get alerts. If team members see an automated message in Slack, what should they do? If they get a phone call, how quickly do they need to respond? Will employees be paid extra if they have to work on a Saturday due to an outage? These are all questions we will address in the *What is incident response* section. Setting up on-call rotations, best practices for working together as a team, and building infrastructure to make incidents as low-stress as possible will also be covered.

♦ *Chapter 4, Postmortems*: The third level is postmortems. Once you have had an outage, how do you make sure the problem does not happen again? Should you have a meeting about your incident? Does there need to be documentation? In this chapter, we will consider how to talk about past incidents and make it an enjoyable process for all involved. Postmortems are the act of recording for history how an incident happened, how the team fixed it, and how the team is working to prevent another similar incident in the future. We want to set up a culture of blameless and transparent postmortems, so people can work together.

Individuals should not be afraid of incidents, but rather feel confident that if an incident happens, the team will respond and improve the system for the future, instead of focusing on the shame and anger that can come with failure. Incidents are things to learn from, not things to be afraid and ashamed of!

♦ *Chapter 5, Testing and Releasing*: The fourth level is testing and releasing your software. In this chapter, we will be talking about the tooling and strategies that can be used to test and release software. This level in the hierarchy is our first level where instead of focusing on things that have happened, we focus on prevention. Prevention is about trying to limit the number of incidents that happen and also making sure that infrastructure and services stay stable when releasing new code. The chapter will talk about how to focus on all of the different types of testing that exist and make them useful for you and your team. It will also explore releasing software, when to use methodologies like continuous deployment, and some tools you can use.

♦ *Chapter 6, Capacity Planning*: The fifth level is capacity planning. While *Chapter 5, Testing and Releasing* focused on the current world, this chapter is all about predicting the future and finding the limits of your system. Capacity planning is also about making sure you can grow over time. Once you are monitoring your system, and running a reliable system, you can start thinking about how to grow it over time, and how to find and anticipate bottlenecks and resource limits. In this chapter, we will talk about planning for long-term growth, writing budgets, communicating with outside teams about the future, and things to keep in mind as your service shrinks and grows.

- *Chapter 7, Building Tools*: The sixth level is the development of new tools and services. SRE is not only about operations but also about software development. We hope SREs will spend around half of their time developing new tools and services. Some of these tools will exist to automate tasks that an employee has been doing by hand, while others will exist to improve another part of the hierarchy, such as automated load testing, or services to improve performance. In this chapter, we will talk about finding these projects, defining them, planning them, and building them. We will also talk about communicating their usefulness to your fellow engineers.

- *Chapter 8, User Experience*: The final tier is user experience, which is about making sure the user has a good experience. We'll talk about measuring performance, working with user researchers, and defining what a good experience means to your team. We will also discuss how the experience of a tool and processes can cause outages. The goal is to make sure that, no matter the tool, or the user, people enjoy using it, understand how to use it, and cannot easily hurt themselves with it.

Nori Heikkinen, an SRE at Google with many years of experience, adds that "the hierarchy does not include prevention, partly because 100% uptime is impossible, and partly because the bottom three needs in the hierarchy must be addressed within an organization before prevention can be examined." (`https://www.infoq.com/news/2015/06/too-big-to-fail`)

The last two chapters of this book are a cheat section and introduction to common useful topics.

- *Chapter 9, Networking Foundations*: This is a selection of tools and definitions of important ideas in networking. We discuss network packets, DNS, UDP and TCP, and lots of other things. After this chapter you should feel like you know the basics of networking, and the ability to research more advanced topics.

- *Chapter 10, Linux and Cloud Foundations*: This is a selection of tools and important concepts involved in Linux and modern cloud products. We cover what the Linux kernel is, common parts of public clouds, and other topics. After this chapter you should feel like you know the basics of Linux and most public cloud products. Afterwards you should feel comfortable researching specific clouds and more advanced Linux topics.

SRE as a framework for new projects

One way to use this book is as a framework for working on a new project. As each chapter is about a different level of the hierarchy, you can work through the book to figure out where in the hierarchy your project sits. If it is a new project, then often it will be right at the bottom of the hierarchy, with no, or very little, monitoring implemented.

At each level, if there are others on the team, then you should begin a conversation to figure out what exists, and if it meets the team's needs. Each chapter will provide a rough rubric for that discussion, but remember that every team and project is unique. If you are the only person who is thinking about reliability and infrastructure, then you may end up spending a significant amount of time proposing solutions and pushing the project in a certain direction. Just remember that the point is to improve the reliability of the service, help the business, and improve the user's experience of the service.

You may find yourself distracted by each thing that you could fix. It is highly recommended to document the problems that you see first before diving in. Documenting first can be helpful in a few ways. Diving in is very satisfying, but it also may lead you to skip over requirements or spend too much time on a solution that doesn't work for your business (for example, integrating your system with a monitoring service you can't afford, or building a distributed job scheduler when you could have just used a piece of open source software).

So, when joining a new project, or evaluating a new service, here is a set of steps to follow:

◆ Figure out the team structure. Who owns what? Who is in charge?

◆ Find any documentation the team has for their service or the project.

◆ Get someone to draw out the system architecture. Have them show you what connects to which service, what depends on the project, how data flows through the service, and how the project is deployed.

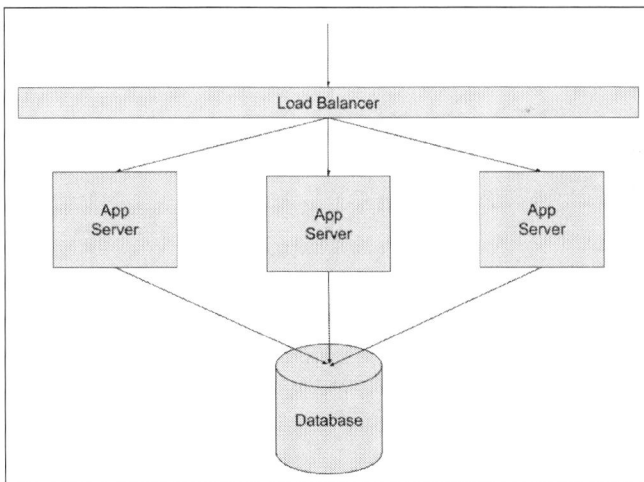

Figure 3: An example system architecture diagram. This is a very simple diagram that someone might draw on a whiteboard. Most companies will have something much more complex or detailed than this, but this is often the level of detail you need. Boxes with names and arrows show what talks to what.

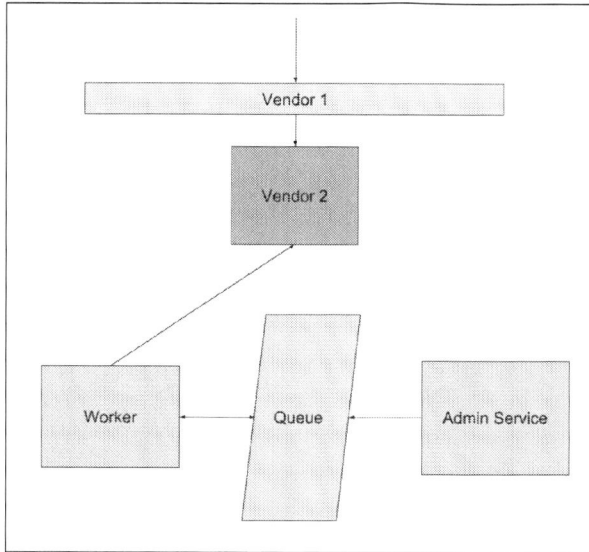

Figure 4: Second example of an architecture diagram. This system is a classic static site generator model. The admin service creates or modifies things and writes update notifications into a queue. A worker reads data from the queue, does work on the data, and uploads it to a static object store, in this case vendor 2. Then, we put in some sort of CDN or serving system, in this case vendor 1 in front of vendor 2.

Name	Role	Manager	Things they know/ specializations
Akil	Junior Full Stack Dev	Jeff	Seems pretty new and jumps around a lot.
Catherine	Senior Frontend Dev	Jeff	Does a lot of initial design prototyping and built most of the frontend originally.
Kareem	Senior Mobile Dev	Melissa	Wrote both mobile apps.
Steph	Senior Backend Dev	Melissa	TO DO: Set up a one-on-one to understand mobile backend.
Suzy	Full Stack Dev	Jeff	Animation wizard who knows the database for CMS better than anyone.

Tom	Full Stack Dev	Jeff	Frontend architecture, made initial protocol buffers and knows sync queue best.

Table 1: An example table with notes on people in the project. With this, we have a reference on team structure. If we need to know who to talk to about mobile apps, we can look at our handy chart and see that we need to talk to Kareem or the manager, Melissa.

Now that you have context for the project, or service, start working through each chapter of the book and ask:

♦ Does the service have monitoring?

♦ Does the team have plans for incident response?

♦ Does the team create postmortems? Are they stored anywhere?

♦ How is the service tested? Does the project have a release plan?

♦ Has anyone done any capacity planning?

♦ What tools could we build to improve the service?

♦ Is the current level of reliability providing a positive user experience?

The trick to note here is that these questions could be asked about a piece of software that has been running for years, as well as one that is just being created.

The service you are investigating could be a large project with many pieces of software (a **service-oriented architecture** (**SOA**) for example) or a single monolithic application. If you are working on a project with many services, then work through each service one at a time. The downside of this can be that if you want to build a framework that will fit all of the services you are interacting with, you will not know how best to solve the problems and needs of them until after you have done a bunch of research and work. The upside is that you will not be pulled immediately in many directions and will be able to focus on one specific service's problems.

Your time and energy are limited resources and, because of this, you will always need to work with more people than you have time for, so make sure to take it slow. Going slow will mean that things do not get lost in the cracks. You also do not want to burn out before each service has its base few levels of its hierarchy filled up.

Summary

Alright! We made it through the introduction. We learned what SRE is at a high level, and we talked about the sorts of problems people in the role tend to focus on. We discussed the structure of the book, and also how to apply that structure to a software project.

In the next chapter, we will be diving into the world of monitoring! Monitoring is the foundation of learning about a system. It is how you record historical data about a system and learn about what is actually going on by analyzing the data you collect. By the end of the chapter, you'll know the basics of instrumenting an application, aggregating that data, storing that data, and displaying it.

References

1. *Oxford Living Dictionary, 2017,* `https://en.oxforddictionaries.com/definition/reliability`

2. *Oxford Living Dictionary, 2017,* `https://en.oxforddictionaries.com/definition/engineering`

3. *Site Reliability Engineering: How Google Runs Production Systems*; *B. Beyer, C.D. Jones, J. Petoff, N. Murphy, 2016, by O'Reilly Media,* `https://landing.google.com/sre/sre-book/toc/index.html`

2

MONITORING

Monitoring is defined by Oxford Dictionaries (https://en.oxforddictionaries.com/definition/monitor) as to "observe and check the progress or quality of (something) over a period; keep under systematic review." This definition points out two crucial details—firstly, you need to define what quality is and make sure that your system is making progress toward, or staying within, a limit of quality. Secondly, you need to be systematic about this work—you should not be randomly looking at your system. Instead, your approach should be consistent. The need for systematic measurements is one reason that your dentist asks you to come in every six months, or a reason why some insurance companies ask you to get a dedicated primary care doctor.

In this chapter, we will be focusing on the tools and methodology of monitoring modern web services. The chapter will include thoughts on what data to collect, how to collect that data, how to store that data, and how to display that data for developers and those who will find it useful. We will also talk about communication about monitoring, why monitoring is essential, and how to get everyone in a company invested in monitoring.

Why monitoring?

Everyone tells you to go to the doctor regularly, but why should you? What are the benefits? My parents would say that you should go to the doctor to catch signs of things that you do not necessarily pay attention to, or notice, by yourself. This could be things like cholesterol levels, blood pressure, and skin cancer. I also like to use doctor visits as a time to think about and talk about changes that I have noticed in my body. For example, if I have had an upset stomach frequently.

These examples work as good comparisons of the two separate types of monitoring that software often needs. The first type is **metrics** and the second is **logs**. Metrics, in this case, are number measurements. Traditionally, metrics focused on performance numbers, like the percentage of disk space used, or the number of packets received, or the CPU load. These days, they can be used to represent just about anything that can be defined as a numerical value. They can come from any piece of software in your system. Logs are events, which can have numbers and other data attached, but are often less structured. Some logs are complete JSON blobs of data, while others are just human-formatted strings of text. They can also be anything in between.

Let's say that I go to see the doctor and my blood pressure is recorded as 120/70 mmHg. My cholesterol is 190 mg/dL. There is also a new mole on my back and my stomach has been feeling upset. The metrics, in this case, are my blood pressure and cholesterol. My doctor collects them every time I visit and there is a documented history of them. They also have simple ranges for the human adult that are considered safe. This fact is not too relevant right now but will be useful later, when we think about alerting in the next chapter. The mole and stomach issues are closer to events.

We are stretching the metaphor a bit thin here, but the mole has data around it and the doctor is making a gut decision based on its size, location, and time present to decide if the hospital should biopsy it or not. My doctor does not have regular data, but he has a one-off measurement. For the stomach issue, the doctor has a few statistics that are partially remembered by me. These are things that I have eaten and approximately how long, how intense, and how frequent the pain is.

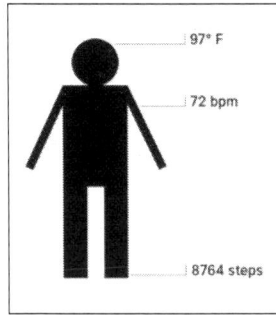

Image of a human with monitoring labels.
Each label is an example metric you might collect about a person's body.

For the metrics, the doctor records them and if they are abnormal, or out of bounds, the doctor may recommend some changes to my lifestyle. For the log data, the doctor will probably start by either collecting more data, by sending the mole to a lab, or by asking me to keep a record of what I am eating.

As much as we might want them to take care of themselves, applications are not humans. So, we measure applications slightly differently. For a web application, the most common metrics are error counts, request counts, and request duration. The most common logs are error stack traces.

If you want help remembering these three metrics, they can be remembered as ERD or RED. Some people also call them **REL** (**requests, errors, latency**).

So, why are these metrics often the starting point? We can increment a counter every time an error occurs and write that error out to a log, with a timestamp. A counter is one of the most fundamental forms of monitoring. We just count the number of times something has happened. Some services let you store metadata with your counter increment, tying the log to the counter, but often you just write the logs and the counter increment with the same timestamp. This counter is useful because you want to know when you are serving an error to a user and to look at your logs to evaluate what the errors are. You increment the counter so that you can calculate what percentage of the requests that you serve are errors, and so that you can quickly view long-term error progress.

A total request count is useful because we know how often our application is being used. I am using the example of a basic HTTP 1.1 web application, so the total request count is an accurate view of how much work a server is doing. If the server is a streaming server, then often a team counts bytes or packets instead of requests, so they have a view of how usage changes over time, because in their case a request can represent more than a single unit of work.

See *Chapter 9, Networking Foundations* for more on how HTTP 1.1 works and how it differs from other versions of HTTP. We also cover what a packet is in that chapter.

In this example, request duration is just the length of a single HTTP request. We are measuring how long it takes the server to process, from when it receives the full request, until it has sent out the full response. Request duration is used for a bunch of things. Firstly, you can use it to figure out whether certain types of requests are taking longer than others. If you tag each duration recording not just with the time it took, but also with the URL hit, the method (GET, POST, HEAD, and so on), and the status code you returned, then you could dig into the metrics.

You could see that, on average, all requests that returned code 404 took one second longer than requests that returned code 200. Secondly, you could use this method to see how similar requests change over time. For instance, you could compare how requests to `https://example.com/` performed in November with how they performed in December.

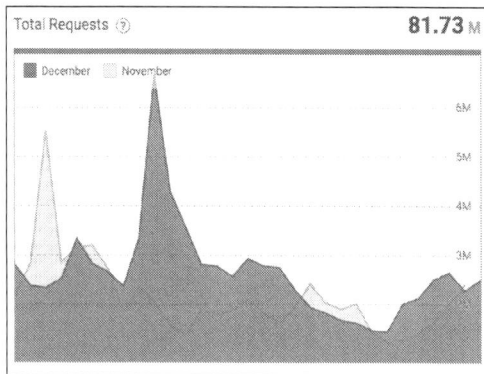

A graph of a service's total request count for the months of November and December. The December line shows traffic was slightly higher than November's traffic for most days. The days where this is not true are a large spike in the beginning of both months, and a slight slump in traffic near the end of the month in December.

We have mainly talked about how monitoring is useful and not necessarily why it is important. I propose some questions for you—how do you know a service is working? How do you know it is not working? How do you define what working is? This is what we are trying to solve with monitoring. Monitoring is important because it provides us with a data-driven view of our application and proves to us it is working, without us having to sit there and constantly check the application every minute of our lives. With that in mind, I believe the best approach is always the practical approach. Let's try creating a simple application and instrumenting it with monitoring.

Instrumenting an application

First, a caveat—there are a lot of programming languages and monitoring systems. We will be talking about various monitoring systems later in the chapter, and there are libraries for all sorts of languages and systems. So, just because I am providing examples here with specific languages and libraries, it does not mean that you cannot do something very similar with your language and monitoring system of choice.

For the first example, we will use Ruby and StatsD. Ruby is a popular scripting language and tends to be what I use when I want to build something quickly. Also, some very large websites use Ruby, including GitHub, Spotify, and Hulu. StatsD is a monitoring system from Etsy. It is open source and used by many companies including Kickstarter and Hillary for America.

I have commented on this simple application as much as possible. However, if you need more documentation than my comments, see the references section.

Sinatra is a simple web framework. It creates a domain-specific language inside of Ruby for responding to web requests:

```
require "sinatra"
```

One of the most popular Ruby StatsD libraries is installed by running `gem install statsd-ruby`. require is Ruby's import function:

```
require "statsd"
```

Logger is part of the Ruby standard library and lets us write out to the console with a predefined format:

```
require "logger"
```

Here, we configure our StatsD library to write debug messages out to the standard output, whenever it tries to send a request to the StatsD server. This is nice for debugging and also for our example application to see what is going on:

```
Statsd.logger = Logger.new(STDOUT)
```

This creates an instance of the `StatsD` class to talk to a StatsD server that is running on port 9125 on the local machine. StatsD traditionally runs over UDP instead of TCP. Note that, because StatsD traditionally runs on UDP, the StatsD service does not need to be running to test our code. UDP does not retry if it fails, so the network requests will just go into the void. While it would be better if it was running, because we are logging all requests to the standard output with the preceding line, we still know what is happening, despite not having set up a server to receive the data. We talk about the protocols of UDP and TCP in depth in *Chapter 9, Networking Foundations*.

```
$statsd = Statsd.new 'localhost', 9125
```

This is a part of the DSL given to us by Sinatra. It says that if the HTTP server receives a request to/of the GET method (which is just a normal page load), we should run the code inside the block. The block is defined between the do and end keywords.

```
get "/" do
```

This StatsD function times the length of the block that is passed to it and, when the block finishes, sends that time to StatsD.

```
$statsd.time "request.time" do
```

This increments the request counter by one. Note that StatsD doesn't natively support tags, or any way to describe this metric. Other implementations of StatsD do, but by default it is not supported. As such, this does not get any of the useful extra data mentioned earlier, such as path, method, or status code.

```
$statsd.increment "request.count"
```

In Ruby, the last line of the block is the return value. In this case, "hello world" is returned from the timing block, then returned by the Sinatra block, and then sent to the user, as Sinatra considers the returned string to be what to return to users in their HTTP response body.

```
      "hello world"
  end
end
```

This is another Sinatra DSL. It is fired whenever Sinatra does not match the URL a user is looking for. So, if they visit any URL besides / on this server, this block will run. We want to know about all types of requests, so we increment request. count here, as well as recording the request.time. The new thing we do here, though, is increment request.error.

```
not_found do
  $statsd.time "request.time" do
    $statsd.increment "request.count"
    $statsd.increment "request.error"

    "This is not found."
  end
end
```

If any other error besides a not found error happens, this block will run. This looks identical to the not_found block, except for the return message, because they are doing the same thing, just returning from a slightly different error.

```
error do
  $statsd.time "request.time" do
    $statsd.increment "request.count"
    $statsd.increment "request.error"

    "An error occurred!"
  end
end
```

While this example is somewhat straightforward, you may be thinking it is annoying to have to write code like this for each route in your application. Also note that this example is being overly explicit. Often, you would want to use a library that gives you these metrics for free, or to use a service like NGINX, in between the user and your application, that records some request metrics. However, the main takeaway from this code sample is the two monitoring function calls:

- ◆ `increment`

- ◆ `time`

With these two functions, you can do a lot. With `time` you could measure how long it takes to talk to a dependency. With `increment` you could do anything you want, from the number of requests received to the number of times a user performs an action. StatsD also supports gauges for numbers you want to take a snapshot of, which is similar to a timing, but without the unit of time. We will be talking later about other things you might want to monitor and how to talk to your team about what is important for them to monitor.

The next example is written in Go, using the Prometheus monitoring library. Prometheus is a relatively new and increasingly popular monitoring system, written by the folks at SoundCloud. It is very similar to Google's internal monitoring system, Borgmon. While StatsD is a push-based monitoring system, Prometheus is a pull-based system. As for the programming language this example is written in, it was chosen because Go has well-written examples and opinionated tools that make development and processes easier.

Like the previous example, for more details please check out the references section, which contains links to the official documentation.

Go files always start with a package declaration. `main` is the package for creating an executable.

```
package main

import (
```

The import section is how Go imports packages. `log` is part of the Go standard library. It lets us write out messages prepended with a timestamp. `net/http` is also part of the Go standard library and includes functions for building an HTTP server. Lastly, `time` is part of the Go standard library and includes functions for dealing with time. We will use it to determine how long it takes for something to run.

```
"log"
"net/http"
"time"
```

The next two libraries are not part of the standard library. `github.com/prometheus/client_golang/prometheus` is the third-party library for building Prometheus metrics. Despite looking like a URL, do not expect a web page there. Go structures import links for external resources as URLs, where the beginning of the path is a domain and path to the source repository, and then the following slashes are directories inside that source repository. To install a package for use, run `go get github.com/prometheus/client_golang/prometheus`. Some domains, such as `gopkg.in`, publish metadata redirecting to another source repository, which the `go get` tool follows to download the code when you install the package.

Unlike StatsD, Prometheus publishes its metrics on the server it is running from. `promhttp` is the second third-party library in this import and its job is to make running a Prometheus metric server endpoint easy for us. It is also part of the Prometheus Go library.

```
"github.com/prometheus/client_golang/prometheus"
"github.com/prometheus/client_golang/prometheus/
promhttp"
)
```

Prometheus requires us to declare metrics before we can write to them. First, we define the request count metric we will be incrementing. All Prometheus metrics require a name and a description to make them more readable. We are also providing an optional list that will describe the required attributes each request increment will need.

```
var (
  httpRequests = prometheus.NewCounterVec(
      prometheus.CounterOpts{
        Name: "http_request_count_total",
        Help: "HTTP request counts",
      },
      []string{"path", "method"},
```

```
  )
  httpDurations = prometheus.NewSummaryVec(
    prometheus.SummaryOpts{
      Name: "http_request_durations_microseconds",
      Help: "HTTP request latency distributions.",
      Objectives: map[float64]float64{},
    },
    []string{"path", "method"},
  )
)
```

On startup, the Prometheus library will make sure all of our metrics are properly defined or the application will die in a panic. This "must" is a common pattern for runtime checks in Go.

```
func init() {
  prometheus.MustRegister(httpRequests)
  prometheus.MustRegister(httpDurations)
}
```

This is a very small middleware, which will wrap any handler passed to it, increment the request count, and record duration. For brevity and simplicity, we aren't recording errors.

```
func MetricHandler(handlerFunc func(http.
ResponseWriter, *http.Request)) http.HandlerFunc {
```

This function takes in a function. It then returns a wrapping function. When this wrapped function is called, we start recording the time by marking what time it is currently. Then, we call the function we are wrapping, which does all of the actual work for the request. We are essentially building a generic wrapping function and this is yielding to the function we passed. The writer variable is what is actually receiving the method calls to modify the HTTP response that Go is building. After the function has returned, we calculate the time passed in microseconds and submit that metric. We then increment the response count with path and method labels:

```
return http.HandlerFunc(func(writer http.
ResponseWriter, request *http.Request) {
    start := time.Now()

    handlerFunc(writer, request)

    elapsed := time.Since(start)
    msElapsed := elapsed / time.Microsecond

    httpDurations.WithLabelValues(request.URL.Path,
request.Method).Observe(float64(msElapsed))
    httpRequests.WithLabelValues(request.URL.Path,
request.Method).Inc()
  })
}

func main() {
```

This is a function, saved to a variable that, when given a request, returns the text "hello world":

```
helloWorld := http.HandlerFunc(func(w http.
ResponseWriter, r *http.Request) {
    w.Header().Set("Content-Type", "text/plain")
    w.Write([]byte("hello world"))
})
```

This says that all requests to / go first to our metric handler, inside of which we have passed our helloWorld function. So the MetricHandler will call the helloWorld function where it says handlerFunc(writer, request):

```
http.Handle("/", MetricHandler(helloWorld))
```

The Handler function provides a default handler to expose metrics via an HTTP server. /metrics is the normal endpoint for that. If you visit /metrics on this server, you will see the current value of all of the metrics this server exports. It is also the path that Prometheus will scrape to store metrics in its datastore. You configure Prometheus to scrape paths in its configuration, so you can actually have this at whatever path you want: /metrics is just a common default.

```
http.Handle("/metrics", promhttp.Handler())
```

This starts the actual server on port 8080, and if it dies, logs the final status to the console:

```
log.Fatal(http.ListenAndServe(":8080", nil))
}
```

The structure of this code is very different to the previous example because it is a different language and monitoring system, but the general philosophy remains the same. Just like with StatsD, you create data sources and, over time, insert data points at timestamps. Whatever you want to measure, there are often many ways to record it, which are available in a multitude of programming languages.

Note that in both of these examples we are ignoring logging. There are lots of ways to log information, including writing to a plain text file, JSON objects written out to the standard output, or even writing to a database. Sometimes, this is called event-driven monitoring. It's just another set of tools and can be used to acquire similar data, just in a different way.

Now that you have a view of the starting point of how to record metrics, we should pivot back to the theoretical. What should we monitor?

What should we measure?

Here is one of my favorite SRE interview questions: "What is your monitoring philosophy?" I find this question fascinating because it tends to spark discussion. A monitoring philosophy is how you decide what to monitor and when. Some people believe in the *monitor everything* philosophy. They think that if something happens, or changes, a counter should be incremented or a log line produced (or both). Another philosophy is a more minimal *wait and see* approach. In this philosophy, if in a postmortem the team wishes they had a piece of data, then it should be instrumented, monitored, and stored.

> Postmortems are retrospectives after incidents. We will talk about them in depth in *Chapter 4, Postmortems*. You can also read a paragraph about them in *Chapter 1, Introduction*.

The only response to this question that I have ever rejected as a valid response was from a friend who was looking to get started in software and claimed his monitoring philosophy was that of On Kawara's, *I Got Up* art piece. Kawara is a conceptual artist and throughout the 1960s and 1970s he mailed postcards from the cities he awoke in each morning to friends and random people, containing a timestamp of when he woke up that day, his current address, and nothing else. So, because it was semi-random, there was no way to view when he woke up over time. Now museums have subsets of this collection, but there are significant gaps. It is fascinating to look at this project as an early view of human logging, but I cannot imagine a more frustrating scenario than having to look at multiple data stores to view a single metric over an irregular period. I am pretty sure the friend was joking, but the idea is still interesting to think about. It is a good reminder that monitoring is not unique to computers.

> Kawara's art is wonderful for envisioning monitoring pre-computers. He also created works of art around the walks he took each day, drew on maps, made lists of who he met for years, and sent telegrams to people telling them he was still alive.

Philosophies aside, if you are new to monitoring a system, it can be hard to decide on what you want to monitor. You may have storage or cost concerns preventing you from monitoring everything, and your service may be too new to have postmortems that provide you with valuable insights on what you are not monitoring.

My recommendations are probably predictable given the previous section and its examples. I always say that it is best to start with the basics. If your service is a web server, then start by making sure error counts, request counts, and request durations are collected. If your service is some sort of data pipeline, batch service, or cron job, then a better starting place is job invocations, job durations, and job successes. If you need a cute little acronym or abbreviation, I like ERD for web servers and IDS for background services.

After you lay those foundations, there are lots of areas you can start expanding. Remember that your goal is to validate that your service is doing what you expect it to. I tend to start recording business logic things, like how many records there are in the database, metrics around connecting to our dependencies, how many types of actions are happening, and so on. After that, I focus on capacity.

> We talk about capacity metrics in greater depth in *Chapter 6, Capacity Planning.*

Capacity is often a recording of the resources your server is using—metrics such as hard drive storage, network bandwidth, CPU, and memory. To provide an example, let us start with an arbitrary image upload service. Maybe it is the server that receives all of the images that users upload to Instagram. Maybe it is the code in your blog that handles uploading images for posts. Whatever the case, this service has a single URL that you post image uploads to. It then writes the images to the local disk, inspects them, and stores the metadata to a database.

The service then uploads the images to a cloud storage service, where we put all of our user images.

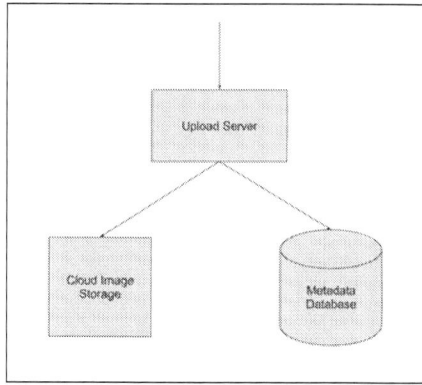

Diagram of the example image upload service

So, what would you monitor? Take a second and try to answer these questions—if a developer introduced a bug, what would you be concerned about? What metrics could tell you that this server is doing its job?

I would monitor the following things:

♦ **Request errors, request duration, and request count**: This is our ERD for the server, since we are a web server. It is at our very baseline of *are things working?*

♦ **Bytes uploaded**: This will account for how much bandwidth we are using. Since some of our requests could be very large, we want to know if we start seeing a spike in how much data is coming into our server, because not every request will be the same.

♦ **Image size in bytes**: This provides the same information but from a different angle. After we have received the bytes and processed them, how big are the final images? This way, if, for example, our upload client changes (such as a new iPhone launches with a more powerful camera, or we change our upload code to compress before sending), we can see the effect versus our network bandwidth.

- **Images uploaded**: This metric will only be useful if we see significant changes. If we get a magnitudinal change in images, it might explain why things fail in the event of an outage.

- **Count of image metadata in database**: We keep a count of this to compare it to the image count uploaded, to make sure we are not dropping image data on the floor if the database is down.

- **Count of images in storage**: This makes sure that images are getting to the data source that we eventually serve images from. If they are not, maybe our cloud storage is down or there is a network issue.

This is not an exhaustive list! You may have listed other metrics, but the key is just to start somewhere. Just because you write monitoring today, it does not mean you are done. This is something you will want to evolve. As your service grows, you will discover what metrics you look at and which ones are useless. As your team grows, some other developer can, and should, add metrics they care about. I like to review everything we are monitoring once a year with the team, to make sure we are consistent with how we monitor. Are metric names consistent? Do the metrics have units? Are we collecting and storing our metrics consistently?

We haven't mentioned it yet, but it is worth at least a shout out that, when thinking about what to monitor, there are often two ways to look at the problem—black-box monitoring and white-box monitoring.

Black-box monitoring assumes that your monitoring tool knows nothing or very little about your application. Often, it is a probe or regular series of requests to check whether things are working the way you expect.

White-box monitoring is the instrumentation of your code. It knows everything about how things work because it is coming from inside of the application. If you were to compare this to something like the electronics of an airplane, white-box monitoring is the gauges in the cockpit. Black-box monitoring is the updates the radio towers send and receive as planes fly over them.

Once you have started to monitor things, you can start working with your product and business team to make sure that your assumptions about system health match theirs.

A short introduction to SLIs, SLOs, and error budgets

At some point, you are going to discuss whether or not it is safe to deploy an update to your software. Change is the thing that improves our software, but it also introduces the possibility of an outage. So, at times of great importance, how do you convince someone in the business that it is safe to make a software change? Can you push a code change on Black Friday, or Singles' Day, to an e-commerce website and know you will not lose the business millions of dollars? We will talk about this in more detail in *Chapter 5, Testing and Releasing,* but a good starting place is figuring out what your team views as its most important metric.

Service levels

A **Service Level Indicator** (**SLI**) is a possible *most important metric for the business*. For websites, a common SLI is the percentage of requests responded to healthily. For other types of services, an SLI can be a performance indicator, such as the percentage of search results returned in under 100 milliseconds. To be clear, an SLI is a metric behind these goals. Request count would be the SLI behind *percentage of requests responded to healthily*. Search result request duration would be the SLI behind *percentage of search results returned in under 100 milliseconds*. For background services, you could do something like percentage of jobs run on time, or percentage of jobs that completed successfully. For some sites, the only metric recorded is the response of a GET request sent every five minutes by a service like Pingdom. This metric of *did we even respond to the request?* can be used as a rough approximation for the backing of a goal like *percentage of requests we responded to*.

A request sent to your service that is identical every time and sent at a regular interval is often called a health check. Many load balancers use this to determine whether a server should continue receiving traffic. We talk more about the basics of load balancers in *Chapter 10, Linux and Cloud Foundations.*

A **Service Level Objective** (**SLO**) is a goal built around an SLI. It is usually a percentage and is tied to a period. It is typically measured in a number of *nines*. For example, time periods are the last thirty days, the last 24 hours, the current financial quarter, and so on. When someone says they have a number of nines of uptime, they mean a percentage of time when their service is available. Without a time-based metric, it is a relatively useless statement, so I usually assume people mean a rolling cumulative average over the past thirty days.

The following are some examples of nines:

♦ **90% (one nine of uptime)**: Meaning you were down for 10% of the period. This means you were down for three days out of the last thirty days.

♦ **99% (two nines of uptime)**: Meaning 1% or 7.2 hours of downtime over the last thirty days.

♦ **99.9% (three nines of uptime)**: Meaning 0.1% or 43.2 minutes of downtime.

♦ **99.95% (three and a half nines of uptime)**: Meaning 0.05% or 21.6 minutes of downtime.

♦ **99.99% (four nines of uptime)**: Meaning 0.01% or 4.32 minutes of downtime.

♦ **99.999% (five nines of uptime)**: Meaning 26 seconds or 0.001% of downtime.

In our modern world of distributed systems, with cheap hardware and constant iteration, rarely do systems operate with reliability better than five nines. Some examples of things that are built with better reliability than this are satellites, airplanes, and missile guidance systems. The point of counting the number of nines, though, is that you usually want to think of things in terms of orders of magnitude.

> Orders of magnitude are usually a multiple of ten. We usually think of things in orders of magnitude because it is at that scale that we start running into issues. For example, if you can do 10 of a thing, you can probably do 40, but it is notably different to do 100 or 1000 of that same thing.

Finally, a **Service Level Agreement** (**SLA**) is a legal agreement a business publishes around an SLO. Often, it provides monetary compensation to customers for the time a business is outside of their defined SLO. This is most common in **Software as a Service** (**SaaS**) companies, but could exist in other places as well.

Companies that publish SLAs often also have internal SLOs that are tighter or more restrictive than the published SLA, so the company can operate assuming some risk but without having to be at the edge of needing to pay customers every time it steps past that limit.

Error budgets

Once you have a rough idea of your SLO, and you have measured it for a bit, you can use it to make decisions on how to do things that are risky. An example of this is something I worked on at First Look Media. We had no significant downtime for a few months and had been sitting at 100% uptime for the previous 30 days. Our SLO had been 99.9% of HTTP GET requests, on a one-minute interval, from an external polling service that needed to return the status code 200. So, we did something risky that we had been putting off because the possibility of downtime was high—reconfigured our services to share clusters, instead of each having their own clusters. In this case, a cluster was a pool of shared servers and each service was a collection of Docker containers scheduled with Amazon's Elastic Container Service. We did this one service at a time, and only had downtime on one service, but we felt comfortable doing this because we had an agreement with our business team as to what was acceptable downtime. The inverse of this was that when we had months when we had many outages and didn't meet our agreed upon SLO, we stopped deploying.

> This is a quick overview of deployments. We go into more details on deploying, releasing, and release agreements in *Chapter 5, Testing and Releasing*.

Not every service needs SLOs and not every organization needs error budgets, but they can be useful tools for working with people when trying to decide when it is safe to take risks. Sometimes, people will say, "Trust but verify," or "Have data to back your claims." When taking risks that could affect your business, this is important. Just like you want to know if and why your human resources team is going to change your health insurance, your coworkers want to know that you are only taking risks in a way that the business can handle. It is not confidence inspiring if you walk into a room with no data and say, "Yeah, everything will be fine." It's much better if you can show up and say, "You can trust us because we have made 100 deploys in the past month with no downtime, and if this does fail, we can roll back and will still be within our agreed SLO. If we do not meet our SLO this month due to a failure, we will stop deploying until things have stabilized and we are back under our agreement."

Services without SLOs run toward the possibility of having customers define what is an acceptable level of performance. That being said, having an SLO does not guarantee that your users will see your service's availability as correct, even if you publish an SLO. For example, Amazon Web Services has an SLA for most services it sells, but customers are often frustrated with the downtime they see. This may be illogical, as customers are using a product that they are being told won't perform at the level they want, and they continue paying for it. However, unless Amazon sees a significant change in user behavior, it has no incentive to update its SLA (and the underlying SLO), because the more restrictive the SLO, the higher the chance it will have to give customers money back. If Amazon were to see a significant number of users leaving, it then might change. If you are seeing your revenue decline due to an SLA, or if your SLO is so loose that customers are implementing solutions to deal with your differing expectations, it might be time to either define an SLO, if your service lacks one, or update your existing one to appease your customers' needs. An SLO can then help you to define the prioritization of work.

In *Chapter 7*, *Building Tools* we will talk more about the prioritization of work. SLOs should never be the only reason work is prioritized. If you are chasing just SLOs, your team may find themselves very disconnected from the business and its needs. If this happens, take a step back and work with the team and management to better define your place in the organization.

As we stated at the beginning of the chapter, monitoring is used to show change over time. People find it useful to prove a history of consistency. Sadly, due to the constraints of technology, we cannot store everything forever easily without a lot of money or resources. So, let's talk about how we collect and store this information.

Collecting and saving monitoring data

Once you have instrumented your application, you will need to store your data somewhere. As I mentioned in the *Instrumenting an application* section of this chapter, there are many possible tools you can use. I will be talking about some of the tools, but be aware that there are many others. Talk to your friends, do research online, and try different tools to figure out what is best for you, your team, and your organization.

I tend to organize monitoring tools into two buckets. This is often a simplification of these systems, but it helps me to think about how they work. These two buckets are polling applications and push applications.

Polling applications

Polling (also known as pull) applications scrape data from a service and then store and display the data. Some of the complaints against polling applications are that you need to keep some record of all of your services to scrape. There's nothing wrong with polling applications, but this is just something to think about: how do you know what services are running on your infrastructure? Polling applications are used by all sorts of companies and individuals around the world, from Google to people who just want to monitor their home Wi-Fi router.

A very simple example is the following Go program:

```go
package main

import (
    "encoding/json"
    "fmt"
    "log"
    "math/rand"
    "net/http"
    "time"
)

func main() {
    rand.Seed(time.Now().Unix())
    http.HandleFunc("/", func(w http.ResponseWriter,
r *http.Request) {
        data := map[string]float64{
            "hello": 1.0,
            "now":   float64(time.Now().Unix()),
            "rand":  rand.Float64(),
        }

        json, err := json.Marshal(data)
        if err != nil {
            log.Fatal(err)
        }

        w.Header().Set("Content-Type", "application/
json; charset=utf-8")
        fmt.Fprintf(w, "%s", json)
    })

    log.Println("Starting server...")
    log.Println("Running on http://localhost:8080")
    log.Fatal(http.ListenAndServe(":8080", http.
DefaultServeMux))
}
```

The preceding code outputs a JSON object that looks like the following:

```
$ curl http://localhost:8080/
{"hello":1,"now":1527602257,
"rand":0.7835047124910645}
```

If you weren't using a monitoring framework or anything similar, you could scrape this data with another service and save it to a database. It wouldn't provide you with much valuable data (as knowing random numbers is not too useful in most cases), but it would serve as the basis for all polling applications. Go actually publishes a package in the standard library, called `expvar`, which publishes memory information about the current application on the path `/debug/vars` in a JSON format, for you to scrape and collect if you want to. It also lets you add in arbitrary data as needed.

Now that you have a rough idea of how polling systems work, let's walk through some open-source polling services.

Nagios

Nagios is one of the oldest monitoring tools. Many of the complaints about polling services come from people who have had bad experiences with Nagios. That being said, Nagios is incredibly extensible and very popular. It runs on just about everything and is very well documented. It is written in C and supports plugins in many languages. There are also a bunch of forks of Nagios out there that have attempted to modernize the system. One of the more popular forks is Icinga, which uses different data storage and a more modern API.

It also stores data in an RRD database. RRD stands for round robin database and uses a circular buffer to keep the database a constant size. RRDTool, the most prevalent implementation of RRD transforms an RRD into a viewable graph. Like other older systems, Nagios has some built-in scraping tools, but more often than not, people end up writing their own scrapers to get the data they want into Nagios.

Prometheus

We gave an example of Prometheus and described its basic attributes in the *Instrumenting an application* section. It is maintained by the **Cloud Native Computing Foundation** (**CNCF**). The CNCF is an open-source foundation promoting software focused at improving infrastructure in the cloud. PromQL (Prometheus's query language) takes vectors of data and uses filters and functions to simplify the data.

```
rate(http_requests_total{environment=~"staging|devel
opment",method!="GET"}[5m])
```

In this example, the metric is `http_requests_total` and, the filter is `{environment=~"staging|development",method!="GET"}`. `[5m]` is bunching data into five-minute intervals, and `rate()` is taking the rate of change between each of those bunches.

If you visit the `/metrics` page for the application, it will be outputting data that looks something like:

```
# HELP http_request_count_total HTTP request counts
# TYPE http_request_count_total counter
http_request_count_total{method="GET",path="/"} 1
```

This is then scraped by Prometheus and saved to the datastore. When you write a query, you are querying the datastore, not the application you are getting the metrics from.

Some find Prometheus's query language to have a bit of a learning curve, but it is very powerful. Prometheus is still young but has a large and active community behind it. It implements its own datastore for storing data but has tools for exporting and backing up data to external datasources. It also has its own alert manager for sending notifications to people who are on call.

Cacti

Cacti is built with PHP and MySQL, but tends to need a decent amount of coding to get up and running. You will need to write scripts to do most of your data aggregation, something that comes for free in many other systems. That being said, it is very popular in smaller setups and in the Internet of Things community. Like Nagios, Cacti stores data in an RRD database.

Sensu

Sensu is often seen as a modern version of Nagios. It is written in Ruby and has a dedicated company behind it, which also sells an enterprise-hosted version with additional features and integrations. It stores the state in Redis but integrates with lots of other backends for actual metric data.

Push applications

Push applications are the inverse of pull applications. Instead of the monitoring application getting metrics from services, services write to the monitoring application. Often, there is an intermediary service, which translates or aggregates the metrics before sending them to the central monitoring application. One of the complaints with push applications is that they can have issues if lots of services are writing to them at the same time. There is nothing wrong with push applications though—they just have different architecture. Like polling applications, many very large and also very small companies use push applications, and they are just as effective.

An example push monitoring system is just a simple application that creates a new row, with metric data in a database, every time you want to monitor data. I've created that in the following Go program:

```
package main

import (
    "database/sql"
```

```go
    "fmt"
    _ "github.com/lib/pq"
    "log"
    "net/http"
    "time"
)

func main() {
    http.HandleFunc("/", func(w http.
ResponseWriter, r *http.Request) {
        db, err := sql.Open("postgres",
"host=localhost
dbname=sretest sslmode=disable")
        if err != nil {
            log.Fatal(err)
        }
        defer db.Close()

        stmt, err := db.Prepare("INSERT INTO data
(metric, value, created) VALUES ($1, $2, $3)")
        if err != nil {
            log.Fatal(err)
        }
        defer stmt.Close()

        res, err := stmt.Exec("GET /", 1,
time.Now())
        if err != nil || res == nil {
            log.Fatal(err)
        }

        w.Header().Set("Content-Type", "application/
json; charset=utf-8")
        fmt.Fprintf(w, "{\"hello\": \"world\"}")
    })

    log.Println("Starting server...")
    log.Println("Running on http://localhost:8080")
    log.Fatal(http.ListenAndServe(":8080", http.
DefaultServeMux))
}
```

For this to work, you'll need to create a PostgreSQL database named `sretest` locally and run `create table data (metric text, value float, created timestamp);` to create the table to insert data into. Then, after loading the page a few times, you can query the database with the following query to get all of the metrics logged today:

```
sretest=# select metric, sum(value) from data where
created >=
now()::date group by metric;
 metric | sum
--------+-----
 GET /  |   6
(1 row)
```

However, instead of implementing this yourself, there are lots of great push-based applications you can use that are much more robust than just shoving time series data into a PostgreSQL database.

StatsD

We gave an example of StatsD and described its basic attributes in the *Instrumenting an application* section. It was written in JavaScript, but its specification has since been reimplemented in many languages to add new features and improved performance. Many companies sell StatsD-based monitoring infrastructure. Traditionally, people used Graphite as the backend storage for StatsD, but as its popularity has grown, people have begun using many different datastores with StatsD.

Telegraf

Telegraf is built by the company behind InfluxDB. It is built to write to InfluxDB and be the T in their TICK monitoring stack. **TICK** stands for **Telegraf, InfluxDB, Chronograf (their graphing and web UI), and Kapacitor (their alerting framework)**. That being said, it supports many different backends and inputs for data. It is written in Go.

ELK

ELK is an acronym for **Elasticsearch, Logstash, and Kibana**. In recent years, this stack has been called the Elastic Stack, as it now includes replacements for Logstash, called Beats. All of these products (and many others) are maintained by the Elastic company.

Elasticsearch is a datastore (it's technically a search engine with a JSON API and a built-in datastore), Logstash is a log processor, and Kibana is a web UI for accessing Elasticsearch's search functionality and turning the output into graphs and tables. I include this because some people enjoy writing log lines for their metrics and then writing Logstash parsing rules to turn log lines into metrics. There are lots of ways to implement this, as Logstash has a bunch of competitors, and you can configure Logstash, or tools like Google's mtail, to write to other metrics services. I personally find log parsing to be fragile, but that feeling comes from the days of having to write parsing logic for lots of different log files that would change without warning and break metric ingestion. Now that people write logs out in various types of formatted lines (such as JSON or Protocol buffers), this is much less of an issue. I still would much rather just use client libraries to write out metrics, but many organizations enjoy log-based metrics, and there can be lots of benefits to having all of the data fidelity logs can provide.

Displaying monitoring information

Now that you are collecting your data and writing it into storage, you can start to display it to users. Many of the previously mentioned monitoring tools provide their own visualization systems. Others recommend that you bring your own. One popular open-source tool for this is Grafana.

Whatever you use to visualize and access your metrics, there are four categories of tools that people often use to get and share their data:

♦ Arbitrary queries

♦ Graphs

♦ Dashboards

♦ Chatbots

Let us talk about why each is useful and things to keep in mind for each of these features.

Arbitrary queries

Everyone needs the ability to create a query of the metrics and logs you are building. The reason is pretty straightforward—metrics are useless if people cannot access them. While you can build people graphs and dashboards, while people are working, they will often have new and exciting questions, which they will need to write new queries against the metric datastore to get answers to. You want to empower your coworkers to be able to do their job without you. If you're the only one who can run queries, your job will quickly become "query executer" or no one will look at the metrics. Both of those outcomes are not great for your sanity.

The most straightforward query is to get the data points for a metric over a period. More complex queries depend on your datastore, what it allows, and how much it stores. Many log systems let you query by a regular expression over a period. Other data stores let you do queries where you do math, such as dividing the total number of requests grouped by a period (let us say five minutes for this example) by the count of errors grouped by a period (five minutes again). This would give you a table of percentage failures over five minutes, which can be very useful.

These adhoc queries are useful because often you have questions that you have not thought of before. Providing a simple web interface, or command-line interface, that lets anyone query the data helps people to find the value of monitoring.

If someone has a question, you can show them how to query the data and provide them with documentation, so they can run any query they want to, and answer their current and future questions. Making it easy for users to query data, and showing people how, will also help them to write more metrics and become better at deciding how and when to instrument their services.

Often, once users have these tables of data, they want it in a graph so that they can visualize large amounts of data. What is the phrase? If you give a mouse a cookie... they will want to graph cookie consumption over time?

Graphs

Graphs are mostly used as a visual representation of data over time. You probably remember making graphs in school when you were younger or seeing them used to show things on television news channels without any labels, or units, or any of the other things your teachers told you were required for a good graph. Graphs are common, and most people know how to interpret them, and while Miller's law states that the average human can hold less than ten objects in their head (thus making long tables of numbers difficult), you can display thousands of numbers at once using a graph.

The classic rules for a graph are as follows:

♦ The x axis (the bottom edge of the graph) contains time

♦ There must be a key for whatever is graphed

♦ All axes must be labelcd

♦ All numbers must have units

Not breaking these rules may be difficult. Some monitoring systems do not support units. Some graph systems only allow you to title graphs, and do not support adding labels to the axes, adding labels to individual lines, or adding keys. The majority of graph systems get the x axis thing right though.

I mention this because, often, after you generate a graph from whatever query you have made, there is a possibility that you will want to distribute it. You might put it in a document, send it in an email, put it in a group chat, or, if you are feeling particularly aggressive, print it out and slam it against the glass wall of a conference room and yell, "How do you like them apples?" as if you were Matt Damon in *Good Will Hunting*. Before you do some or all of these things though, remember that the graph will live on, often without you there to explain it. Working at Google, I often read through postmortem documents that had graphs that broke these rules, and the person who made them had left the organization long ago. With no way to know how to interpret a graph, it loses its original value.

I also suggest that if your graphing service can output static copies of graphs, you share the static image of the graph, along with a link to the query. As we will mention again in a bit, often, data will be lost or sampled down in a way where you lose the granularity, or accuracy, of your graph. If someone tries to figure out what you were talking about six months from now, even if your link to a graph no longer works, they will have the static image available. Also, it's worth mentioning that if you are going to share a link, make sure it is to an absolute time, not a relative one, so when people click on it, it links to the same time you were talking about.

Sometimes, you do not want to link to a single graph though. You want to share a collection of graphs. Alternatively, there are certain queries that you always want quick access to. This is what dashboards are for.

Dashboards

Dashboards are a collection of graphs that are usually all synchronized around a certain period. There are a lot of philosophies and opinions on what makes a good dashboard. Should a dashboard be on a TV? Should it be readable on mobile? Should there be more than five graphs? All of these questions are up for debate.

The best rule for building dashboards is to let your users see the data they need. If you are designing dashboards for yourself, or your team, here are some suggestions and things to keep in mind:

♦ If you are going to put a dashboard on a television, make sure it only has a few graphs and can be read from far away. If you have to run across the room to see what is going on, it probably isn't fulfilling its role.

♦ If you can, make a mobile-friendly version of your dashboard. More and more engineers first check outages and graphs on their phones before pulling out a laptop.

♦ There is a suggestion from some folks that you should limit your dashboards to five graphs at a time. I often end up with dashboards with a lot more than that. So, as a slightly more achievable metric, I suggest keeping the first three graphs to showing the most important things about a service. This way, when the page first loads, the stuff at the top is where you can focus. One good trick is to have links to other dashboards. If you have a graph about network traffic, below it have links to dashboards with more details about networking, in case the graph shows that something is wrong.

All of the suggestions from the graph section still apply. Make sure your graphs have units and labels if you can. You often will not be the only person looking at your dashboard. Your dashboard will probably last longer than your employment in the job.

Chatbots

I live in chat. I am often idling in Slack, IRC, Signal, Keybase, and Google Hangouts. One very useful tool for me is for graphs to appear in chat, or to have the ability to have a graph be requested from chat. GitHub writes in its blog `https://githubengineering.com/deploying-branches-to-github-com/` that they can just type `/graph me 20150517..20150523 @github.deploys.total` in Slack and get an image with a graph of the metric `github.deploys.total` for May 17, 2015 until May 23, 2015.

In past jobs, when an outage happened, we had the alert email include an image and link to the graph in question. For my personal websites, I get a message in a private chat once a day, with a graph for each of my sites telling me whether things are working properly. This is a pretty simple bot, which just runs on a `cron`.

Cron is a service that runs jobs at regular intervals. We talk about it in depth in *Chapter 10, Linux and Cloud Foundations*.

Chatbots that provide graphs are not a required part of the monitoring infrastructure, but over the years they have become one of my favorite ways to start an investigation or to begin digging into an issue. They provide a quick snapshot and are often very useful in conversations with coworkers about outages, especially when not everyone is in the same room, or you want a record of the conversation.

Managing and maintaining monitoring data

OK, now you have the basics of a monitoring system all set up. You have data flowing from your service to a datastore. You can visualize how things change over time. As you accumulate data over time, you are going to have to maintain that service. There are a few tricks for dealing with that.

The first way is a classic, tried, and true method—pay someone else to do it. There are tons of companies that sell hosted monitoring software. Datadog, Honeycomb, GrafanaCloud, InfluxCloud, Librato, Instrumental, New Relic, and many others, sell products with all sorts of features and tools where you do not have to host your monitoring tools.

Sometimes though, you do not have that kind of money, you have special security requirements, you cannot deal with the restrictions that hosted services impose, or you have some other reason not to relegate your monitoring infrastructure to someone else. In that case, first and foremost, you should monitor your monitoring.

Saying it seems straightforward, but if you run out of space, so that you stop storing monitoring data, you lose six months of monitoring data due to successive server failures, or something else, you will be sad. Monitoring is one of those systems that people forget about. Often, it gets spun up and just ignored because it *just works*. Make sure you keep an eye on it so that it does not fail when you need it most. As we've said many times through this chapter, make sure your service is doing the thing it is supposed to. In this case, it should be storing metrics.

Storage tends to be the thing that bites people about monitoring tools. This is because, often, people don't realize how much data they are collecting and how quickly they can use up all of their storage. If you have a limited amount of space, and you are monitoring many things, you will want to start deleting data at some point. The two common ways to deal with this are sampling and archiving. Usually, what this looks like is changing the granularity you can look at the farther you go back into history or requiring the monitoring system to get data from a slower data source if it is past a certain time in the past. Some services have this built in, but with others you will have to deal with it yourself. Thankfully, you can also just throw more storage at the issue, as hard drive prices have dropped consistently year over year.

Communicating about monitoring

We have talked a bit about communicating about monitoring to others throughout the chapter, but let's focus in on it for a minute. Firstly, if you have spent all this effort spinning up a monitoring system, make sure other people can access it. If you are going to go about spreading the gospel of your new monitoring system, make sure to test it. Otherwise, when you get them interested with all of your well-crafted emails, and poking and prodding, they will give up immediately if they cannot access it.

Do they even know there is monitoring?

They can be your boss, your product team, your engineering team, your friend who runs her website on the Raspberry Pi cluster sitting in the closet of your sister's house with a fiber connection, or anyone else you think should care about your service. The first thing to do is tell them about the new monitoring system. A well-written email with example graphs, links to documentation, and your favorite dashboards goes a long way. Yet far too frequently, this is ignored. The next step is sending messages in a positive tone showing a useful graph or dashboard. An excited statement like, "Did you see how many requests the site got last month?" with a link to the graph in a text message can do wonders. This is different than the first step. The first step is education by showing that monitoring exists. The second step is integrating it with your life and showing its usefulness constantly to another employee.

Another useful tool is carrying out lightweight user studies. Take a coworker out to coffee and ask them what they think of the monitoring. Do they find it useful? Is there data they wish they had but don't know how to get? This can inform the documentation you can write for your team or get you to pair program with another engineer to help them implement a new metric in a service. Avoid just doing it for someone. Instead, figure out how to help them to help themselves. Also, make sure you share what they learn with the rest of the team. If one person has a question, very often someone else has the same question.

> We talk about user studies in depth in *Chapter 8, User Experience*.

As monitoring becomes more widely used, people may start using the monitoring system in new and exciting ways. Monitoring graphs may be used in executive summaries presented at board meetings. Developers may ask to integrate not just production data, but also to monitor data from their development environments to help debug performance issues.

Keep an eye out for new use cases, as you want to make sure the tools are performing at a level your teammates find useful. Also, this is a good time to remind you to continue to perform quarterly audits of the things you are monitoring. If you find issues with how queries are using the system, work with them to understand misconceptions and to fix bugs that might exist in their code.

Your monitoring service is just another product. This is true for all of your infrastructure. It will improve with market research, usability studies, and constant iteration based on feedback from your *customers*.

References and related reading

Related to the code in this chapter, the following are links to documentation for frameworks, programming languages, and other code.

1. Sinatra is a web framework for Ruby and has excellent online documentation at `http://sinatrarb.com/`

2. The StatsD Ruby library documentation is at `http://www.rubydoc.info/github/reinh/statsd/Statsd`

3. I am using Ruby 2.5.0, whose documentation is at `https://ruby-doc.org/core-2.5.0/`

4. An overview of StatsD—`https://github.com/etsy/statsd/`

5. The Prometheus Go client documentation—`https://godoc.org/github.com/prometheus/client_golang/prometheus`

6. The Go language documentation—`https://golang.org/doc/`

7. An overview of Prometheus—`https://prometheus.io/`

8. Oxford Dictionaries (`https://en.oxforddictionaries.com/definition/monitor`)

Future reading

No book should ever be the sum of all knowledge. It is impossible. As I mentioned earlier, there are many monitoring philosophies, and while the following books and websites touch on some of them, neither my chapter, nor these other books are the be all and end all.

♦ *Distributed Systems Observability, Sridharan Cindy, O'Reilly Media*, 2018, `distributed-systems-observability-ebook.humio.com/`

♦ *Monitoring, the Prometheus Way, Volz Julius*, YouTube, 8 May 2017, `www.youtube.com/watch?v=PDxcEzu62jk`

♦ *Think Stats*, 2nd edition, *Downey Allen, O'Reilly Media*, 2014

♦ *The Art of Monitoring, Turnbull James*, 2016

Summary

Now that the metrics and logs are flowing, and people love this new system you set up, it is time to start using it for what it was meant for—waking people up at three in the morning because of an emergency.

In this chapter, we learned about a variety of tools that you can use for monitoring, plus why monitoring is useful and important.

In the next chapter, we will be talking about alerting team members about outages and how to run incident response in such a way that people will not be afraid of responding to an incident. Let's make sure that everyone will be laughing and hugging, instead of running for the doors!

3

INCIDENT RESPONSE

Incident response is the next level in the hierarchy we introduced in *Chapter 1, Introduction*. While introducing monitoring into your organization, or project, is mostly a technical exercise, incident response is almost all process and people. Incident response builds upon the world of data that we built using monitoring and starts our feedback loop, helping us to find and tighten our monitoring for our services. This shows us what is important, because if we do not get an alert and someone tells us that our service was not working, then we were not monitoring the right things.

The inverse of this is also true, although rarer—when we do not launch or deliver new features because we spend all of our time trying to reach a level of reliability that our service has trouble reaching.

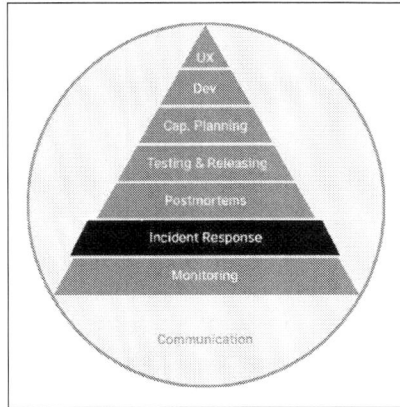

Figure 1: Our current position in the hierarchy

In this chapter, we will define incidents and explain how to respond to them. The chapter will help you to establish processes of alerting and communicating during an incident. This will set you and your team up for success when responding to the fact that everything is broken and no one is happy.

What is an incident?

Let us start with the basics—incidents are scary. They cause our bodies to produce adrenaline and make our hearts race. They force us to stop what we are doing and reevaluate. Commonly, when responding to incidents, we try to figure out what is going on and what is not working while in a panicked state.

An incident is when something significant happens and it requires you to change your path and normal actions. It could be a cup of coffee spilling on you and you need to change your clothes. An accident could happen during your commute to work, causing you to have to take a different route.

You could fall and break your arm and have to spend the next three months wearing a cast. All of these incidents require you to do something immediately and then, often, make longer-term changes to your plans.

In software, incidents can be similar. They tend to be a failure due to a change in the system (either in the system itself or the input the system is receiving) or something changing about the environment the system runs in. The system itself changing is usually due to the deployment of code or a change in scale that the system operates in.

Figure 2: In this example diagram, we have a load balancer sending traffic to four identical pieces of software. The load balancer is sending equivalent traffic to all four. However, because of a bug, some requests are returning invalid results. To all automated systems this service looks healthy, but it has bugs that are causing real damage to the business by giving users undesirable results.

The input to a web server changing could be due to many different types of changes. It could be a malicious user sending millions of corrupted packets to your server. It could be an article in The New York Times about your service that means you get a million new users. It could also just be the launch of a new feature that adds new types of connections to your servers.

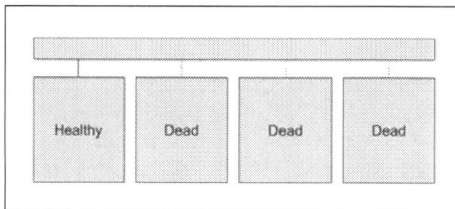

Figure 3: In this diagram, increased traffic has caused three out of four of our pieces of software to die. The fourth one is probably about to fail. The software likely did not have enough memory or CPU to handle the requests, so stopped being able to respond to health checks and the load balancer marked them as unhealthy or dead. The dead tasks are no longer receiving traffic.

The environment changing could be a database upgrade, new hardware with faulty RAM, a Linux kernel upgrade that accidentally changes the permissions of some files, or even a classic network partition. An environment change could even be your database no longer being available.

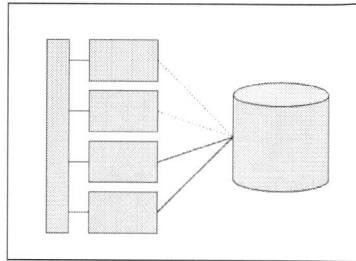

Figure 4: In our third example diagram, there is some sort of network instability, so two of the pieces of software cannot talk to the database on the right. The load balancer in this case is not including database connectivity as part of its health check, so the task is still in service. That being said, 50% of requests are probably incorrect, as the tasks cannot talk to the database.

The fact that the world is made up of constant chaos means that change can come from any direction. The above are some possible examples and are just a subset of the infinite number of things that could go wrong. Incidents are often proof that we, as humans, are not omnipotent. We write the software and do not know everything, so events happen that we have not planned for, which can often cause software to act in ways that are not to our liking.

What is incident response?

Incident response is responding to an incident that happens. A shocking revelation and wildly unpredictable definition, I know!

Incident response is usually a set of a few actions:

♦ Noticing that something is not right

♦ Communicating that something is not right

♦ Doing something to make things right

Noticing comes through alerting. Sometimes that alert is like a 911 call—an SOS message from a human who has seen an error in your software. A human alert could come in the form of a text message from a friend, an email from a coworker, a ticket to a support system, or even a yell from across the room. Human escalations can be useful, but usually it is preferred to receive alerts from automated systems. Automated systems are preferred because, unlike humans, they are consistent and can be defined in a consistent manner. Humans will come up with new and unique ways to break your system. Automated systems will use your system consistently. When I say automated systems, I mean monitoring like we described in *Chapter 2, Monitoring*. Monitoring sees that systems are not okay and fires off an alert requesting that a human look at a part of the system.

Figure 5: A drawing of someone staring at a computer that is literally on fire. Usually, when we say something is on fire, it's a simile for something that is broken.

One of the most human things to do is to communicate with others. When you receive an alert, or realize an incident is in progress, you must ask yourself a question—how do you tell other humans that everything is okay? Usually, you do this with body language, but in the software world, often, no output means the software is working correctly. If an incident is not going well, you want to let your team know that someone is looking at things and they should not be worried. In your own words, you should try and promote calm like a parent does to a child with an injury—in a soft and soothing way. You reassure the child that everything will be alright. With grown-ups though, you need to skate a fine line—be soothing, but also make sure people know when you need help. On top of presenting this calm demeanor, you still need to keep people updated.

If they are dependent on you, they need to know you're still there and working on fixing the system. You need to make sure that you acknowledge their concerns. When everything is back to normal, you often need to calm the nerves of the people around you that an outage like this will not happen again. Your goal is to present confidence, reliability, and honesty to the outside world. This is important because you are showing that you know what you are doing and giving customers a reason to trust you.

Figure 6: A drawing of the same computer on fire, with caution tape surrounding it and the person yelling into a megaphone.

During all of this communication, you need to resolve the incident. You need to make sure that you quickly recover and also that the incident never happens again. The goal is always to have the shortest downtime, and because of this, the incident responder tries to put out the fire before figuring out what started the fire. This is not always possible, but many organizations have quick fixes available to make sure outages are short. For example, if broken code is released, many organizations have a one-click button to undo a code release.

Figure 7: A drawing of the person hosing down the computer with a fire hose and water. While the computer would probably not work after this fix, it would stop the fire from spreading.

Now that we have set the stage for what incidents and incident response are, let us dig into the details of how to notify our team of an incident's occurrence with alerting.

Alerting

Alerting is a contentious topic. It is contentious because no one wants to be alerted. An alert is a queue that requires you to work, so if an alert is implemented poorly, or without thought, it can quickly disrupt your life and sour your relationship with a project. It is such a common problem that almost every field, company, and person has an opinion on the topic. Doctors have policies that state how long they can work for, along with when and how they can be paged. The **Federal Aviation Administration** (**FAA**) of the United States has requirements for pilots and many countries keep a close eye on the health of their military units that work in high-stress situations.

> Being paged is an old but common term. It refers to the act of someone trying to alert you. It comes from the days when, when someone was oncall, they carried a physical device, called a pager, that would display a phone number you needed to call and make noise, so you knew you had to do something.

As we have become more connected online, some organizations have come to expect you to answer every email quickly, no matter the time of day. This can be overwhelming to you as an individual. When do you disconnect from work when you have a device with you all the time that can pull you back into work? Defining what your relationship is with work and making sure that your employer agrees with that relationship, and that it is at the right level for you, your family, your product, and your team is not trivial.

When do you alert?

This all leads to the question of when to alert. What is the query that forces someone to get notified that something is wrong? We start with this question and not with who we alert, or how we alert, because of the question we asked in *Chapter 2, Monitoring*—is our service working?

If the answer to this question is often no, then it should create the most serious of alerts. You want someone to know and react. Often, this means a customer is affected. I usually think of a serious incident as being something that a customer will see and that prompts them to get in touch with us because our product is broken. For a media website, example queries are:

♦ Can our viewers see our content and access our website?

♦ Can our content creators create content?

For an infrastructure project, an incident could be that jobs are not running, data is being lost in the database, or services are not able to talk to each other. You want to focus on symptoms (things that are actually broken) and not things that could be causing an outage. We call this category of failures "page-worthy," "wake someone up," or "critical" alerts. I will stick with the term "critical" for the rest of the chapter, but I tend to think of this category of alerts as the ones that I would want to be woken up for at three in the morning.

The second category of alerts is the "eventually," "this will probably hurt us soon," "oh, that is weird," or "non-critical" bucket. I will stick with "non-critical" for the rest of the chapter, but this category is everything else you might worry about that doesn't have to be dealt with right now. Certain organizations might separate alerts in more detail and specify reaction times based on the type of alert:

♦ **Critical**: Respond within 30 minutes

♦ **Non-critical, today**: Respond within 24 hours

♦ **Non-critical, eventually**: Put into the ticket work
   queue for someone to pick up in the next few weeks

This categorization is an example. Whatever your
categorization is, it will probably come from your team's
SLIs, SLOs, and SLAs, if you have them. For example, you
are breaking an SLO or SLA, so that is probably worthy
of a critical alert.

The key to this bucketing is defining what type of reaction
is necessary for the person who is reacting, and also making
sure that the person responding agrees with the level. If you
send an urgent alert to someone and there is nothing to do,
or they do not believe it is urgent, then when something that
truly is urgent comes up, the chance that they will ignore it will
increase dramatically. See the story of the boy who cried wolf
for an example: a shepherd lies to his village about there being
a wolf attacking his flock. He repeatedly lies about the wolf.
The villagers stop believing him. When there finally is a wolf,
the wolf comes in and kills the shepherd and his flock. No one
from the village comes to help him as he cries for help and is
eaten alive. This is dramatic, but if a service keeps notifying
you about things that you do not care about, you will ignore
it. This is human nature.

One trick to solving this problem is to have a weekly email
thread, or discussion, about all of the past week's alerts:

♦ Did we respond appropriately to all alerts? If we
   received an alert, did we care? If not, we should
   probably change the alert, or delete it, because we
   aren't reacting to it.

♦ Was each alert at the appropriate level? If we were
   woken up for something that we could not act on, was
   it worth waking up for? Should we have just waited
   until the morning to look at it? The inverse is true
   as well—did a subtler alert need to be more critical
   to gain more immediate attention?

♦ Should we keep this alert? Alerts take time away from the receiver. Alerts often cause adrenaline surges and interrupt everything. If this alert is not important, or a good use of our time, we should delete it for the sake of our sanity.

♦ Should we change this alert in any way? Maybe the text of the alert does not tell us what to look at or is not worded in a way that everyone understands what it is trying to tell us.

♦ Did things happen that we wish we were alerted about? Should we create new alerts for things that we should have seen but didn't?

These questions let us evaluate each alert that fired and decide as a group whether the alerts that fired were useful. This is where you can find out whether one engineer feels that an alert is too sensitive and he or she was never able to correlate the alert with a problem. You can also decide to adjust the thresholds for an alert that is valuable but doesn't work properly during off-hours because of low traffic.

In essence, like monitoring, alerting is a constantly changing thing. Be wary of alerting too often, because you will lower the effectiveness for whoever receives the alert. Constant evaluation is needed to make sure that alerts are useful and reacted to correctly.

How do you alert?

Once you have defined when to alert, it is time to decide where alerts will go and how they will get to people. You can send them in many ways. Some common ways to notify people include:

♦ A phone call

♦ An SMS message

♦ A dedicated app that makes loud noises

♦ A group chat message

♦ An email

♦ A loud siren in an office

Some delivery methods are better than others. Choosing a delivery method depends on the frequency and volume of your alerts, and also on how people are expected to respond to an alert. A loud siren would probably result in everyone quitting if you were at a small software start-up, but for software running a nuclear reactor, maybe a loud siren isn't a bad idea. An IRC channel is an excellent place for a constant stream of alerts but can also be a place where you might miss some things. Google used to have a channel that was a stream of every alert, for every service across the entire company. This was great because you could see when similar failures hit teams and know if there was some dependency issue hitting lots of teams. The downside of this channel was that there were always alerts firing, so you couldn't easily follow anything.

An email can be great because you can include graphs and longer descriptions. More modern group chat applications, like Slack, allow you to embed images with messages from bots, so you can push alerts that have context for them. Phone calls can be great because you can configure most smartphones to always ring when calls from a certain number come in. Equally, mobile apps like PagerDuty and VictorOps can override system volume levels on a user's smartphone and make loud noises when things are critical. Sometimes, just a text message will do. You can use a service like Twilio to send a text message when there is an issue. One of the world's simplest monitoring and alerting systems is the following script on a one-minute `cron`:

```
#! /bin/bash

DOMAIN="fake.example.com"
status_code=$(curl -sL -o /dev/null -w "%{http_
code}" $DOMAIN)
if [[ $status_code -ne 200 ]]; then
  echo "$DOMAIN is down!"
  curl -s -XPOST https://api.twilio.com/2010-04-
01/Accounts/$TWILIO_ACCOUNT_SID/Messages.json \
```

```
    -d "Body=$DOMAIN%20is%20down!" \
    -d "To=%2B$MY_NUMBER" \
    -d "From=%2B13372430910" \

    -u "$TWILIO_ACCOUNT_SID:$TWILIO_ACCOUNT_TOKEN"
fi
```

Tip: It is not advisable to store passwords or tokens in code. This is because tools such as TruffleHog scan source code looking for things that look like passwords or account tokens. Instead, you can use external configuration tools or environment variables to pass in sensitive tokens to your application.

A quick explanation of this Bash script: `#! /bin/bash` is the shebang, sha-bang, or hash-bang. When a text file starts with a hash (#), a bang (!), and a path to an executable (/bin/bash), that executable is used to interpret the file. This is only true in Unix-like operating systems. In this case, we are writing code for Bash, a common shell and scripting language:

- `DOMAIN="fake.example.com"` is setting the variable `$DOMAIN` to the domain we want to check.

- `status_code=$(curl -sL -o /dev/null -w "%{http_code}" $DOMAIN)` is setting the variable `$status_code` to the HTTP status code of sending a GET request to `$DOMAIN`. The `-sL` flags tell `curl` to be silent and to follow any redirects. `-o /dev/null` tells `curl` to send its output to `/dev/null`, a special Unix file that throws away all of the content it receives. `-w "%{http_code}"` is telling `curl` we only want to save the HTTP response code. The `status_code=$()` is telling Bash we want to run the command inside of the parentheses and assign it to `$status_code`.

- `if [[ $status_code -ne 200 ]]; then` is checking whether `$status_code` does not equal 200. If it does not, then we need to alert. The `fi` a few lines later closes this `if` block.

♦ The final large `curl` command is sending a POST request to Twilio's API. `$TWILIO_ACCOUNT_SID`, `$TWILIO_ACCOUNT_TOKEN`, and `$MY_NUMBER` are expected to come from the environment this script is being run inside of. Each of the `-d` flags are telling `curl` to send that piece of data in the post body. We are URL encoding the data we are sending, which is why we say the `From` field is `%2B13372430910` instead of `+13372430910`. It is also why we say `Body` equals `$DOMAIN%20is%20down!` instead of `$DOMAIN is down!`. `-XPOST` and this tells `curl` to send a POST request instead of the default GET.

> **NOTE**: We talk about URL and HTTP encoding more in *Chapter 10, Linux and Cloud Foundations*. We also talk about `curl` in *Chapter 9, Networking Foundations*.

The key to all of these systems is to find a system that is affordable, reliable, and something that whoever is receiving the alerts will look at. If no one at your work reads their emails, then don't send them alert emails. Also, speaking of reliable, you can always send multiple copies of an alert. I like sending one to chat, one to SMS, and one to email. I will get it somehow!

As we mentioned for monitoring systems, alerting systems are software too and are not always reliable. How reliable they are is up to you and your team. How dangerous is it if an alert doesn't reach you? You can diversify your alerting tools to improve the chance of an alert being delivered. You could use Twilio to send a text message, Google Mail to send an email, and IRC to deliver a chat message. The message system could be set up so that if one fails, another can pick up the slack. It all depends on what you pick, but often alerting systems operate using "Master Election" or "Leader Election". This is a process, usually built on top of the Paxos or Raft algorithms for a set of identical servers to decide on who is going to be the leader and do the actual work.

Alerting services

There are a lot of ways to send alerts. We have mainly been talking about the interface that developers have to send the alert. You also need to think about how the alerts will flow to the actual user. As with monitoring, there are a bunch of companies that you can pay to funnel your alerts from your monitoring system to a device of your choice:

♦ PagerDuty

♦ VictorOps

♦ OpsGenie

There are also open-source solutions and you can always write your own system. As I mentioned earlier in this section, there are services that deliver messages for you, so it all just depends where in the pipeline you want to stop being in control of things and when you want to delegate to others. I generally suggest companies do not handle alerting delivery if they can help it, because building a very reliable alert delivery system can be difficult and the consequences of not delivering an alert can be very severe.

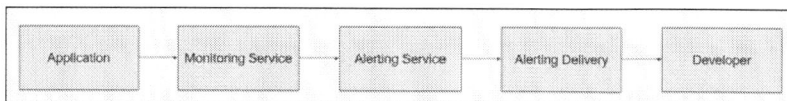

Figure 8: A simplification of an alerting pipeline. The application streams metrics and events to the monitoring service. The alerting service queries the monitoring service for the status of things and if they are out of bounds, sends messages for alerting delivery. Alerting delivery then gets alerts to the developer (or whomever).

Let's look at an example alerting pipeline if you're building it yourself: if you use Amazon CloudWatch as your monitoring system, CloudWatch Alarms, its alerting service, is recommended to pipe that data to other places. How CloudWatch Alarms works is that it shoves all state changes around an alert into Amazon's **Simple Notification Service** (**SNS**). Amazon SNS is a hosted Pub/Sub service. Amazon gives you email delivery for free of all the notifications that come from an SNS topic for free.

You could also have a piece of software that turns SNS notifications into API calls to Twilio or you could run something like Plivo, which is an open-source piece of software that lets you make phone calls with code and have a small piece of code that subscribes to your SNS alert topic and pipes alerts into phone calls.

NOTE: We talk about queues and Pub/Sub in *Chapter 10, Linux and Cloud Foundations.*

All of this is to say that you need to find the pipeline that is right for your company. Often, for many smaller companies, finding a cheap pipeline that keeps your engineers notified is all you need. For very large companies, you may want to build and control the entire pipeline, so you can have specific delivery guarantees. Google, for example, has custom software for every layer of its stack, from monitoring software to how it delivers alerts. Google has a global system that can essentially page any engineer using email. Each engineer determines how they want their pages delivered and specifies that in a config file. So, you send an alert email to a service target, which then looks up the schedule for that service, then alerts the on-call engineer in the way that the engineer prefers. This works for Google but that is three separate pieces of software that a team has to maintain. That might not be good for you and your constraints. At one job I worked at, we just used a piece of software to pipe alerts into Slack and two of our employees had notifications set to "always" for that channel. It wasn't great but it worked. The next step we were looking into was piping all of those alerts into a larger alert system, but that would have cost us around $200 USD a month, which is money that we just did not have. Find the balance that's right for you between cost, energy to maintain, and reliability.

So, what do we want to include in our alert? Once we know how to deliver it, we need to know what to say.

What is in an alert?

The first thing to think about is the initial string. This is often the subject of the email, the first message in a chat, or the alert header. It should be short and descriptive. Tim Pope, a prolific software developer in the Vim open-source community, has some formatting suggestions for committing messages in Git, a version control system, that I like for alerts as well (`http://tbaggery.com/2008/04/19/a-note-about-git-commit-messages.html`). Most of his advice is hyper-specific for Git, but there are some things that we can take away that are very useful:

♦ Subjects should be less than 50 characters. This provides a quick understanding of why the person is being alerted.

♦ Use the imperative. This is important especially because you will often want to give instructions on what to do if this error fires. For example, saying, "Go to AWS console and terminate instance i–1234567890."

♦ Provide an extra explanation after the subject. If your alerting service allows it, include live details like graphs or evaluations of metrics. Also, include links to documentation that would be useful to the person responding to the alert.

If you're receiving a phone call, often the software will read just the subject line of the alert into the call. As the receiver of the call, you will just hear a computer voice describing the alert. In comparison, an email or text message may have the full description and images. Other services just send a link to the description.

Who do you alert?

Now that we are sending alerts that are easy to understand and can get to people, we have to decide who should receive our alerts. Remember how, earlier in the chapter, I said that alerting is a contentious issue? This is because people often want alerts to be sent, but they do not want to be the person who receives the alert.

By definition, an alert is interruptive. The need to do incident response is very rarely something that you know is coming, so you are forced to drop everything immediately. It is also often the case that incident response is not a primary part of a person's job, so they also have to push off deadlines and stop what they are working on.

Usually, you create a schedule for who is on call. Sometimes this is a schedule per-service, whereas other times it's just a pool of all engineers. Two of the most well-known schedules for on call are "rotate once a week" and the "three-four split". On "rotate once a week" every seven days the current on-call (often called the primary) person is taken off-call and the on-call backup (often called the secondary, on call partner, or buddy) person becomes the primary. Then, a new person, who has been off call the longest, becomes the secondary.

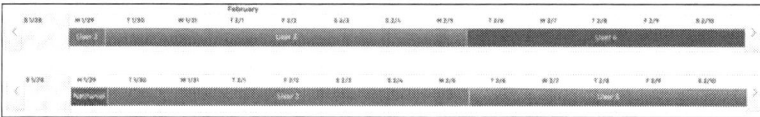

Figure 9: Example of a weekly on-call rotation schedule. This image shows two weeks of an on-call schedule. The first row shows a primary on-call schedule and every seven days the person on call changes. The second row is that person's secondary or on-call partner. Usually, the same people are in both the rotation for primary and secondary. The same person should never be both primary and secondary, so secondary follows a similar but different schedule.

In the three-four split, Monday through to Thursday, person A is primary and person B is secondary. On Friday, Saturday, and Sunday, person A is secondary and person B is primary. On Monday, both primary and secondary change to new people.

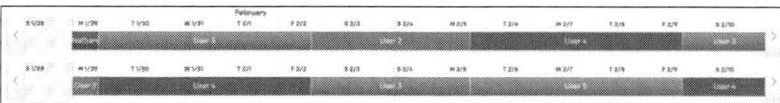

Figure 10: Example of a three-four split rotation schedule. Like the weekly schedule, the same people are in both the primary (first row) schedule and the secondary (second row) schedule, but the same person is never on call for both rotations. This image shows two weeks of on-call schedule. The shorter bars are the three-day weekend portion of the rotation, while the longer bars are the four-day weekday portion.

These are just two example schedules you could use. There are a million different schedules that you can use and the key is just figuring out a schedule that people are happy with. The options also change if you have multiple teams. If you have a team in London and a team in Seattle, then each office can do 12 hours and pass responsibilities back and forth. You can also have new people added only to the secondary schedule at first and then, after being secondary on-call once or twice, promote them to being in both schedules.

Whatever schedule your team picks, make sure that it works for everyone on call and people understand when they need to be available. If you can help it, try to avoid getting a message saying, "Oh shoot! Am I on call? I just sat down to watch a play and I don't have my laptop, so can someone else get this?"

Being on call

On-call life can be very stressful. The stress comes from not knowing what is going to happen, plus not being able to work on the projects that you actually enjoy. To make it a better experience for those involved, the following are some tips and general policies for keeping everyone happy:

♦ When deciding who to alert, do not alert everyone unless you have less than three people to alert. If you alert everyone, then you are alerting no one. I say less than three because with one or two people, in a rotation that has a primary and a secondary, you both are always on call anyway. You can do a rotation, but it might be just as easy to alert you both. Once you have three people, then one person can have time off.

♦ Make sure there is an on-call schedule and people know when they are the on-call person. People should know how long they will be on call and when they next need to be on call. Usually, it helps to have the next three months of on call scheduled, so that people know if they need to be available and they can schedule life and work time.

Not having on-call scheduling ahead of time can be frustrating for employees and tends to mean that people take less vacations because they don't know when they will be needed at work.

♦ Provide people with a backup when they are on call. As humans, we have lives outside of work. If an on-call has a backup, then they can feel less stress about spending an hour on the subway without cell service or not having coverage when they see a movie. It is completely possible to have a single person on call for a service, but having a backup provides that person with support and makes sure they aren't alone.

♦ Create an explicit escalation policy for on-call folks (and alerting systems) to follow. If there is only one team, that is usually the on-call person, their backup, and then the rest of the team. If there are multiple sites (for example, one in Asia and one in the Americas), then often, after the backup, the on-call person at the other site is alerted before everyone else. This is important so that if a person is not available, the alert system has someone else to contact. For example, I take the subway to work and it doesn't have Wi-Fi or cell phone reception. During my commute, I am not contactable. As such, if an alert fires during this time, the system won't be able to reach me and instead it will try to reach my on-call partner. If they are asleep or also on the subway, it alerts the rest of the team.

♦ Escalation policies for other teams should also be visible. This isn't that valuable for very small companies, but once you have multiple engineering teams, making it easy for one team to send an alert to another team and land on the correct person is incredibly important. It is important because a team designates an on-call person and that person is aware of the current state of their software and is also set up to be responsive during that time period.

If you were to message a random person on a team, instead of their dedicated on-call, you might not get an answer or you might get an incorrect one. If someone reaches out to you and you are not the on-call for your team, you should probably redirect them to the correct person and also send them the information of where to look so next time they escalate to the right person.

♦ Define what a person's responsibilities are while on call. Are they expected to still do normal work? Do they need to travel with their laptop and a wireless internet connection? What is an acceptable response time to alerts? Do they need to write up any documentation after an alert or incident? Also, make sure the hours and times of responsibilities are addressed. For example, some services have different SLOs during business hours and at night. So maybe an on-call person can mute all alerts that happen between 10pm and 6am, or maybe the allowed response time is longer at night. If there is a team in a different time zone, as we mentioned above, the on-call may need to be less available at night because they go from being the primary to the tertiary on-call because the primary is now someone else in another time zone.

♦ Compensate people more for being on call. That is, if possible, pay people extra for being available outside of traditional work hours. My general philosophy is that you should get a 15% pay bump while on call. This number is pretty arbitrary, so could be anything, but 15% assumes that you're working six hours extra over the normal 40 hours per week in the US. This pay increase is not always feasible and I have seen managers find all sorts of ways to compensate employees for their time on call. One friend gets a day off for every ten days he is on call. Another friend gets extra stock options. A third friend, at a very small start-up, just gets taken out for a very nice dinner once a month because she is always on call.

Adding new people to a rotation takes time. Make sure that you provide people with support as they are ramping up to being on call. Let someone shadow a primary on-call person to see what receiving an alert is like, without having to do the response work. Having a seasoned secondary around when someone has their first primary shift is great; just make sure that the seasoned person doesn't try to do things for the new primary person, unless they ask for help. Often, a more seasoned developer tries to do things for someone while they are trying to learn because they get frustrated with the newer person going slowly or doing things slightly differently. You can also use tools like Wheel of Misfortunes and DiRT to train new people before they join a rotation. We talk about these practices in *Chapter 5, Testing and Releasing*.

Communication

Once someone has been alerted, and they have acknowledged or "ACK"ed an alert, they need to start communicating. My rule of thumb is that you should send a message, no matter what, to all stakeholders every 30 minutes. If nothing has changed, then tell them. Know your audience, so do not go too technical if you do not need to, but if your audience is technical, then share what you can, but keep it brief. If it is an internal communication, then make sure to tell people where to go if they need to know more:

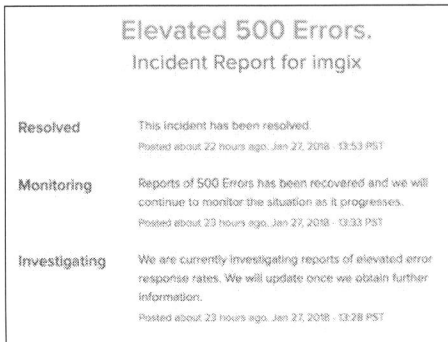

Figure 11: Screenshot of an Imgix (an image CDN company) outage status page. It shows updates from the company to the public in reverse chronological order. The oldest message, at the bottom, is when it first notified the public about the outage, then five minutes later it provided an update. 20 minutes after that, it posted the final message saying the incident was over and had been resolved.

Outside of your 30-minute updates, explain what you're doing in your team chat so that people can follow along and you have a log for the future. You should also do this so that work is not duplicated and people who are helping can contribute with educated questions and suggestions. Even if no one else is awake, it can be helpful for people to read your log when they come online, to understand the current status of the incident.

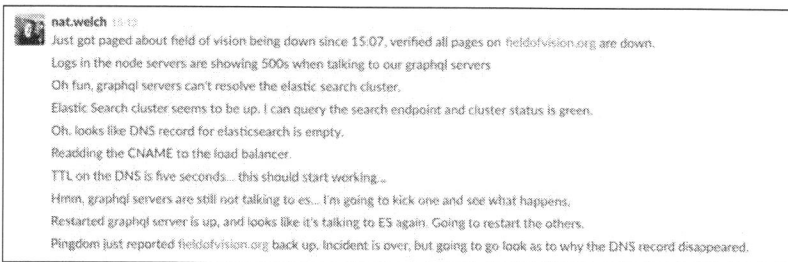

nat.welch 18:13

Just got paged about field of vision being down since 15:07, verified all pages on fieldofvision.org are down.

Logs in the node servers are showing 500s when talking to our graphql servers

Oh fun, graphql servers can't resolve the elastic search cluster.

Elastic Search cluster seems to be up. I can query the search endpoint and cluster status is green.

Oh, looks like DNS record for elasticsearch is empty.

Readding the CNAME to the load balancer.

TTL on the DNS is five seconds... this should start working...

Hmm, graphql servers are still not talking to es... I'm going to kick one and see what happens.

Restarted graphql server is up, and looks like it's talking to ES again. Going to restart the others.

Pingdom just reported fieldofvision.org back up. Incident is over, but going to go look as to why the DNS record disappeared.

Figure 12: Example of talking to yourself during an outage

A good setup is often two channels. One channel can be used for discussion by people working on the outage and one channel can be used for people affected by the incident. Two channels split the discussion but keep things focused in their respective rooms. Having just the person on your team in charge of communication in the customer channel will also keep messaging consistent and give customers a single point of contact to send information back to the group of folks responding to the incident.

If you use just a single channel to discuss things, then make sure you set the mood as serious and create the expectation that it's a serious discussion place only, so you can keep things on topic and not too noisy. If you don't set this mood, you can get lots of chatter and conflicting information, which may make your incident last longer than it needs to or create extra confusion.

After you are alerted, and you are trying to figure out how to fix things, make sure that you keep talking to your team and also set a time to ask for help. A coworker once suggested that if you still have no idea what is wrong after 10 minutes of working on an issue, then start asking for help. Usually, at 10 minutes I start to ping my secondary, because then I will know whether I can handle it by myself or whether I will need a second pair of hands. If they do not know either, then bring in other people. Slowly grow those involved until you know what is not working and how to make the system healthy.

Incident Command System (ICS)

One important aspect of communication is who is in charge. With all of the communication and the work needed to actually repair a broken system, during a large incident a single person can get overwhelmed. I mentioned bringing people in to help and that's when it helps to have trained your team ahead of time in the **National Incident Management System's** (**NIMS**) ICS. ICS is a system from the 1970s, built for combating California wildfires. It focuses on making it easy for many different organizations to work together to deal with an incident. NIMS is a system designed in the US, which adopted and expanded ICS after 9/11. It has been used to respond to all sorts of national disasters across the country.

ICS is often used in the SRE world because of its focus on growing and scaling an ad hoc organization of people responding to an incident, or series of incidents, as the incident grows or continues for long periods of time. This is really important in larger organizations that have lots of teams that may be affected by an outage. For example, a networking outage causes a cascading set of failures across the company. Each team needs to work together to stop more services from failing, to make sure work isn't done twice, and to coordinate messaging to those affected who cannot do anything.

The first rule of ICS is that whoever is on the scene first is in charge. This is almost always the on-call person and they call the shots. If anyone else shows up, then until the role is delegated, no matter the seniority or organization, the first on the scene is in charge. The point of this is to formalize the structure of the incident to make sure no one has multiple bosses. You can imagine the results of this in the scenario of a wildfire. A crew of fire fighters arrives on the scene and they are dealing with the fire. Then, both a police chief and a fire chief show up, then a group of police officers shows up. This is a fire, so people might think that it's best to listen to the fire chief, but the normal structure dictates they must follow the police chief.

Thanks to ICS, the officers don't have to think during the incident because only one person is in charge. That person is the incident commander, who was the initial person to show up on the scene. In this case, it was probably the most senior person of the first fire crew on the scene. However, let us not forget about delegation. There will be tasks that, as the incident commander, you need to delegate away. In our example, you could put the police chief in charge of communication, the fire chief in charge of personnel and supplies, and ask the officers to work on evacuations and appoint one officer in charge of the evacuation work.

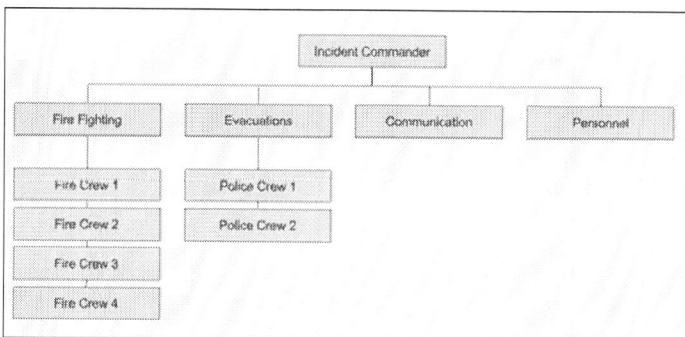

Figure 13: An example ICS structure for responding to something like a wildfire

For software on-call rotations, delegating through communication is often a good first step. Make sure that you tell everyone that this delegation is happening. For example, say, "Chris is now the communications commander and all updates will be coming from him." Then, if an incident goes on for a long time, you may delegate the commander role to someone else, so you can get some sleep. This should be clearly communicated to all and usually included in your next 30-minute update.

Many people have trouble with delegation, or taking charge, when they first go on call. For delegation, if I am the secondary, then I will offer to take over communication by saying something in chat along the lines of "@primary, you seem busy. Would you like me to take over communication and send an update email out?" For dealing with who takes charge, I usually show up with offers to help, but don't do anything until asked.

Often, messages like "@primary, I am online if you need a hand," or "@primary, I saw this graph, would you like me to dig into it?" can help to lower stress for people. Knowing that the primary has help available if they need it often makes people feel more at ease and lets them focus more on the problems at hand. If you go rushing in, trying to help before being asked, people can interpret that as a lack of respect. Other times, they may start interpreting it as you thinking that you are the only one who knows how to do something. Neither of these outcomes are good. You want to support your coworkers. You also want your team to be able to survive an incident, no matter who is on call. This requires everyone on the team to be able to fill roles and feel comfortable filling roles, as needed, during an incident.

Where do you communicate?

The key for where to communicate is to always be consistent and share the location of where the communication is happening often. If the outage is being debugged in lots of places, then people will often make the problem even worse by doing things that do not need to be done. As an example, at one point, I was on an SRE team supporting three separate products. This was not a great situation, but the real issue was that no one knew where to contact us, so often issues would get raised in other teams' channels or in private messages with other people, and this information was not shared with the person who was on call. Outages would then be ignored and would only make it to our on-call person when a customer reached out after noticing an issue.

So, instead, we published an IRC channel and to all three teams we said, "If you need help, come here and we will all talk about it." It took a bit of time, but people started slowly bringing all new issues to that channel and we started delivering a consistent level of quality response to all three teams. This consolidation also helped to fix an issue that was hidden to us until it improved—people on our team felt like they were never able to disconnect. No one voiced this issue, but when random people stopped receiving private messages whenever there was an incident, or question, many voiced a sense of relief and an improvement in their ability to focus during their day.

Outside of internal communications, it often helps to publish public status pages. Things like `https://status.cloud.google.com/` or `https://www.cloudflarestatus.com/` are useful because your external customers need a place that they can go when there is an issue. Often, linking to these pages from places like Twitter or Facebook will lower the number of emails that your support team receives along the lines of "is something broken?"

Recovering the system

One thing that we have yet to touch on is how to debug your application and do the technical work of responding to an incident. This is the third pillar of the initial three pillars we mentioned when defining incident response. We were alerted that things were not great. We communicated that we were on the case. Now we need to make things better.

How do we do that? We will be talking about **measuring mean time to recovery** (**MTTR**) in *Chapter 4, Postmortems*, but the strategy that we kept mentioning earlier in this chapter was bringing the system back to a working state. That's because you don't necessarily want to immediately go into bug-hunting mode. Instead, you want to find what has changed in the system and revert back. Let us walk through the common first steps in trying to track down a broken system.

Step zero is to take a deep breath. Force yourself to slow down a little. I prefer to count to six while inhaling, count to six again while holding my breath, count to six again while exhaling, and finally count to six before beginning this loop again. Doing this just a few times causes me to relax a little. I am still freaking out because I just got paged and everything is broken, and I do not know what is going on, but breathing slowly forces me to check myself before I wreck myself, as they say.

> This method of breathing is called box breathing. Apparently, it comes from the US Navy SEALs. How you calm down doesn't matter because the key is to just find a way to calm yourself a bit, so you can think clearly.

Once I have calmed down, the first thing I always check is if there was a deploy recently. A graph that I have had in past jobs is a percentage of servers running a version of our application. With that, you can see the number of servers running an old version decrease and the number of servers with the new version increase.

If there is a new version appearing on the graph, then code was probably recently deployed. You can then try and correlate whether the errors you are seeing match with the appearance of a new version. If that is the case, then you should revert the deployment and roll back to the previous version.

NOTE: We talk about deployments, rollbacks, and related concepts in *Chapter 5, Testing and Releasing.*

If the application didn't change, or if the rollbacks did not fix the issue, the next area to look at is whether our environment has changed. Have our inputs changed? Have we started receiving a large amount of traffic? Are we being sent a bunch of traffic that is nonsense or corrupted? Do we need to start blocking a certain IP address or user-agent while we figure out how to change our application to handle this type of bad traffic better? Is this valid traffic? If so, can we increase the number of things we have running to increase the number of resources that we have to deal with this increase in traffic?

Dropping, or stopping, to respond to traffic to a web server that matches some sort of filter is called load shedding. It is often viewed as an aggressive tactic, but it is very useful when a certain category of traffic is causing your application to fall over.

If user inputs have not changed, then maybe one of our dependencies has changed. Is our database up? Are services that we depend on running? Have they changed, without telling us, in a way that our application is not compatible with?

Often, external dependencies will publish public status pages, or post on Twitter, announcing that they are having an outage. You can also message their support emails, or Twitter, if you have reason to believe they are down but are not publishing an outage on their status page (or they do not have a status page).

Very rarely does this list of areas to check (code change, input change, and dependency change) result in finding something that you cannot quickly change and bring the system back to a healthy state. In cases where you cannot find something, it is a great time to call in other coworkers and start digging deeper. Start checking everything, finding graphs that look unusual, starting to dig through the logs, and exploring weird theories. Remember, this is not meant to be a permanent fix but more of a way to bring the system back to a place where most customers can use it. Then you can let your customers keep using your service, while you work with your team to come up with a longer-term plan to prevent this from happening again.

Calling all clear

The first step of declaring *all clear* is making sure that your app does the thing it should. Then you can begin solving the root cause. Note that your first goal is always to bring the system up. Your first goal is not to fix things or to figure out the root cause.

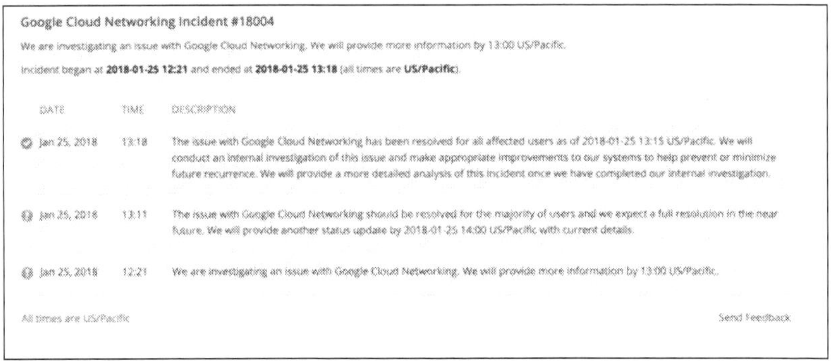

Figure 14: Screenshot of https://status.cloud.google.com/incident/cloud-networking/18004. Notice the two separate messages calling all clear: the first saying things should be becoming healthy, and the second saying that everything is all clear and defining when further communication will happen.

Once you have verified the solution, then post an update saying that things are resolved and mention whether there will be a follow-up. Post at least one more update when you have found and fixed the root cause of the outage. Often this is immediate, but sometimes it takes hours or days to figure out why something happened in your system.

Summary

In this chapter, we talked about incidents, incident response, and alerting. We focused on figuring out when to alert, who to alert, and how to alert. We then talked about what to do once you have acknowledged an alert. We discussed how to communicate and then how to finally close the incident with an *all clear* message.

Having proper incident response set up will help your team to shorten the amount of time it takes to resolve incidents and promote a level of competence to the rest of the company. Your team will be able to show that it knows how to respond when things are bad, and keep its cool and bring the system back to a healthy state.

In the next chapter, we will talk about postmortems. Postmortems are the act of documenting and looking back at the work you did, and working as a team to reduce future incidents.

∾ 4 ∾

POSTMORTEMS

What is a postmortem?

A postmortem is the act of holding a retrospective after a service incident. Depending on the organization, a postmortem is called by many names—retrospective, **root cause analysis (RCA)**, incident review, and others. The idea is to create a document that records why an incident happened and discuss what happened with those involved.

The term postmortem is usually connected to the medical or judicial professions. It is defined by the Oxford English Dictionary as "an examination of a dead body to determine the cause of death." This definition is the reason that many people in software use the term postmortem. Some view software processes as living things and so, when a process stops, it is described as dead. Those who find the idea of ascribing life to a machine to be problematic often use the terms incident review or RCA. Whatever the term used, the goal is to create a historical artifact and discuss the incident that happened.

I mentioned the term retrospective, which a postmortem is, but retrospective is often a more general term used for any process that looks back on a period. A typical time to have a retrospective is at the end of a quarter, right before a planning meeting, or at the end of a week. Many people also do personal retrospectives. This can involve looking at their lives and deciding what they can improve, what they want to keep the same, and what they want to stop doing. Postmortems are more focused, dealing with a specific event, but they follow a similar structure of evaluation.

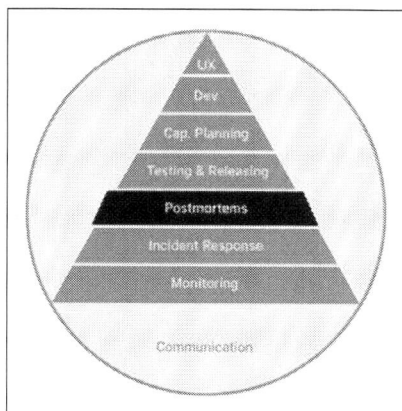

Figure 1: Our current position in the hierarchy

Postmortems, understandably, follow incident response. In this chapter, we will talk about why it is important to write a postmortem document after an incident, how to write one, and how to hold a postmortem meeting.

Why write a postmortem?

In the previous chapter, we talked about incident response. When responding to an incident, we mentioned that you need to focus on bringing the system back to a healthy state as quickly as possible. This need often prevents you from finding out the root cause of the incident. The writing of a postmortem document is the right time to figure out what happened. How did the process die? What part of the system caused instability? How long after the incident began did we notice this? Why did other systems fail?

We carry out a postmortem separately from the initial incident so that we can be thorough and meticulous. We must make sure that we have all of the data and that we fix the issue entirely. Often, during an incident, adrenaline is flowing and quick gut decisions are made. This is because there is very little time to think and weigh decisions. If we do the analysis and research afterwards, we can talk to more people, the stress of the outage is not upon us, and we have more time to make a calculated decision. From this analysis, we can decide to create a document to summarize our findings and share the incident with our teammates. To write a postmortem, analysis is required no matter what. You need to know why something failed. Choosing to create a document is optional and we will cover that decision next, but a report will be useless if you do not analyze the incident and figure out what happened.

A postmortem is also a historical document. It is very likely that you will not be working for an organization forever and that you will have people in your organization who were not involved in the incident or the service that broke. A postmortem document lets you record what happened, how you resolved the issue, and what your team learned. You can then share the document and archive it so that people in your organization can reference it and learn what types of actions your team took to respond to this sort of incident. This sharing will not be as useful if your organization does not have a transparent culture. Personally, I think that I learn most by trying things and reading, so I find the act of creating a postmortem very useful. However, an organization will not be helped by a document if you cannot share what you work on between teams. I have never worked for an organization like this, but they definitely exist. A culture of transparency also tends to promote trust. If you are able to see the work others are doing (and how they handle emergencies), you're more likely to trust them to do the right thing and also value their advice in the future.

As already mentioned, often people will use postmortems for future reference, for example to help them to decide future priorities or planning. By having an archive, you can see whether a particular type of problem happens across multiple pieces of software that your organization runs and decide to work on a unified fix. It is said that you should automate yourself out of a job. Postmortems provide that at an organizational level, as you remove the burden of having to remember the precise details of what went wrong and can move forward onto other things while still improving organizational knowledge.

Outside of postmortems about incidents, you can also write documents about events. These tend to be a little more freeform but provide the same benefit. An event can mean something like a product launch, a significant new feature, a complex integration, the changing of vendors, or something similar. Documenting a significant business event lets you point to past events and reference them when making future decisions. This documentation can prevent future teams from implementing a new feature in the same way or from trying the same product strategy over again. It can also help you plan for similar events based on how your team dealt with past ones.

You can also write a postmortem for the public. Often, these documents are for internal usage, but sometimes companies will publish a version of the postmortem for the public or for customers to promote trust. If one of your vendors explains why it couldn't deliver your emails or process your requests, you are more likely to trust it in the long run than if it has an outage and does not acknowledge that it happened. This transparency is a mutual thing. You want your dependencies to explain why problems arise and how they are fixed. These outages and their responses go into your evaluation of the dependency and whether you should keep using it or replace it. The same is true for your services. Someone is using them and sometimes that person is technical and other times they are not.

Providing them with assurances that you are doing your job and that they should not expect this type of outage again will improve their trust in you and will help lessen the hesitation when a customer is using or paying for your service. In my opinion, the more transparent the company, the better. That being said, sometimes you cannot share everything because of legal or financial restrictions.

Besides trust building, sometimes there is a responsibility to publish a postmortem because a service broke a published SLA. A classic example of this was when Amazon, which traditionally does not publish detailed postmortems, wrote one when it had a very large S3 outage in 2017 (`https://aws.amazon.com/message/41926/`). Outside of public and private documents, there are also documents that are shared between businesses that have service contracts or relationships. Sometimes an organization does not want to publish its postmortem to the public, but it is willing to send you a detailed document because you are an important customer.

When to write a postmortem document

One question I often get from people when starting to document postmortems in an organization is "should I write a postmortem?" There are many different ways that organizations decide on when to write a postmortem, but I have a simple rule I like to follow—if someone asks for a postmortem, you should write one. In a large organization, this works great, because someone will often ask, "What was that incident last night all about?" or "Will there be a postmortem for last week's outage?" These are cues that a document should be created.

In a smaller organization, it is more difficult because, often, it will be you deciding whether you should document the incident. To determine whether you should, you could come up with an internal metric. For example, saying, "If it took us more than 10 minutes to recover, we should write a postmortem." You can also keep it casual and only postmortem things that feel abnormal.

This can be dangerous though. Over the years I have developed a bit of a gut feeling for when something is postmortem-worthy. On reflection, though, I have found that because of this I do not document some of the smaller outages I am involved in, but I do document similar-sized outages that other people are involved in. This realization tells me that I should come up with a more specific metric for when I should write a postmortem. The metric I have been using recently to solve this is two-fold:

1. If the incident happens twice within a few days, I should write a postmortem

2. If we are down for more than 30 minutes, I should write a postmortem

An example of the first one might be a bad code push, followed by a rollback, followed by another release that didn't fix the initial bad code push correctly. Another example is a series of bad configuration changes that cause similar and related outages.

An example of the second one might be a 30-minute period where an application's SLI is outside of normal bounds. See *Chapter 2, Monitoring* for a description of SLIs. Another example could be if the customer couldn't access the app for 30 minutes.

I use these metrics because they match the level of severity that First Look Media (my employer at the time of writing) is currently operating with. We have smaller incidents due to bugs, or carelessness, or other things. At the speed we are operating at, we cannot stop and document everything, but incidents that hit these metrics seem to be the same sort of incidents that concern a broader number of people. When multiple people (engineers, product folks, customers, and so on) are concerned, we have to manage their expectations and produce documentation to calm them, and also reach out to them and make sure our service fills them with joy, not dread.

Carrying out incident analysis

Incident analysis is complicated. Sometimes you know the answer right away and sometimes it takes hours or days of research. You should approach the system like a paranoid Sherlock Holmes. Start at the scene of the crime and then dig deep into every aspect. Be wary of your preconceived notions, be aware of red herrings, and always test your hypotheses.

> A red herring is something that is misleading or distracting from the task at hand. It is often an attractive answer or problem unrelated to the actual issue.

The scene of a crime for an outage is often the thing you rolled back. It may be a bad config or buggy code. Was the outage caused by the change your team was trying to deploy or was it caused by a system interacting with that code? You can then start reading through the code that changed or the code that interacts with the code you deployed. If there wasn't a rollback, then you've probably already figured out the issue, as you will have had to figure it out during the incident to solve the issue, unless it solved itself. We haven't talked yet about reverse engineering systems, and that is often an important tool, so let us delve into it.

Reverse engineering is the act of starting with a system and figuring out how it works by interacting with it and seeing how it responds to inputs. If I have a system that I do not know anything about, and I cannot ask anyone about it (because they are asleep, no longer an employee, or for some other reason), I start by looking at how things interact with it. This could be by opening up a browser's development tools and looking at the requests made, looking at client libraries, or running something like Charles Proxy (`https://www.charlesproxy.com/`) or `tcpdump` to see what network packets are being sent. Once you know that and you know what software is running (which you can discover with tools like `strace`, `netstat`, and `ps`), you can go find the code and start reading through it, knowing what inputs are going into it.

> We talk about how to use `netstat` and `tcpdump` in *Chapter 9, Networking Foundations* and we discuss `strace` in *Chapter 10, Linux and Cloud Foundations*.

Reading code is a skill that many people do not have when they start in programming. I highly recommend that you practice by doing code reviews, reading through software you didn't write, or just reading code you wrote a long time ago. I personally love reading code in languages I do not know well, because it forces you to go extra slow and question everything. If you can read a program in a language you do not know, then reading code in languages you do know becomes easier.

As you are reading through the code, try to build a function graph. I often keep a large notebook nearby and list the functions called by functions as I read them. This helps me to remember things I still need to look into and functions I have already read. Be careful of getting lost though. Remember the goal here is not to understand the software completely but instead to figure out how it does the thing you are having problems with. Does it call other external or internal supporting services? Does it store data? Can it do both of these things? Are there comments and do they match what the code actually does? As you discover this, you can draw up a system diagram of either how functions or how services interact.

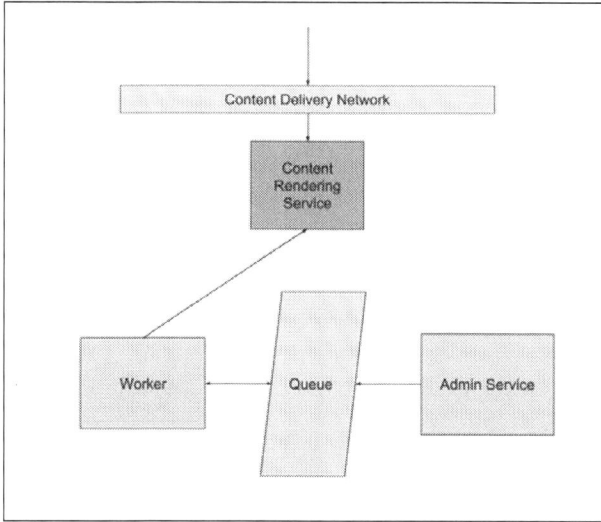

Figure 2: This is an example diagram I drew for an approximation of an old CMS that I worked on. The admin service was where users created content. As updates were made, notifications were added to the queue. The worker then rebuilt the pages that had been modified. The content rendering service would then receive the updated pages, store them, and clear any related caches in the Content Delivery Network (CDN). When an external user viewed the website, they visited the CDN, which then queried the rendering service only if nothing was in the cache.

Besides looking at the code, and the inputs and outputs of the system, you can also look at the logs and the metrics the system generates. If the service has some, you can also look at related dashboards. Searching through code to see what generates certain log lines, and also what changes certain metrics, can be super insightful for figuring out what was happening. Also, you may see nearby log and metric statements that can help you to search for other things and generate other hypotheses.

How to write a postmortem document

The incident has happened and you've decided to write a postmortem document. You have done your analysis. What do you put in it? My rough template tends to be as follows— summary, impact, timeline, root cause, action items, and appendix. As long as you capture the incident in detail, you can put whatever you want in a postmortem document. I usually aim for a few pages, but depending on how complicated the outage was, it may be as short as one or two pages or as long as 20. The following is the template I usually use as a starting point to help me to organize my thoughts. Staring at a template after (or during) analysis is a helpful framework compared to just looking at a blank page and debating what to write. There are many other templates available online and one repository of templates is at `https://github.com/dastergon/postmortem-templates`.

At the top of the document, add the names of those involved, the date of the incident and when the document was last modified. If you store your postmortems in some sort of online system, you could add keywords or tags to help organize the document.

Summary

The first section should be an executive summary. This means that no matter who opens this document, they should have a rough idea of what happened, when it happened, and who was affected. It tends to be short and a statement that gives the reader a snapshot of the incident.

An example:

> On February 22nd, 2016, there was a bad configuration change pushed to our edge routers. Our edge routers distribute requests to our various backends for all applications. This caused 20% of requests to our website to fail for 30 minutes. The failed requests all returned 500 responses to customers.

This example covers the basics. It summarizes what broke, how it broke, and what the effect was. It doesn't point fingers, it doesn't go too deep technically, and it is not very long. If your summary is longer than two paragraphs, then it is probably too detailed.

Impact

I do not always include this section, but it is helpful for determining what the customer service response should be or whether there will be any external fallout from the outage. The impact section is a great place to describe customers who felt the outage, any public news about the outage, a discussion on how this affected your service's SLA, and maybe a graph or two. You can also include statistics about the time to recovery or on-call response speed, if those are things that your organization is interested in measuring.

Product teams find this section useful to gauge how much they should care and this helps management to determine the priorities of the action items later on.

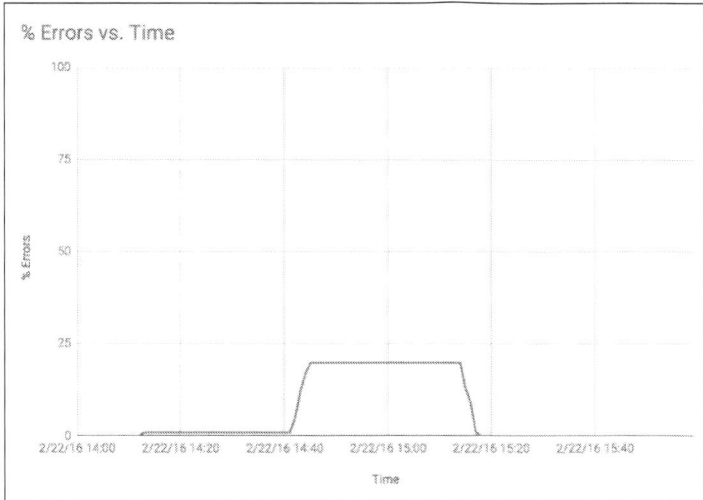

% Errors vs. Time

Figure 3: An example graph of % errors over time

> **This graph shows that for 30 minutes, 20% of all requests to all of our edge routers returned 500 errors. We saw no mention of these external failures, but there were 15 related support cases filed by customers during this outage. We have decided not to publish a public postmortem but have responded to the 15 cases.**

This explanation is light, as it could include a lot more detail, but it is important that readers of the postmortem understand the impact of the incident outside of just request failures, or failed jobs, or whatever the technical failure was. If you have access to a customer support team, they can provide lots of insight into what their incoming requests looked like during the outage.

You can also search social networks and news sites for mention of your outage. Alternatively, you can dig through logs and try and make an estimated guess about how many unique clients saw the outage. It will not be perfect but could give you a better understanding of the impact. Another way to measure impact is to look at the traffic to an external status page. If you host something like `status.cloud.google.com` or `status.github.com`, you might be able to extrapolate interest in your outage based on increased user visits. It will be less informative than more direct metrics or customer notifications, but it could help guide an understanding about how many people care about your system's performance.

Timeline

I love this section, as it gives a minute-by-minute explanation of what happened. Each line is a timestamp and a description. In the description, links to code changes, event timelines, and the deployment of services provide extra insights and details to the document. This is useful for tracking down what happened as a reader because you can click and see the context or look at the appendix to understand what the person who responded to the incident was seeing. As someone who is learning to be on call, this section can show you how your teammates respond to an issue. As a manager, you can get a sense of who was involved in the response to an issue. As another team member, you can see the methodologies that coworkers use and you can compare them to how you might respond when you see something similar. One of my favorite questions is "why did you do X when you saw Y?" Sometimes it's just intuition, but often it points to something that can be fixed or automated, or at least documented for future responders.

An example:

All times EST

16-02-22

14:04 - – Commit abc1234 was made to configuration repository introducing new routing path for upcoming project launch.

14:12 - – Release is canaried with one percent of edge routers. Errors begin appearing but do not trigger alert. [Outa Begins]

14:42 - – Release is rolled out to 20 percent of edge routers.

14:45 - – Primary on call, Nat, is paged for elevated request failures.

15:00 - – Nat discovers he does not have permissions to rollback routing config. Pages routing parser owner Sarah, hoping she has permissions.

15:15 - – Sarah begins rollback.

15:17 - – Rollback is complete. [Outage Ends]

This timeline is very brief, but it hits a few good points. First off, it defines when the incident began and ended. It shows who responded to the incident and performed actions, so they can provide more detail about what they saw if needed. Postmortems do not blame people for the initial cause. Also note that while you can place people's names here, you should not attack their decisions. By giving someone the responsibility to respond to an incident, you must trust their decisions and support them, if only so that they will do the same for you in the future. If you do have criticism that comes up from reading the timeline, then I suggest you highlight it in a friendly and suggestive tone. Instead of asking, "Why didn't you...," or saying, "If I was on call, I would have...," try asking, "Could we have made X work better for the on call person?" If your statement or question is accusatory or aggressive, it does not need to be said. Sometimes, if it looks like someone doesn't know about something, you could mention it in passing after the meeting. You could say, "Hey, I noticed you didn't use tool Y while debugging. Have you used it before? If not, I'd be glad to show it to you some time, as it's great for showing things like Z."

Root cause

The root cause is probably the most important section of a postmortem for an engineering team. It describes what caused the outage. Previous sections describe what happened, or how they happened, but not why. If we want to prevent future outages, then we need to know why they happened. The goal is not to say that an outage was a single person's fault but rather to find how the systems failed, why they failed, and how to prevent that in the future. The root cause is the main result of your analysis.

An example:

> The configuration change that was made triggered an unknown bug in the edge routing code. There was an assumption made in the routing code that only ASCII characters would be allowed in configured paths. This assumption is not defined in the validation code, so when a new route was defined with the prefix of /☺, the routing parser raised an exception. The edge routers did not catch this exception and instead started crash looping, as they read the configuration at boot and would crash as soon as they parsed the configuration with the non-ASCII character.

Root cause sections can be huge if there is a very surprising discovery as to why the system broke, but more often than not the issue boils down to something small. You can use this section to explain how you came to your discovery or why you are sure you are correct. This can often be the section you need to defend, so try to be succinct while still covering your bases. Sometimes, there are processes that failed and those can be brought to light here as well. However, be wary—your goal is not to assign blame while describing what happened. "Chris committed a software change that broke everything," is not good, so instead say, "A change was made that introduced a new route that caused an exception in our parser." Often, it is good to run your postmortem by one or two people before sending it out to a wider audience, to make sure what you want to say comes across well.

Action items

Action items are a list of actions to take after the incident, usually with tickets or some tracking attached. Tickets are good because they attach accountability and prioritization to fixing the issue. Action items make sure that a group of people are working to prevent this outage from happening again, and having accountability in place is important. That being said, avoid piling all of the work onto one person. No matter how the issue occurred, the team should be working together to make sure it does not happen again. An example:

♦ #1234 - – Add test for incompatible routes

♦ #1235 - – Tweak the first canary to be large enough to trigger alerts if there's an issue

♦ #1236 - – Make sure all current members of on-call rotation have the ability to roll back routing configuration deploys

♦ #1237 - – Add check to on-call member onboarding for permissions to do rollbacks

This example shows new issues that were created for this specific incident. Often, you'll also link to existing issues that would have helped to prevent this incident or improved recovery. Linking them here as well helps to make sure they are visible to stakeholders and your teammates.

When trying to design and pick action items, focus on things that could have prevented the outage, that will improve the response and recovery time, and that will fix the current issues. Usually, adding tickets to automate responses for this class of incidents is a good step. Improving tooling to make it easier to debug an issue like this is also very useful. Stay away from "adding another graph to a dashboard" tickets and instead look into improving tools that let you go from the very general to the very specific. An example of this might be a system that lets you single out queries or systems that are performing very differently to the majority.

Note that action items are pointless if you ignore them once they are in your ticketing system. There is no point in putting action items in your postmortem if you do not think anyone will ever do them. There are some groups that like creating tickets and then just constantly adding new postmortems to the bug. This, as well as a postmortem that has 40 action items that no one will ever touch, is useless. Action items that won't be done are useless because they imply that the SRE (or whoever is driving the postmortem) is not a priority to the company. One of the jobs of an SRE is to promote reliability throughout the organization, and so it requires constant vigilance, and working with those in charge of scheduling work, to make sure action items get done.

Postmortems without action items

When writing a postmortem document, you may run into a classic problem—there are no immediate action items. This usually happens when there is an outage related to a dependency and you are a smaller organization. As mentioned earlier, an example that hit many was when there was a massive Amazon S3 outage on February 28th, 2017. S3 is a blob storage system where many companies store lots of things, such as images and random files. When S3 went down, there were many organizations that could do very little about it. It can be dangerous for your business to try and build a solution where you are not dependent on a system if you are still young and do not know whether your business, or the data you have stored, will be useful in six months. You will often want to spend time focusing on figuring out your business, not building up resiliency. This is a difficult decision for a business, but your team can work together to decide whether solving this type of outage is important enough to spend time on and build a solution for.

In these cases, you usually want to replace the action items with a paragraph on the cost evaluation of doing something versus doing nothing. Is this the first time this dependency has failed? What would it cost to move to another dependency? Should we duplicate the dependency so that if it fails again we have another option? Providing a system you can failover to is the preferred resolution to a large dependency failing, but that can be expensive. It can also often take a lot of time or money to implement, which could be time or money you don't have.

Once you have evaluated possible directions you could go in, decide based on these facts. A postmortem document will probably be more useful for senior engineering leadership because you are explaining the cost of fixing a dependency. Do we want to pay for storing all of our data twice? Was this a one-off change? We cannot just pray that it doesn't happen again, but we can evaluate the cost of it happening again versus the cost of dealing with it. If we go down for two hours but save lots of money every month, and thus can keep the company running for another few months, maybe it is worth rolling the dice. On the other hand, maybe the downtime will happen during our biggest event and that will hurt us as an organization.

Some say that postmortems cannot exist without action items. In a well-funded organization, I think that is true. If you have lots of resources, action items are important. On the other hand, if you are a three-person engineering team, then just leaving some notes about things you could have done with more resources might be enough for now. When your team and business grow, it is a good idea to revisit some of these decisions, but until they do, never forget to be realistic.

Appendix

The appendix is the section where you add all of the things related to this incident. Adding chat logs, relevant service logs, screenshots, graphs, external URLs, and the like is a great way to make sure that the document will be able to stand on its own in the future. Each item should be labeled so that it is easy to find.

The appendix is useful in the same way that the timeline is—it gives context to how you reached the root cause and provides visual displays to go with the text. The appendix is also important because the tools you use now may not be around in the future and you very rarely keep monitoring data at the same fidelity forever. By taking a snapshot of things, you can provide your team with a look into the past, without needing to store high-resolution monitoring data forever.

Blameless postmortems

A topic we have touched upon is the key adjective usually attached to postmortems—blameless. Postmortems used improperly can lead to really dangerous and toxic cultures, where people are afraid of outages or feel incapable of doing their jobs because of the fear of failure. Start with a fact—we all fail. As humans, failure is one of our most defining traits. One of the key tenets of SRE is that if you are going to fail, set up your organization so that it is not a big deal and you can quickly recover and learn from the failure. Another tenet is that reliability is a team sport. Everyone needs to feel comfortable raising issues, responding to outages, and working on improving the system. Fostering that level of psychological safety is difficult and constantly needs reinforcement and help.

Note that, in the *Root cause* section, we did not point out the person who made the change that broke the system, nor the person who wrote code that couldn't handle the user interaction we had. On top of that, no one got fired, no one was yelled at, and no one was blamed.

We need our employees to feel comfortable to take risks, and also that they can comfortably fix things when they fail and talk about why they failed. This sounds simple, but when an outage causes major damage to an organization or business, it is not a trivial thing. If you are a manager, you may be put in the position of needing to explain why you shouldn't fire a person. You may even be asked to provide a sacrificial lamb. I used to think that this situation only happened in movies, but often an organization wants to be able to blame a problem on a single person. Stay in the industry long enough and you will hear stories of people doing all sorts of things so that they can keep their jobs and claim to a customer that something will never happen again.

If you're having trouble not blaming a person, I have some tips. First, go through your document and replace all names with "we," then start going through the timeline. Instead of blaming the human, figure out every step where a tool could have prevented a human from making a mistake. Could automation save a person from skipping a step in a checklist? Is there a checklist? It is well known that checklists save lives (this was discovered by medical and aeronautical professionals years ago `https://ti.arc.nasa.gov/m/profile/adegani/Cockpit%20Checklists.pdf`), but as computer programmers, we can often turn processes into code. The reason we do this is that there will come a day when someone doesn't even know that the checklist exists. So, instead of requiring the human to do something, figure out where the human shouldn't have had to do anything.

> The importance of the checklist is often connected to the large crash of a Boeing plane in 1935, where the crew forgot essential steps in preparing the plane for take off. After implementing a checklist for take off for the large B-17, there were no other incidents for 18 million miles. Robert L. Helmreich, Ph.D. is often considered the reason that checklists have continued to gain such reverence. He wrote extensively about how they lower accidents in hospitals and aeronautics in the 90s.

Next, ask whether your service had trouble dealing with a dependency failing. Cascading failures are one of the most dangerous types of failure in service-oriented architectures. You can often recover from one service failing but recovering from all of your services failing is much more difficult. An example was a chat service that Google was running. It had a bug in its retry logic, so if the mobile service was down for long enough, the retry polling started lining up. All of a sudden, there were millions of devices polling servers at a synchronized time. This increased traffic, causing other services to go down as the ingress network became overwhelmed. These outages continued until they were able to shed some of the load to deal with increased traffic. There were lots of issues with the mobile app, the chat service backend, and the generic frontends, which weren't ready for that kind of traffic pattern. Any one of these teams could have pointed the blame at each other.

I should mention that I was not on any of these teams; this is just one of those stories that gets passed down. The goal is that all pieces that had an outage or failure should change their behavior. At Google, the frontends needed a way to shed traffic faster, the backends needed better testing to prevent code bugs ending up in production, the mobile clients needed to randomize their connection retries, and some services needed to remove dependencies they didn't even know they had.

The point of all of this, though, is that people need to feel safe to raise issues. People in the organization, no matter how large it is, need to work together to fix issues. Everyone needs to feel safe to fail and safe to discuss their failures with others. If people don't feel safe, they will often not be honest or may try and hide things. Even worse, they may just leave.

Holding a postmortem meeting

A postmortem meeting is the follow-up to the document. It often finalizes action items, discusses the findings of the root cause, and offers a safe setting for discussion. Usually, the best set of people to invite to a postmortem meeting are those involved in the incident—the tech lead for services affected, the product manager for the affected services, and any interested engineers. Finding the right balance is hard, because if the meeting is too large, you will not get much done, but if the meeting is too small, knowledge won't be disseminated well.

It's a good idea to have those involved in the incident present because they will know what happened in case data is missing from the document. Tech leads from affected services should be there in case assumptions are made about their services that aren't true and to accept responsibility to make sure that the action items get implemented. Product managers for affected services are important because they can help to describe business needs related to the service and work with the tech leads to make sure that the fixes get prioritized. Allowing interested people to attend is important to promote knowledge transfer.

The incident commander from the incident should lead the meeting. While the incident commander doesn't always write the entire postmortem, they are often the most knowledgeable about the event, and those involved, and can direct conversation. Open the meeting with a statement requesting that those who have not read the document excuse themselves from the meeting or agree not to participate. The thinking here is that those who have not read the document will ask questions or make statements that might be already answered in the document. The meeting should not cater to those who couldn't take the time to be informed about the incident for the sake of wider learning. Following that, try sticking to the following agenda:

- **A brief timeline and incident summary**: This should take no more than five minutes. Remember that, since everyone has read the document, this is more to refresh people and point out any particularly noteworthy facts. You do not need to go minute by minute, so just give broad strokes.

- **Discussion of the root cause**: This is usually the most variable of sections, as sometimes people do not understand how the root cause could have been possible. This is also an area where people can get defensive if they feel they are being attacked or blamed. Try to keep discussions civil and try to redirect any accusations of blame toward working together, as we are all responsible for each other's success. Also, be careful not to go too deep into discussions on how to engineer a solution to the root cause. If there is not an obvious fix, a follow-up meeting should be created for engineering a solution, which should be an action item.

- **Questions**: This section will often bleed into the previous section, but you can have people pre-submit questions if it is a large group or go over any concerns people might have.

- **Discussion of action items**: The previous discussions may have made extra action items, so make sure that all tasks are properly documented. If you have an issue tracker, make sure issues are logged and linked from the document. Also, make sure that someone is responsible for the bugs. We don't want to blame people, but we do want to make sure that fixes get implemented. One of the most annoying feelings is participating in multiple postmortems that all have the same action items but no one makes sure that the fixes get done.

This schedule works great for larger organizations. I have worked on teams where we ran a postmortem meeting once a week and would go through every outage from the past week in this format. In smaller organizations, it is often useful to be less formal and go faster. In these cases, I like a quick discussion about a postmortem or incident:

♦ What worked? Go around the room and ask each person to list up to three things that worked during the incident.

♦ What didn't work? Have each person state what they felt didn't work well.

♦ What should we start doing? This time, have people list one thing they think the team should start doing. This is often a good way to figure out the prioritization of action items or to generate new ones.

♦ What should we stop doing? Instead, focus on what the team should stop doing.

♦ What should we improve doing? Finally, go around focusing on things to improve.

For this more informal rotation, you should try and only spend a minute or two on each person for each question. That way, the whole process takes less than half an hour for a team of five.

Analyzing past postmortems

Once everything is said and done, it is good to go back and review past postmortems. Once a quarter, or once a year, collect all of the postmortems and try and pull together some metrics. These metrics can help to give you an insight into what your team is doing to respond to incidents:

♦ Time to recovery

♦ Time between failures

♦ Number of alerts fired versus postmortems generated

♦ Number of alerts fired per on-call rotation

MTTR and MTBF

Outside of incidents, two metrics that are often talked about are **mean time to recovery** (**MTTR**) and **mean time between failures** (**MTBF**). Looking at these numbers across a year can show how your ability to respond to incidents is improving or changing. Note how the goal is to minimize the time until recovery, not necessarily to minimize the time until the cause of the outage is fixed. If MTBF is low, it might mean that your team is not investing in testing enough, and this is also probably draining your team. If MTTR is high, it probably means that your team does not understand how to respond to incidents, or the tooling for doing things like rollbacks and other recovery actions is poor or slow.

Alert fatigue

Figuring out what percentage of alerts were actionable is important for the health of those responding. As we mentioned in *Chapter 3, Incident Response* responders need to know whether, if they get alerted, they need to respond. Having a historical record of alerts that turned into postmortems, alerts per rotation, and actionable alerts can help you to determine whether responders are overwhelmed, and whether they are getting interrupted by things that matter. If you have engineers who know they will get woken up at three in the morning every time they are on call, they may not stick around long or may just stop responding.

Discussing past outages

Once you have collected data about your past postmortems and outages, you should share it with the team. After circulating the data, it can be useful to have one-on-ones or a team meeting where people share their concerns about the current health of incident response. Sometimes the team may feel fine, whereas other times they may feel there is something missing—maybe too many alerts, poor monitoring, or they feel fixes from outages aren't being prioritized enough.

Other times, a single member of the team may be having issues. I remember very clearly that while I was at Google, I was completely burned out because we were a four-person team responding to the alert load a team of six should have been responding to. I worked with my manager to take two months off from being on call. Others weren't as overwhelmed as me, so I appreciated that they were able to cover for me. That time off allowed me to recover, and if my manager hadn't checked in on me, I am not sure I would have taken the time off. Making sure your team is healthy and that incident response is not a burden is important for the long-term survival of developers. This is often not visible at the single postmortem level but can be seen when you look at things in aggregate and talk to your team.

Summary

In this chapter, we talked about what postmortems are, when we should write them, and how to write, discuss and analyze them. We also talked about keeping blame out of postmortems and helping your team to prevent future issues by prioritizing what comes out of the postmortem process.

As an SRE, or as part of an organization that wants reliability, postmortems are the transition from dealing with the present to dealing with the future. Everything above postmortems in the hierarchy is about the future—planning and improving processes. Everything below (monitoring and incident response) is about dealing with the present. Postmortems allow us to look at the past, before we start thinking about the future.

In the next chapter, we will talk about testing and releasing, where we think about code we have written and how we introduce it into the world. We have finished looking at incidents and now will move on to the constant evolution of our products and services.

References

Dan Luu's postmortem list—`https://github.com/danluu/post-mortems`

~ 5 ~

TESTING AND RELEASING

This chapter could easily be two books, as testing and releasing are both very complex fields. There are folks, who refer to themselves as software test engineers and release engineers, who specialize in both these fields. The two topics are very closely integrated when it comes to reliability. They form the first layer of preventative reliability. While *Chapter 2, Monitoring* and *Chapter 3, Incident Response* were about reacting to the current state and *Chapter 4, Postmortems* was all about looking back, this chapter focuses on looking into the future.

Testing and releasing are processes that are often set up early in a project and then are forgotten. Many engineers assume that tests will just run and code can be released. However, processes that are built for a few engineers don't necessarily scale to larger teams. For projects that last a long time (years for example), improving the releasing and testing process is often ignored until an organization is much larger and scale begins to cause issues with the existing processes. Improving a team's developer tooling can often lead to productivity and developer happiness, and make it easier to release fixes for issues found in incidents.

That being said, both testing and releasing are very large topics. We will be approaching them mainly from a reliability aspect. You will learn how to invest in them and how to work with your teammates to make them valuable tools.

This chapter will focus on what to test and how to test it. It will also take a look at releasing software and the strategies and timing around releasing. After this chapter, you should have ideas about how to improve the experience of the teams you support as well as how to deploy code in a safe and stable way.

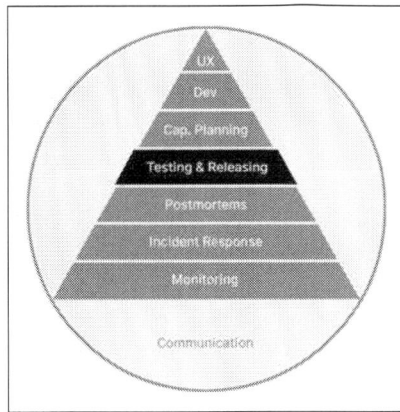

Figure 1: Our current position in the hierarchy

Testing

To test something is to verify that it works as expected. You can test just about everything and in a sense, testing is very similar to the analysis mentioned in *Chapter 4, Postmortems*. However, instead of coming up with a hypothesis, you are taking something that you want to exist, creating it, and then verifying that the thing you created does what you want. Be aware of the famous Dijkstra quote: "Testing shows the presence, not the absence of bugs." This is another way of saying that whatever hypothesis you test, you will not necessarily invalidate other hypotheses.

Some people ask why you should bother with testing. There is a belief that often exists, when people haven't done much programming with larger groups, that testing is pointless. This belief often comes from being told that testing is important but not seeing any immediate benefits. Testing can be frustrating and daunting, but it is not pointless because, as we have mentioned, humans are flawed. We misremember, misread, and misunderstand all the time. When we are programming and working with humans, we must not ignore this fact. When you write code, you make assumptions. Testing is important so, when someone else is working on code you wrote, they can verify that they did not break any of the assumptions that you made. For example, if you assume your function for putting sprinkles on ice cream will always be called after ice cream is put in a cup, someone will undoubtedly call it when there is no ice cream in your cup. Your code will then probably break. Instead, you need to add tests to validate that your code is only called at the right time and that it responds correctly when called with state or arguments that you did not expect.

As an individual developer, a common feeling is that you do not need anyone else to understand your code. You can keep all of the code you have written in your head. You wrote most of the code you are interfacing with, and you know how the code is used, so it will probably not break. This belief is not wrong. Smaller projects or features are often worked on by individuals, but holding this belief assumes two things—you will be the only one who works on that piece of code and that over time, you will not forget what you did. I cannot speak for every human, but my memory is horrible. I rely heavily on computers to show up at places on time, let alone to remember every piece of work I have ever created.

My brain, like most people's, often misremembers things or completely forgets them. Outside of my many abandoned side projects, most of the code that I have written has been picked up or modified by someone else. While these examples are from my own life, most software developers forget things and most software is touched by multiple engineers, if you look at the industry. Most software is written by teams.

On average, software engineers stay at a company for four years in the US, according to a study by the Bureau of Labor Statistics in 2016 (`https://www.bls.gov/news.release/pdf/tenure.pdf`) (according to other studies, it is much lower (`https://hackerlife.co/blog/san-francisco-large-corporation-employee-tenure`). This implies that if your code lasts for a few years, your team structure will change, as will who will work on the code.

Regarding memory, I propose a simple test. Try and remember everything that was in the room you slept in last night. If it was destroyed, could you recreate a list of everything in it to send to an insurance agent? While I don't doubt you could get the broad strokes (your bed, maybe some things on the walls and the stuff on your nightstand), getting a list together of everything under your bed or in drawers or closets gets more difficult. This may sound like a false dichotomy, but the point is that human memory is flawed. To assume you will remember every bit of code you have ever written, and how it works, forever, is just an absurd proposition.

One of the great quotes that I heard while learning to code is that software is 20% creation and 80% maintenance. Dr. John Dalbey told me this originally and although there is a lot of argument on the internet as to whether this number is made up, it's still interesting to think about. More likely, it comes from the idea of the Pareto Principle, which says that 20% of the causes create 80% of the effects. All of that aside, you can take away the idea that in a professional setting, software is usually created for something that will exist for a while.

If you are working on the initial 20%, there is a high chance that there will be maintenance required further down the line because of changes in your organization, environment, or requirements. Software, despite all of our hopes and dreams, is not static. Requirements always change because humans have no idea what they want and have a severe inability to describe and outline what they want accurately.

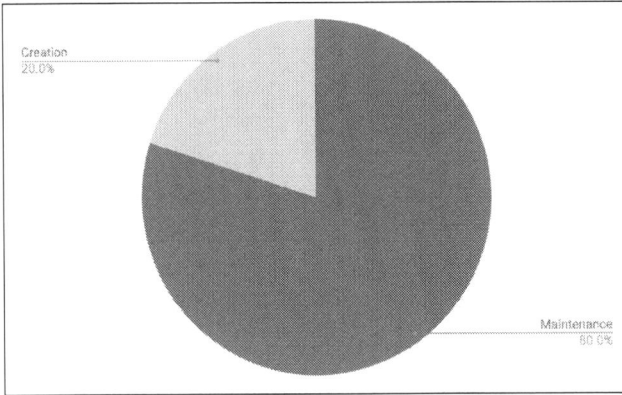

Figure 2: A graph of software development time

On top of an almost guaranteed need to change software as its definition and requirements change, there is the fact that software testing can be more fragile than the software itself. One of the more famous problems in computer science is the "halting problem". It says that we cannot know whether a program will finish or run forever, given a random program and inputs. This is actually a semi-complicated piece of mathematical theory but, basically, there is no one test or function you can run that will prove whether any program will finish. You can write a test for a single program, but you can't write one test for every program. Alan Turing proved this in 1936 in his paper *On Computable Numbers, with an Application to the Entscheidungsproblem*. So, given this, tests need to be written uniquely for each piece of software. This is annoying (how great would it be to have a test that worked on all of the code ever written?), but it allows us to write down our assumptions, so that when we need to maintain our software, or someone else's software, we can have some degree of assurance that our changes will not break the system.

Smaller organizations may also want to ignore testing because it slows them down. They have to take the time to write the tests, then they have to run the tests and that can be slow. Some companies believe that a far better idea is to just have one person who has all of the test cases in their head and can click through the website or decide whether the code has bugs in it or not.

That is ridiculous. Based on our previous statement, that is not possible. No one person should be held accountable for verifying whether software is correct or working properly. Your team should not just be writing code and throwing it at someone and saying, "Hey, does this work right?" Instead, if you do not want to write code tests, then work as a team to create a verification checklist. For every release, have everyone who has code in the release go through the checklist. This checklist can then also be grown and modified based on postmortems and new features.

I mentioned earlier that reliability is a team sport. Writing software is a team sport. Building things is a team sport. If you do not understand how to verify whether what you are building is correct, then expecting someone else to do so is just absurd. This is not to say that everyone should know everything, nor that everything should always be tested, but being able to write code that proves what you wrote works is just a good idea. Like most of SRE, testing is an exercise in finding the right balance between effort and risk. Your team needs to figure out what to test and what you can ignore testing, so that your team can move at the appropriate speed and also not have code failing all of the time. If you are too risky, people will burn out reacting to failures. Inversely, if you are too safe, you will not release new things fast enough for your small business to survive in the market.

Larger organizations are essentially just lots of small organizations unified together under similar goals. They need to make the same evaluations as small organizations do, but they often need to weigh the company's external reputation as well. Google, for instance, cannot launch new things as easily now that it is so large because customers expect the same reliability and polish from products that have existed for years. New products, then, have to include that reality in their evaluation of how much risk they can take. The upside, though, is that they usually have more infrastructure and support available to them to make testing easier and faster.

With larger organizations, you might also find yourself shunted into a specialized role. It might feel like testing is not your responsibility. Just remember it is not only your job to fight fires, but it is also your job to prevent them. We have mentioned this a few times but it bears repeating: an SRE is not just a sysadmin, nor are they just a software engineer. As an SRE, you can and should help those you support to write code, write tests, and promote reliability. Just as people should not be relying on a single person for testing, you should not be relying on others to be the sole developers of application code, nor should they expect you to be the sole owner of infrastructure. All of this requires teamwork.

As you make the argument to your team to write tests, or improve testing, it often helps to have a few suggestions on what to test. Let us talk about that next.

What do you test?

Hopefully, you now think that testing is important or at least not a waste of time. So, what do you test? There are many philosophies on this topic and I urge you to do lots of research, but I will try to provide some guidance on how to think about what to test.

First, let us ask a question: what can we test? We could test every line of code. We could test every piece of infrastructure. We could make sure that every random piece of user input does not break us. We could even test ourselves, to understand where our processes fall apart. Which of these should we invest our time and energy in? Deciding how much to test is an evaluation between risk and time. Only you and your team can figure out where the line truly is.

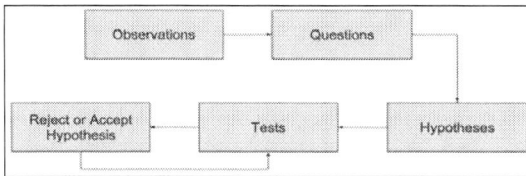

Figure 3: The scientific method

Whatever you do test, it will be iterative and should roughly follow the scientific method. For those who do not know this method, or if you have trouble applying it to software, the rough steps are as follows:

1. **Observe**: This is often seeing an outage, getting a requirement, or just writing the software.

2. **Question**: Ask yourself, what happens when software gets this type of input, or this dependency goes away, or the software gets into this state?

3. **Hypothesis**: Come up with a hypothesis. In code, this is more asking what you want to happen.

4. **Test**: Do the thing and ask, does the code react in the way I want?

5. **Reject or approve**: If your test failed, then you need to modify something (tests, code, infrastructure, processes, and so on) to meet your expectations.

Testing in the software world differs from normal scientific testing because often, instead of trying to figure out how something works, you are instead trying to verify that things are working the way you want them to.

Testing code

Testing code is often the most laborious type of testing, but it is also where people frequently start their testing. This is because it is the most obvious work output for most software developers. They are tasked with writing code and want to make sure they have done a good job. They also want to make sure a user's random inputs do not break things and that the code works properly with everyone else's code.

Code reviews

The most basic type of code test is a code review. Code reviews are not what people think about when they think of testing code, but they are a second pair of eyes validating your changes. For those that do not know much about code reviews, they are the act of taking a set of changes before they are released and having a coworker read through them. That coworker will make suggestions on code style, logic, and implementation. The two of you will then go back and forth, iterating until you are both happy with the code, and then release it. Releasing, in this case, is done by merging code into a shared repository. GitHub provides this to developers through pull requests. Git itself uses email to do this. Other systems people use include Trac, Gerrit, GitLab, and Phabricator.

If you are asked to be a code reviewer, try to be thorough and find code paths the developer may have overlooked. Make sure to read the surrounding code and understand how this change interacts with the rest of the system. Also, be sure to read the messages left in the code review by the developer, and any related issues or tickets, to make sure you understand the context of this change.

My aim, when I am a reviewer, is to reply to code reviews in one business day, assuming that the changes are not gigantic. Asking reviewers to shrink the size of their changes is always a good idea if they are too big. The goal should be to have related code in a single change set, but to make the chunk of code as small as possible to still be easily understood in a quick reading. Try not to be a jerk. As software development is a team exercise, you will often need to work with the person whose code you are reviewing. They will also probably review your code in the near future. Be nice, be courteous, be understanding, and provide constructive feedback. The point is to work together to make better code, not to belittle the other person or prove that you are somehow smarter.

As a code submitter, be considerate of the reviewer's time when requesting a review. Make sure things are well documented and that you have done the basics, such as validating that you have passing tests and passing any lint checks you might have. You can automate lint checks and test running using tools such as Git commit hooks. Many source code repositories can also be configured to automatically run tests when sent new code.

> Linting is the act of making sure that your code matches a specific style. It is great for helping projects with lots of developers to stick to a consistent code style. Linting and test running are useful processes to automate. We will talk about this in a bit, but anything you want someone to do before requesting a code review can usually be automated.

It's important to not take offense when reading code reviews. Rarely do code reviewers mean you any ill will. Instead, assume that your colleagues have the best intentions when suggesting changes. If their changes are significant, talk to the reviewers about the changes and see if waiting would be fine. I often file tickets from a code reviewer's suggestions if they request that I rewrite a large section of code. First, I try and understand why the request is being made and evaluate it. Not all suggestions are good, but it is useful to work with your reviewer to find a common ground. Is it just a difference in style or is there a deeper unaddressed concern? The filing of the ticket lets me return to the code, but I am still able to move forward. If there is something important though, such as a security concern, I will take the time immediately to fix the code, instead of delaying.

The goal of code reviews is to work together with another person to make sure that your code does what you want it to. Together, you can find the oversights and weaknesses of an individual's work and create more robust software.

Unit, feature, and integration tests

There are many types of tests for code, but I tend to group them into three categories:

♦ **Unit tests**: Used for making sure functions and methods are working properly

♦ **Feature tests**: Also called smoke and acceptance tests. They validate that a feature is working correctly

♦ **Integration tests**: These tests are for making sure features and systems work together correctly

I will go into some detail on these three categories but first a caveat: do not get too hung up on writing the perfect test in each category. It's more important to test the thing you want to test. Do you want to test what happens when a user creates a username with an emoji in it? Find a level of testing that makes the most sense to you, instead of getting hung up on making sure that you stick perfectly to any one model of test category.

Unit tests

Unit tests tend to be small and some of the most prolific tests in existence. **Test-driven development (TDD)** is the mentality that you should write a test for every feature before you write any code. Those who follow TDD often write thousands of unit tests to make sure that the code they are writing sticks to their initial specification. I personally find TDD exhausting, but it is very popular and a great way to make sure that what you are writing is tested.

What is a good unit test suite? It is something that validates that your function performs correctly when given valid input, but also tests failure conditions when bad input is given. If the function is dependent on external factors, such as a database or external API, then it mocks that service, so only the local code is tested. If there are multiple types of responses that the function can respond with, making sure that the suite includes tests for all states is important. For example, if there is a user modification function, make sure to test that it can create a user, modify an existing user, or produce an error if the user does not exist.

One thing to note is that mocking (or stubbing or faking) external services is not required for unit tests. If your system has a lot of networked dependencies, it might be a good idea to not stub your dependencies but instead to guarantee that your code deals with network latency correctly. This is up to you and your team though. The reason people usually recommend that you mock your dependencies in unit tests is that you just want to be testing the logic inside of your method and not your dependencies. The problem with this is that you also often get people who only write simple mocks that don't deal with edge cases of services being disconnected or sending in corrupted data. You are probably seeing the problem with my statement though. Your dependencies will not always be in good or bad states, so you are not testing those either. There is not a good answer here. Testing every state for every dependency is hard and takes a lot of time. Finding the right solution is difficult and so far, I have not seen great answers. Some people suggest recording states using VCR tools. VCR is a library from the Ruby world that saves the response for a request into a file and then uses it for future tests. Others suggest using complicated mocking frameworks (which use code to imitate external systems), while some people advise not using any mocks.

Feature tests

Feature tests are for testing features, as you might expect. I tend to group feature tests into two groups: smoke and acceptance tests. Smoke tests should be run always and are often the very core features that you do not want to change. Smoke tests should be fast and easy to run. Acceptance tests, on the other hand, are often in-depth tests that will test many features. They tend to contain lots of edge cases. The goal for all feature tests is to make sure that features for a part of a service are working. You still should mock out external services (such as databases, external APIs, and so on) like you do in unit tests, but instead of testing a small function, test the business logic, user interactions, and data flow through multiple functions. Often feature tests will test an API, for example, making sure that it conforms to a published specification.

Integration tests

Integration tests, on the other hand, test the entire flow of data between services. They do not mock anything. They fire off an initial request and monitor to make sure everything happens correctly. An example integration test might be an API request to a virtual machine creation service that waits for a virtual machine instance to spin up and then tries to SSH into the machine to mark the test as passed. Another example is making API calls to add a product to a shopping cart, checkout with the item, and then cancel the order. Integration tests are sometimes not run as part of development because they tend to be slow. Instead, they are more often run as hourly or daily cron jobs.

Integration tests are complicated, though, because as your systems become sufficiently complex, the chance that one of your services is always acting in a degraded state increases. In these cases, more often than not you are testing how your error handling works as systems and dependencies are in various states of health.

If you have tests that require everything to be working properly to pass, then you might want to think about your systems architecture. When one of your dependencies fails, are you okay with that level of outage? Your integration tests' fragility will often reflect the fragility of your architecture and users' experience.

There are other ways to test your code, including static analysis and fuzzing, but the above strategies are great starting points. If you are doing code reviews and have some degree of tests at all three levels, you will be well on your way to more stable code.

Negative testing

While not necessarily a type of testing, negative testing is an important methodology to keep in mind. The theory goes that people will always input data that you are not expecting. This could be input with unusual characters or code meant to cause a security vulnerability, or your users could just be doing things in an unexpected way.

When testing, try to come up with as many unusual cases for input as possible. Your users will often think differently than you and there will always be users who do not have good intentions or send you unusual input.

Testing infrastructure

Another area to test besides your code is the infrastructure that your code runs on. When I talk about infrastructure, the line is becoming more and more blurred, as now everything in your datacenter can be software defined if you want. So, I will start with this—if you write code to maintain your infrastructure, such as a job scheduler or a vulnerability scanner, that code should have similar testing just like application code.

Testing infrastructure is interesting because there are multiple layers. One aspect is making sure that your infrastructure is configured correctly. Another aspect is ensuring that your infrastructure deals with single pieces failing at any one time. Finally, testing is important to make sure that new code can handle production's level of operation.

Configuration testing is often the easiest. It depends on your tooling, but whether you are using Chef, Puppet, Ansible, Salt, or Terraform, all these tools have a way to validate and test their configs. Once you have tested the actual configuration, you can test its application to a similar environment. Often, people will have a staging environment which is a clone of their production one but with slightly less resources. This is easier in setups where you use cloud infrastructure but finding ways to run your infrastructure configuration in a separate environment is very useful.

After verifying that your infrastructure is configured correctly, it can be a good idea to have some sort of regular verification that things have not changed. Monitoring server health, system configuration, and general infrastructure changes can keep your mind at ease. You can monitor lots of system metrics, from the classics like CPU, memory, disk space, and network traffic, to the number of applications deployed on a system or the number of applications behind each load balancer. One of my favorite metrics is bastion SSH logins by a user. You can watch to see who is actually connecting to your infrastructure in unsafe ways. If you are running in a cloud service, they often also provide audit logs, which let you see what API calls people are making against your infrastructure. If you run some sort of service discovery system, you can record the metrics of how many instances of a service are discoverable, compared to how many are configured. It all depends on how you have your infrastructure set up, but pulling in metrics about what is currently available, versus what is configured, can be very useful.

Once you know that your environment is created and configured correctly, you can start testing by removing pieces and testing failover. One of the more prominent tools for testing failover is Netflix's Chaos Monkey. The idea is that you can have a piece of software constantly killing or disabling software throughout your environment. By assuming this chaos is always there, you will, in theory, start writing software which is defensive and not as delicate as software that assumes things will always be working. There are other pieces of software that do this, but you can also do the same thing yourself. The key is to make a plan, have a recovery plan in case things break, and then execute it and monitor the results. An example experiment might look like this:

> **What if we remove access to memcached? We could test it by spinning up an extra server, sending fake traffic to it, and then turning off its access to memcached. Now, because it's not a normal production server, we don't need an off switch there, but if we need to cancel the test, we will stop sending traffic to the test server. We will look at error counts before, during, and after memcached removal to see how the system reacts.**

This example may seem contrived, but in comparison you can also probably imagine the outage that might happen if one of your dependencies just dies and disappears in the middle of the night. Maybe your system is incredibly well architected and nothing bad happens, but often when your organization is building things and moving fast, you skip this part until it becomes an issue.

This field is now called **Chaos Engineering**. There are automated tools to kill Docker containers, add network latency, cause issues with CPU and RAM, and really cause chaos at every level. One of my favorite implementations was at Google where for a while it had a separate wireless network that acted like a 2G EDGE cell phone connection. You could connect to it and see how different the network speed made your browsing experience.

Another area which is often ignored is data recovery testing. I usually view this as the inverse of testing absence because this is testing your backups of stateful data systems to make sure that you can come back from a catastrophic failure. This usually involves three steps for everything you consider to be a datastore or database:

1. Are you backing up your data regularly?

2. Are you regularly testing restoring your data?

3. Are you validating that restored data?

You cannot easily test backups if they do not exist, so that's usually a good starting place. The next test is trying to restore one of your backups. You can do this test manually, but make sure to have someone try to do the restore who is not the same person who set up the backups. Does everyone know there are backups? Do they know where the backups are? Do they know how to restore the backup? Once you have restored the backup, how do you verify that all of the data is there? Is there another source of truth you can look at or does it require you to look at your working database to verify the restore? Once you have done all of this manually, automate the test! Have it run regularly.

Since you have tested how things deal with the possible chaos of the environment, you should also test how they deal with real-world traffic. One way to do this is to write load tests. These are scripts that create artificial amounts of traffic. Often, they generate spikes of traffic that all match a certain pattern. There are lots of pieces of software which will do this for you, including:

- ◆ Apache Bench
- ◆ Siege
- ◆ wrk
- ◆ beeswithmachineguns
- ◆ hey

Most of these tools work in a similar way. You provide them with a URL, a number of connections to make, and a test duration, and they will send many HTTP requests to the URL in the duration. These HTTP requests are network traffic to your application. My personal favorite is hey, mainly because I like the name. That is not a great reason for choosing a piece of software, but since most of these tools act in the same way, it serves my needs. hey is also interesting to me because it is written in Go, so it's easy to read the source code, and it runs locally. All of the provided scripts above run locally as well except for beeswithmachineguns, which actually creates virtual machines in AWS and then runs there.

The default way to run hey is just with a URL:

```
$ hey https://etsy.com
Summary:
  Total:        15.4234 secs
  Slowest:      7.3585 secs
  Fastest:      0.9804 secs
  Average:      3.1290 secs
  Requests/sec:    12.9673


Response time histogram:
  0.980 [1]    |■
  1.618 [12]   |■■■■■■■■■
  2.256 [47]   |■■■■■■■■■■■■■■■■■■■■■■■■■■■■■■■■■■■■■
               ■■■■■■■■
  2.894 [43]   |■■■■■■■■■■■■■■■■■■■■■■■■■■■■■■■■■■■■
               ■■■■■
  3.532 [37]   |■■■■■■■■■■■■■■■■■■■■■■■■■■■■■■■■
```

```
4.169  [17]  |■■■■■■■■■■■■■■
4.807  [17]  |■■■■■■■■■■■■■■
5.445  [13]  |■■■■■■■■■■■
6.083  [5]   |■■■■
6.721  [6]   |■■■■■
7.359  [2]   |■■
```

```
Latency distribution:
  10% in 1.7135 secs
  25% in 2.1085 secs
  50% in 2.8585 secs
  75% in 3.8118 secs
  90% in 5.1091 secs
  95% in 5.8204 secs
  99% in 6.9235 secs
```

```
Details (average, fastest, slowest):
  DNS+dialup:  0.2798 secs, 0.0000 secs, 2.8845 secs
  DNS-lookup:  0.1346 secs, 0.0004 secs, 1.1582 secs
  req write:   0.0001 secs, 0.0000 secs, 0.0003 secs
  resp wait:   0.4646 secs, 0.2297 secs, 2.2864 secs
  resp read:   1.4861 secs, 0.2546 secs, 4.4335 secs
```

```
Status code distribution:
  [200]        200 responses
```

By default, `hey` sends 200 requests at a concurrency level of 50. This means that it opens 50 channels and sends 200 requests as fast as it can. In this example request to `etsy.com`, hey made on average 12 requests per second. Next, we will tell `hey` to send one request every second, on a single channel, and only send 20 requests. Math says that this should take only 20 seconds (20 * 1 * 1 = 20), but because of network latency, and how long requests take to complete, it may take a longer or shorter time.

Also, because requests per second is an average over all requests, we will actually see a QPS less than one because of server processing time and networking transfer times. Note the `Details` section, which shows how time was spent by the client when sending and receiving HTTP requests:

```
$ hey -q 1 -c 1 -n 20 https://etsy.com
Summary:
  Total:        27.8880 secs
  Slowest:      1.9484 secs
  Fastest:      0.9688 secs
  Average:      1.3444 secs
  Requests/sec:     0.7172


Response time histogram:
  0.969 [1]  |■■■■■■■■■■
  1.067 [4]  |■■■■■■■■■■■■■■■■■■■■■■■■■■■■■■■■■■■■■■■■■■
             ■■■■■■■■
  1.165 [2]  |■■■■■■■■■■■■■■■■■■■■
  1.263 [2]  |■■■■■■■■■■■■■■■■■■■■
  1.361 [3]  |■■■■■■■■■■■■■■■■■■■■■■■■■■■■■■■
  1.459 [2]  |■■■■■■■■■■■■■■■■■■■■
  1.557 [1]  |■■■■■■■■■■
  1.655 [1]  |■■■■■■■■■■
  1.752 [1]  |■■■■■■■■■■
  1.850 [1]  |■■■■■■■■■■
  1.948 [2]  |■■■■■■■■■■■■■■■■■■■■


Latency distribution:
  10% in 0.9828 secs
  25% in 1.0822 secs
  50% in 1.3048 secs
  75% in 1.6352 secs
  90% in 1.9073 secs
  95% in 1.9484 secs
```

```
Details (average, fastest, slowest):
  DNS+dialup: 0.0428 secs, 0.0000 secs, 0.8559 secs
  DNS-lookup: 0.0209 secs, 0.0017 secs, 0.3805 secs
  req write:  0.0001 secs, 0.0000 secs, 0.0002 secs
  resp wait:  0.3897 secs, 0.2737 secs, 0.5480 secs
  resp read:  0.3370 secs, 0.0763 secs, 1.0449 secs


Status code distribution:
  [200]      20 responses
```

While load tests can be useful for understanding how a service handles large amounts of requests, often this is unrealistic compared to normal web service traffic. Normal web traffic is very diverse and we will never see a uniform distribution of traffic. You get normal users trying all sorts of things all at the same time, plus random users driving by hitting random URLs and sending you arbitrary payloads.

To deal with this, people often test with production traffic. This concept scares people, but the two most common methods, shadow testing and canarying, are very useful. They scare people because you are putting services into production that you know could have bugs. The usual answer to this is that your code should deal with any system failing, but also that would be true of any code you launch into production because it all could have bugs.

Shadow testing is the act of recording requests to a service and then replaying them to a new version of the app, as a way to test it. This lets you take production traffic and have it tested against new code, without the cost of running it in front of actual production traffic. This can be difficult to set up but can be good for validating in certain types of scenarios.

Some tools for shadow testing include:

♦ For HTTP requests there is vegeta (`https://github.com/tsenart/vegeta`) and goreplay (`https://goreplay.org`)

- For raw TCP there is tcpreplay (`http://tcpreplay.appneta.com/`)

- For database queries there is query-playback (`https://github.com/Percona-Lab/query-playback`) and mongoreplay (`https://github.com/mongodb/mongo-tools/tree/master/mongoreplay`)

There are other tools as well, but these are just a sample.

A much simpler and more common method of testing against production traffic is canarying. Canarying is the act of introducing an instance of a service that is new and having it get a small portion of traffic. So, for instance, you have new code, or a new type of server or something, and you slowly divert traffic to it. You first send 1%, then 10%, then 50%, and finally 100% of traffic. This is the equivalent of putting your foot in the pool to see if it is too cold. It lets you verify that the code can handle normal traffic patterns, without exposing every single user to the new code. If you are doing a canary, make sure that the traffic you send to it is representative. For many services, 1% of traffic is not enough to effectively test your application.

Monitoring is what makes something like canarying work. When you have insight into your entire system, you can know whether there are bugs firing from the new code. Another testing methodology, that only really works when you have extensive monitoring, is feature flags. Feature flags work like canarying, but instead of using the deployment to separate the new code from the old, you use code. Feature flags let you surround new features or code paths with a Boolean statement. This Boolean statement says whether this feature is enabled for this user then continues. So, you can do things like only letting 10% of logged-in users see a feature or only letting employees see a feature. With monitoring, you can then see whether certain code paths are erring more than others. Feature flags can make debugging more difficult because if a user is seeing unusual things while using your service, then you may need to first figure out what features they are enabled for, before you can properly debug their experience.

Without monitoring, testing in production like this is very dangerous because you have little or no visibility of the effect your changes are having on everyone. The whole point of testing is to verify your hypothesis. If you have no way of seeing the results of your test, then you cannot verify anything, thus you are not actually testing anything.

Testing processes

Outside of testing computers and software, it is important to test processes and humans as well. The first process I want to bring your attention to comes from Google and has a rich history. The process I am referring to is DiRT (`https://queue.acm.org/detail.cfm?id=2371516`). DiRT is a yearly exercise where Google plans for large outages to see how teams react. **DiRT** (**Disaster Recovery Testing**) examples include making Google headquarters unreachable, shutting down systems that large numbers of teams are dependent on, taking a datacenter offline, and planning unified outages across multiple teams.

What makes DiRT particularly useful is not the scale of the outages, but that it prompts teams to plan their own training exercises during the week and provides resources to help teams to have successful experiments. Some experiments are purely theoretical, some are against testing servers, and some are against actual production systems. DiRT also tests people and systems. So, if everyone is forced to evacuate the building, can you still respond to an incident? Are there certain processes that only have one person who can do the thing?

The idea of such large-scale testing is very similar to the idea of a military exercise, where you get multiple arms of the military to work together to practice a war. Modern versions of this apparently came from the RAND corporation after World War II but can be traced as far back as the 19th century Prussians, who ran practice war simulations under the name of Kriegsspiel. Similarly, schools in California regularly have earthquake drills. On an even larger scale, Mexico holds a national public earthquake drill every year on September 19th.

This has been happening since 1985 when an 8.1 magnitude earthquake killed tens of thousands of people. It has led to heightened preparedness among the populace and is believed to be one of the main reasons that a similar 2017 quake killed approximately 200 people, instead of two magnitudes more.

While DiRT is a yearly large-scale test, like the Mexico drill, a much smaller but lighter weight test is the Wheel of Misfortune (also known as a WoM or Gameday). A WoM is a role-playing exercise, closer to the scale of a school earthquake drill. A WoM is where a person comes up with a scenario and then has someone pretend to be on-call and respond to the scenario. In most cases, the on-call person receives something like an outage notification and then talks through the scenario with the person running the scenario (the game master or GM). The GM will provide example graphs or describe what the on-call sees when they run a command or look at a tool.

A WoM is best done in a room with others watching and not talking. After the fake incident happens, which should be limited to a certain amount of time to respect everyone's time, open the floor for questions. Often, people will wonder why an on-call person tried something or how to do something in real life. Attendees might also want more detail about the incident. If it is based on a real outage, providing the postmortem or explaining how this scenario relates to real life is helpful.

Finally, you can test things before they are ever created. You can do this by holding design reviews. A design review is a meeting held in a similar way to a postmortem meeting (see *Chapter 4*, *Postmortems*), but instead of discussing a document talking about a past incident, you talk about the design of a piece of software you want to write. The document should be sent around ahead of time and include what problem you're solving, how you're solving it, other possible solutions you're not using, and anything else you think is important. A design review meeting then lets people poke holes in your design and talk about possible outages and problems that might arise.

Sometimes, no one sees anything wrong, while other times they will correct assumptions about dependencies or talk about possible concurrency issues. Design reviews aren't perfect because they often talk about theoretical software, but they can help you to move in the correct direction and also prime people to think about how new code will interact with the rest of the system and maybe cause other outages.

Releasing

Releasing or deploying is the act of taking a bunch of code, bundling it up, and distributing it to users. It can take lots of forms, from copying a lot of individual files to a running server, to building a package and publishing it to a repository for users to download, or even creating some type of physical media and putting it in the mail. Getting software to this state of "done and shipped" has changed dramatically over the years. Where we used to hand friends copies of floppy disks (books like this used to come with 3.5-inch pieces of square plastic that contained software on them), we now visit websites to download software or more commonly, the website is the software itself. When you were shipping software on physical media (which people still do, especially in the video game and movie industries), you would deem software "gold" and that was the version that was burnt to disk and sent to customers. Now, more commonly, we release software to a server or have various ways of delivering iterations of code to people remotely. This increases how often we release and decreases the time we spend on each individual release. Determining the perfect release is no longer the goal, instead we just want a good release, so we can keep iterating and growing the product.

What makes a good release? How do we have confidence in what we are delivering? How do we make sure we do not break things by deploying? How do we know if the release worked? There are a few things in these questions. First, is verifying the code beforehand, which is what a lot of the testing we talked about is for. Next, is making sure our distribution is consistent and stable. Finally, we need to verify that our deployed code is healthy after our release.

Making sure the build and distribution are consistent and stable usually requires the release to have three properties:

◆ Repeatable

◆ Tested

◆ Idempotent

Repeatable is actually the most controversial of these three. Repeatable builds mean that if you build the same code twice, it gives the exact same output. Traditionally, very few builds were this way, which meant that if two people built the same code, they could not both take the hash of the output and compare. This was problematic mainly for security. You cannot guarantee that you have the correct binary, and that it has not been tampered with, if you cannot say that it has the correct hash. This is easier to do if you are just compiling code, as most compilers output the same binary consistently. It is much more difficult if you are building something like a Debian package, a Docker image, or an Amazon Machine Image. This is because often, steps require getting up-to-date dependencies or writing out files that change with time. It is not impossible and the Debian team has been making huge strides to make every Debian build deterministic and reproducible. You can verify that your build is repeatable by building on two different systems and comparing a checksum (such as the SHA256) of the output. They should be equivalent if they were built in similar ways (two different Linux machines for example).

Tested is pretty straightforward. You want to make sure that your tests are passing and that they actually test something. One of the dangers here is a reverence for "green". Green means that your tests have all passed. If your tests are not testing much, then having a green build does not mean anything. This is a fine starting place, but it also means that you probably should not deploy whenever your build is green if green does not have much meaning. We will talk about verifying a release soon, but less testing done upfront usually means more validation after release.

Idempotent is very similar to repeatable but focuses more on the deployment and distribution phase of a release, and less on the building aspect. Idempotent is a term from mathematics that means if you do the operation multiple times, it will have the same output. For example, if you have the equation x = x * 1, x will always be the same. If you have y = y * 5, every time you run the equation you will get a different y. The x equation is idempotent, whereas the y one is not. This is important because of scaling. You need a deployment system that no matter what the state is of the system passed in, you will always get the same resulting system. For example, if you start with three servers running version 1.0.0 of your code and you deploy 1.1.0, you expect them all to get 1.1.0. Then if you need to scale up, the same process should be able to take an empty server and get it to the state of running 1.1.0. This is an important metric to record, by the way, so you know what version each piece of software is running. That way you can graph your rollout of your software and understand what is running where and when. However, the point of idempotent is that if you were to run the deploy script over a server every hour, no matter what, you would always get the server to the same state. Idempotency is the basis for most configuration management tools, such as Chef and Ansible, as their goal is to be able to take a system in any state and bring it to an identical final state.

When to release

We mentioned earlier in the book the idea of an SLO—we do not even need to always have a service that is healthy. Instead, we need to have a metric for when we've been healthy enough recently. If we are within SLO, we can release. There are a lot of caveats to that statement, but at the very core fundamentals, that is what we are aiming for. However, lots of services do not have SLOs and there are lots of risks associated with modifying a service that has users.

To circumvent modifying a service with active users, we can start by first changing different environments. In this modern world, where new virtual machines can be created in minutes and the cost of infrastructure is constantly plummeting, it is a good idea to have at least three environments. The first is on your development machine. It does not have to be a perfect replica of production as some people want (having everything running on your laptop gets very difficult when you have a larger infrastructure with lots of moving pieces), but should at least let you have a view of the code you are working on running. The next environment should be something like "test", "dev", or "staging". You can have multiple of these, but the idea is a production-like environment. These environments should have new code deployed to them often. They can be used for testing and playing with code running in a production-like environment. You might want more than one for testing different configurations or to have systems in certain states. Another popular thing to do is to spin up a new environment for every code review of a service. This lets you have a single instance of a service with new code running, to make sure it interacts correctly with other services.

Releasing to production

Next, and finally, is production. Production is the environment that holds the services that users actually talk to. While every other environment can be released whenever, production is where you need to take risks into account. Let's start with the easiest risk to manage—people. Think about your organization—are there people around to deal with outages or problems if you release now? For many US-based organizations, that means only releasing between 10 am and 4 pm local time, Monday through to Friday. For larger organizations, maybe you'll have people available at all times of the day. If you have an office in Tel Aviv, your weekend may be Friday and Saturday, instead of Saturday and Sunday. Releasing outside of the hours that people are available is doable but not recommended if you can help it.

If you are releasing code that other people wrote and you do not have any way of getting hold of them, then there is always the risk you will have to roll back if something goes wrong. This is not a problem if rollbacks are easy but if they are not, this is a much bigger issue.

Beyond having people available at deployment time, the other reason to limit when you deploy is to allow for the software to bake. This idea is that software sits in production and receives traffic, and if it is going to have issues, the chance of that will decay exponentially. Obviously, this isn't true because very little software exists in a static system, but the chance of an issue happening is greatest when a change occurs. It decreases quickly after that until the next change happens.

To limit this people risk, some organizations set up a policy where you can only release outside of the allowed release window once a month. This is hard to deal with because the chances of there being an emergency need to release need to be considered. Instead, if you are intent on making your release schedule a thing, try enforcing postmortems for releasing outside of the schedule. What caused it? What benefit did it provide? That way, you can discuss as an organization, or group, whether this was a valid reason to deploy out of schedule or if the schedule even makes sense.

The next kind of risk is a risk of full introduction. This is the risk of the first time you introduce code being at 100%. It is like giving a gift to a stranger because you have a limited idea about what will happen. There are lots of strategies to deal with this. We've talked about canaries, which help, but there are also blue/green deployments (also sometimes called black/red deployments). There are other strategies as well, but these two are the most popular deployment strategies. In a blue/green deployment, you spin up a whole new copy of the service, while leaving the old version running. You then point the new load balancer at the new copy and then once you verify the new copy is running well, you turn down the old copy. In blue/green deployments, the blue copy is the old one and the green copy is the new one.

blue/green is useful because it lets you jump back to the running service quickly, which is especially useful if rollbacks are slow. You can even combine the idea of canaries and blue/green deployments by slowly migrating traffic between the two clusters! One note about these strategies is that they can be very expensive in terms of time and resources to set up. Make sure that you have the monitoring and insight into your platform before setting it up, or these strategies will not help you much because you will be unable to validate between the different systems.

Some people ask how often you should release. I personally like to release as often as possible because the smaller the code changes between release, the easier it is to track down what is causing an issue if there is a problem. Others go for a more scheduled approach, such as every Tuesday or the second to last day of a sprint or any other number of arbitrary choices. All options work. It's best to work with your team to find a schedule that works for your team.

No matter how often you deploy, though, I recommend making sure that there is some way to surface the difference between releases. That way you can see what has changed between releases when you are trying to track down an issue. On top of being able to see the code differences between releases, also keep a change log with human-parsable changes. A change log lets you track down which release something was introduced in and code differences then let you dig into how it was introduced. This is not only important for your team to debug releases, but also for people who integrate with your software and for management to see how the service is progressing. Communicating on how your service is changing is important, just like communication at all other levels. Communicating how a service is changing helps people to debug their own issues and also understand the work that other people are doing.

Validating your release

After you put your release out into the world, you need to validate it. All sorts of things can go wrong in computers, so being able to verify a service is running the correct version and working properly is important. This should not be just waiting to see whether errors come in because unless you have a large user base, you cannot assume users will hit all features and edge cases after a release. Make sure that someone is in charge of validating that the changes that went out actually work and the deploy went out well.

That being said, monitoring and error tracking is probably the best way to validate a release over time, after you check the new changes which were released. Having your alerts and monitoring tuned makes knowing whether a release is stable, and that you did not introduce any regressions into your code, easy. I have had jobs where the on-call person is in charge of doing releases, which lets a single person be the knowledge repository for the code going out and the incidents it causes for any given period.

If you are using a system that deploys using canaries or deploys in a pipeline first to one environment and then another, have a button or something that lets the person in charge of the deploy click and say, "I have validated this portion of the release". You could even have an automated system do integration tests and then if no errors occur, continue through the workflow pipeline.

Outside of keeping an eye on errors, another common cause of outages is when you break compatibility with an older client. For lots of web services this is not an issue, but for those that work in the mobile application space, this is a constant problem. Some companies do this by creating many API versions, others by just obsessively testing existing client code with new backends. Some just define a maximum number of versions they support, pop up a message to a user, and tell them to upgrade to keep using the service. Every service is different, so figuring out what you support is a business decision but making sure that that is part of your release validation is important.

Rollbacks

I have mentioned rollbacks a few times so far without really describing them. A rollback is the idea of reverting a release. The faster and easier your rollback is, the more risk you can take on with your releases. This is because if there is a single button someone can press to rollback to a known working version, someone who is on-call can just press that button if they see anything bad and ask questions later. This is not always possible. If your deployment process is to just `rsync` some files to a server, it is often harder to revert those files to a correct version. If you are stuck with just uploading files, I would recommend installing your version control software on the server and have it checkout a tag when you want to release. That way all files are changed to the correct version.

Along with making your rollbacks speedy, also make sure to test your rollbacks. This is very similar to testing your database backups because if you do not test your process, it is very possible that it will break when you need it most. However, you do not need to just test to make sure your rollbacks happen. When you rollback, you need to do a validation as if you had just released because you have essentially done that.

Automation

Automating releasing and testing is a common task. Both tend to have a lot of steps, so creating a consistent place and way to run tests and releases can improve overall reliability. Without this, a build or test could happen on a differently configured machine each time and introduce unknown variables. Incomplete configuration, steps done out of order, or incorrectly typed commands have caused many an outage, so automating this process is incredibly valuable.

Automation of testing and releasing usually requires automating three things:

♦ **Building**: The actual creation of an artifact from source code

♦ **Testing**: Validating the created artifact

♦ **Distributing**: Sending the artifact to the user

Automation exists because people are forgetful. All three of these things can be automated using similar tools. Almost all of these tools are essentially job runners that run on an event queue. That queue can be filled by actions, such as code committed to a version control repository or a button click. The queue can also be filled with events based on time, like an event every hour to run integration tests. There are many tools that can do this and many are hosted services. The top three that I have used and enjoyed are:

♦ Travis CI

♦ Circle CI

♦ Jenkins

Each has different features and is changing constantly, but all of them operate on the same methodology—reading events and running jobs. Travis and Circle are hosted services that are configured with YAML (a whitespace sensitive markup language). Jenkins is an open-source piece of software that people can run and maintain themselves. It's a pain to configure and run, but it's very powerful if a hosted service doesn't meet your needs.

How you design your automation is up to you and your developer workflow. Sometimes you will have to build twice—once with options for testing and once with production optimizations. Sometimes you will need to build a binary and then build a package around it to distribute it. You can also cache your builds, so maybe your test runner just needs to go and get the most recently built binary to do the test. Most services even support defining workflows, so you can do many different things in parallel or in sequence.

The point is, just automate your tests and releases. You are going to have an emergency and need to push out a quick hot fix, or someone new is going to need to push out a deploy and they aren't going to know what to do. By automating these steps, you can make it so all the person has to do is trigger an event and they can just sit back and watch things happen.

You can also add automation to other places in the stack. One common trick is to have things like lint checks run and automatically comment on code reviews. You can also move a lot of your automation into chat. This allows for things like sending group chat messages that tell the service to deploy, thus informing everyone that a deploy is happening and also making the deploy happen at the same time.

Continuous everything

One last subject I would like to talk about for testing and releasing is the continuous category. There are a lot of words that people like to put after continuous, and often they cause arguments that are incredibly pedantic. This is usually just describing the three steps I described above in the *Automation* section. Some call the whole thing continuous integration, which is what most of these job-runner service providers name themselves. I have also read many think pieces, each trying to define very subtle differences, none of which matter. Terms I have heard that all seem to be very similar are:

- Continuous integration
- Continuous release
- Continuous deployment
- Continuous delivery
- Deploy on green

The overarching point is that things are tested, built, and delivered all with automation. Some systems add human checks into pipelines. Some allow for automated rollbacks if issues arise. Some have buttons that need to be clicked or test conditions that need to be passed. I highly recommend staying out of pedantic arguments about naming your integration and instead focusing on finding the workflow that works best for your organization and the levels of risk your coworkers are comfortable with.

That being said, each of these ideas and their subtle differences can be useful. Continuous integration is the idea that on every commit a set of tests should be run to determine whether code has bugs or not. Continuous deployment is the idea that every commit should be deployed to production automatically. Continuous delivery is similar but instead focuses on the idea that once you decide to deploy code, the entire deployment happens automatically. Deploy on green is the idea that continuous deployment should happen whenever the tests pass.

All of these different definitions (and the many more I didn't touch on) each have long books and blog posts written on them. More often than not, especially for smaller organizations, knowing the difference doesn't matter. Instead, focus on consistency. As you discover problems with your existing processes, use the ideas in those long writings to figure out ways you can improve your process. It's rarely worth starting from scratch, instead just keep iterating as you would with any piece of software.

Summary

We covered a lot in this chapter! We talked about various types of testing—the differences between unit tests, integration tests, and many others. We covered a few tools you can use to help with those tests and also how to think about what to test.

We focused on releasing code and validating those releases, before touching on canaries, blue/green releases, when to release, and what makes a good release. We also discussed automating both your testing and release processes. Finally, we looked at the different terminology people use in this space and things to think about when coming up with a workflow for your organization.

In the next chapter, we will be talking about capacity planning and how to grow your infrastructure over time.

~ 6 ~

CAPACITY PLANNING

Capacity planning is the art of predicting the future. It is the process of figuring out how you take your view of the past as metrics and apply it to future planning. As a field, capacity planning has significantly changed over the years. It has been around for centuries, because as long as humans have been able to, we have planned for the future. Where does our food come from? Where are we sleeping tonight? How much food do we trade and how much do we keep for our family? How do I surround myself with people who respect me? Can my tribe survive by hunting this herd? Where has the best jobs? Even today, we are constantly evaluating how our current situation will change and whether we can survive within it.

Capacity planning grew throughout the industrial age, as people learned that they had to hire workers based on demand, their output speed, and how many materials they had. This is how things stayed for a long time and it is still accurate today, whether we are building data centers or making products such as chairs. In terms of data centers, something I learned from Google is that filling a data center is easy but finding the space for one and building it is not.

Starting in 2012, it took Google around three-to-five years to find a plot of land to build a data center, persuade the local government to sell it the energy it needed, and get all of the appropriate paperwork signed. It would then take 18 months to build the building and wire it up. Finally, it would take six months to fill it with servers and be online and working. These long timelines require Google to always be planning for growth. If it will take five years to make a significant growth in capacity happen, careful planning is needed.

These sorts of timelines used to be more common in the engineering world. Imagine how long it might take to build a bridge or look at the release cycle of Apple laptops. With software, though, we are quickly moving away from long timelines. Now, we have moved to a world where you can create servers almost immediately. Software-defined networks are becoming the norm. Often, you are running on other people's computers in *the cloud* or are in the process of building a platform for other people to run on top of.

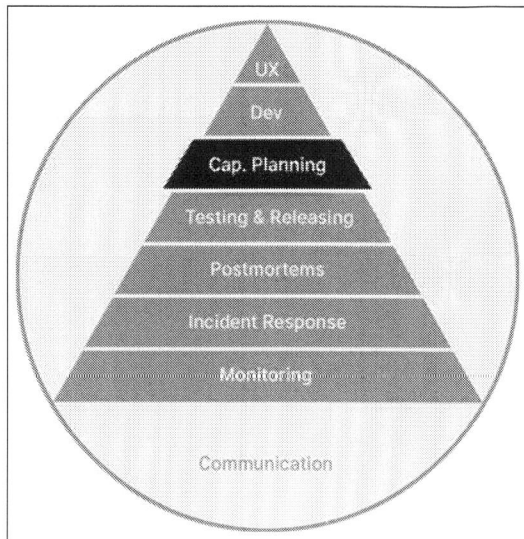

Figure 1: Our current position in the hierarchy

Capacity planning is incredibly valuable, because growing capacity can be a slow and expensive process, even given the advent of modern technology. As we continue to move up our hierarchy of reliability, we are now talking about the future. How do we plan for it, shape what it may look like, and assess the risks and problems that may appear? In this chapter, we will be talking about how to plan for growth, some basics of finance, how software architecture changes affect capacity planning, and how to communicate within your business about growth.

A quick introduction to business finance

Often, engineers think about things such as software performance, metrics, servers, hard drives and network bandwidth. Instead, we will first dive into some business finance. I have found that many software developers are interested in finance (see cryptocurrencies, flash trading, gambling, and so on), but it took me a long time to be turned on to it. As such, people would speak finance jargon and I would smile and nod. Frequently, I did not realize what was being implied about how the business thought about my team or about how our CEO viewed economics. I bring this up now because one of the most significant aspects of capacity planning is figuring out money: discovering how your business deals with money and how to acquire it for your team. Can you ask your CEO to approve a $50,000 purchase or do you need to work with the finance department? Does your company have a budget for increases in infrastructure costs? Often, you will interact with someone who will use terms you have never heard of, which will make discussing money difficult. Knowing jargon and language is vital to working with people. It sets a baseline to start discussions.

> This is not legal, investment, or financial advice, as I am just an engineer. Talk to your accountant, bank teller, financial planner, lawyer, CFO, or anyone who has a degree in these things before making financial decisions.

Here is a list of some economics jargon that I have found useful when thinking about businesses:

♦ **Cash flow**: This is how you describe how much money you have, where it comes from, and where it goes. It consists of *revenue*, which is incoming money, and *expenditures*, which is outgoing money.

♦ **P&L**: **Profits and losses** or P&L is a description of how much money you have and how it changes, usually on a quarterly basis. You get these figures by subtracting your expenditures from your revenue. If the result is greater than zero, you have profits. If the result is less than zero, you have losses.

♦ **Balance sheet**: A balance sheet is a list of assets, liabilities, and equity. Basically, it is what the company owns, whom it owes money to, and who is investing in it. The backing equation for the sheet is *Assets = Liabilities + Equity*. The money you have spent (your assets) is equal to the money you have borrowed from the bank (liabilities) and equity (money you got from investors).

♦ **Capex** and **Opex**: Capex is capital expenditures and Opex is operational expenditures. Capital is a term used to define the value of stuff or assets that an organization owns. Capital could be money, intellectual property, real estate, physical goods, and so on. Capital expenditures are investments made to increase the amount of capital you have. Often, it is said that Capex is money spent directly correlated to bringing in more revenue. Opex is everything else.

These are investments that you will not get back, such as insurance, labor, people costs, infrastructure, and so on. If you were a gardening service, purchasing the lawn mower would be Capex, while its fuel would be Opex.

♦ **Return on investment**: This is also called **ROI**. In the finance world, this is usually a percentage. To calculate that percentage, you take the money you made, subtract the initial money you invested, and divide that number by the initial money invested. This is the same as saying *ROI = Net Money / Initial Investment*. It is also often used to ask, "Why are we doing this and what do we expect to get in return?" The answer to that is not always money: sometimes it is opportunities or physical goods.

♦ **Cost center versus profit center**: Cost centers and profit centers are usually split similarly to Opex and Capex. Both cost centers and profit centers are groups of people. Investment into a profit center translates to the product we sell. Inversely, a cost center is everything else. So **human resources (HR)** is often a cost center, because it is necessary for the business but not for the creation of the product. Depending on the company, software developers may be considered either a cost or profit center.

Public companies on the New York Stock Exchange are required to share a lot of this financial information with the public every year. Specifically, in the US, they must file a P&L statement, a cash flow statement, and a balance sheet. Some companies also share the information quarterly. Unlike many educational systems (which often have arbitrary periods to define quarters and semesters), businesses usually have financial quarters that are exactly three months long. That means that if your company's fiscal year lines up with the US tax year (which is January 1 to December 31, although tax periods are different depending on the country), then your quarters will end on March 31, June 30, September 30, and December 31.

Private companies can do whatever they want fiscally, but it is pretty standard for private companies to have quarterly board meetings where they discuss their finances with their board. Some companies share board meeting notes with their employees, which is where this data may come up. Note that every company is different, and every country is different, so depending on where you live and where the company you work for is based, all of this may be very different. I have mainly worked for US companies, so my explanations may be imperfect or biased based on that fact.

You should figure out how your organization operates as a business. To do that, you need to understand the flow of money and how to talk to the people who deal with making sure your business has balanced books. While you do that, you can start planning how your software will operate inside that world. Capacity planning is a never-ending task, so you will have to create plans and then adjust them based on how information changes.

Businesses often have a business continuity plan. This is a plan for how the company will deal with significant change. If a business is taking a large risk, this may be written up so the company has a plan for how to recover after a tragedy. This is similar to capacity planning but is designed for the business heads to deal with unforeseen actions. Some businesses and governments even run **Business Continuity Plan (BCP)** as if it is an incident response team. There is constant evaluation of the plan and practice table-top sessions to make sure it would work and people know their roles. All of this is to hedge against the risks that a company constantly faces.

Why plan?

One of my favorite things to read is a good tell-all article about how one decision caused a series of cascading failures. Seeing humanity respond to a crisis brings me great joy and, because of this, I have often been described as a proponent of chaos. What is more chaotic than the reactions of people (and systems) to failures? When I tell people that I enjoy planning and organizing, I usually get at least one raised eyebrow in response. I believe deeply in the Scout motto of *be prepared* and capacity planning is just that: being prepared for eventual change. The theory behind the Scout motto is finding the balance between having all of the tools necessary to deal with problems and the mental fortitude to improvise to deal with the fact that you did not bring all of the tools you need. You can never be fully prepared for risks that you do not know about. So, instead, you should build a plan that has rough edges, that has room for improvisation, and that also solves the issues that you currently know about. The further in the future your plan will take effect, the more room is needed for improvisation. For example, if you are planning two or three years in advance, you may not know even what products your organization might be supporting by then, while if you are planning a month ahead, you probably have a pretty good idea as to what will be happening at a business level.

The reason we do this planning and getting prepared is because running blindly down a dark road is not fun. It may be the true definition of chaos, but it is preventable. If you know you are going hiking at night, bring a flashlight. Likewise, if you know you have a large event coming up, such as the FIFA World Cup, and you know that your data center is running at 40 percent capacity, and the traffic of the event has the possibility of taking you to 240 percent capacity, you should invest in more infrastructure.

Planning is a pain. It requires your monitoring systems to be reliable and comprehensive. It requires having done some amount of load testing. It requires talking with every relevant person in the business, from the developers writing the code, to the product managers and executives planning the direction of the company, to sales people (to understand the flow of incoming customers and how the scale of the product is going to change), to finance, to understand how much money we have and how much we can spend. However, if you can get past all of the hurdles and get everyone to speak the same language, you can prevent serious outages and problems that occur when your infrastructure cannot handle the amount of traffic it is receiving.

Managing risk and managing expectations

The main goal of planning is managing risk and expectations. Arguably, this is also true for the entirety of life, which involves managing other people's expectations and examining the risk of doing things. For capacity planning, it is about expanding that to the entire business. The expectations you are focusing on are how people expect the service to respond when the business sees growth, especially spontaneous growth. The risk you are evaluating is spending time and money on the extra infrastructure to deal with that.

In our discussion of **Service Level Objectives** (**SLO**s) in *Chapter 2, Monitoring*, we talked about different levels of reliability. Some services need to be up more consistently than others for the business to succeed. For example, Casper is a mattress company. Hypothetically, we can assume that Casper always wants to be able to sell mattresses, but if its order fulfilment software fails, as long as it does not lose orders, the order fulfilment system can be down for an hour. That is to say, if you can decouple the flow of incoming orders taken at the store from the process of actually fulfilling the order from the warehouse, the user's experience is not blocked on order fulfillment and will not be affected by short bursts of downtime.

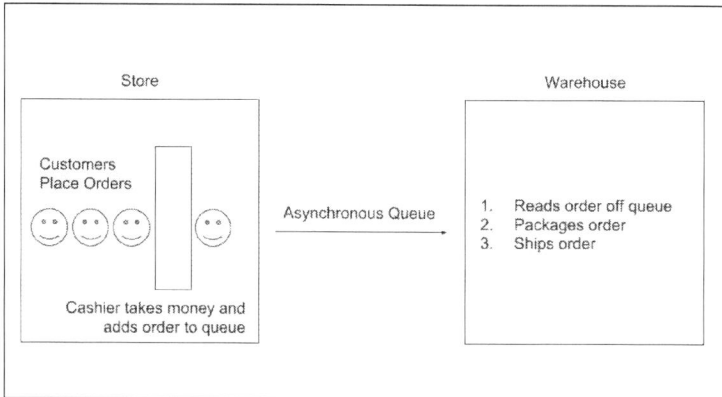

Figure 2: A rough architectural diagram of a mattress store system

The majority of large web companies have migrated to service-oriented architectures or microservice architectures (two phrases that mean the same thing: a bunch of different pieces of software that work together). The business as a whole probably does not care how your system is architected, though, as it just wants to assume that all systems will stay up and be healthy. However, because we are now seeing an increase in the number of systems, and those systems can have different levels of reliability, each system may also need separate capacity plans. Having a discussion with your business partners about how your team views reliability can be important because some business partners can be disconnected from your capacity planning. Sketching out a user experience like the one above can help people outside of your team to understand the engineering decision you are making. By working with business partners and understanding their expectations of the service, you can set yourself up for success in the future when you ask those same people for money or need people to support your budget plans.

Defining a plan

Defining a plan is a series of steps. Each step requires the evaluation of a question to discover the answer:

1. What is our current capacity?

2. When are we going to run out of capacity?

3. How should we change our capacity?

4. Execute plan!

Let us work through each step. Note that I am using long periods of time in a lot of the examples below. If you are using systems that can automatically add and remove capacity, you may be working with data on the scale of minutes instead of days.

What is our current capacity?

There are lots of ways to define the capacity of your infrastructure. You can use aggregated metrics such as CPU usage, disk storage availability, requests per minute, packets per second, or any application metric. Usually, the metrics you want to focus on are the resources that you use the most or the resources that are most important to you. What is most important often comes from your SLOs and the SLIs (Service Level Indicators) behind them. Note that the metrics do not have to be server-side metrics. Companies such as Netflix use the number of people browsing their UI to gauge how much content they may end up serving soon.

Picking metrics for defining your capacity is important because you will want to store them for as long as possible, arguably much longer than you might normally store a metric. Having data to analyze is a requirement for attempting to predict the future. This need is why capacity planning is higher up in the hierarchy than monitoring. Newer companies often have trouble defining their current capacity due to poor metrics collection and monitoring. Without data, capacity planning is just going to be guessing.

If your company is so new that you have no metrics (or just haven't been collecting them), you might instead focus initially on people planning. People planning is a complicated topic, but I would suggest looking at metrics for your team's efficiency at writing code, developing new features, and fixing bugs. Then, once you have started to retain some history of system metrics, you can connect it to people planning.

The other important detail when picking a capacity metric is finding a metric that matches system usage. People often use aggregated CPU usage or aggregated memory usage because computers often have trouble working if there is no CPU or RAM for them to use. As the percentage of available CPU drops while traffic increases, your system gets closer to the total amount of capacity it can handle. One way to hunt down the metrics that correlate to usage is to isolate a single instance of your service and slowly increase the amount of traffic it receives until it stops working. Watching which metrics increase as traffic increases can help to show you what correlates to capacity. This should usually be done with production traffic or at least traffic that looks like production.

We talked about this a bit in *Chapter 5, Testing and Releasing*. Production traffic is helpful because it maps to reality. If you are generating fake traffic, there is a possibility that you are not testing with workloads that match your normal traffic reality. If your tests do not match reality, then you may end up with incorrect capacity plans. One way to do this effectively is to have your load balancer duplicate the traffic, so that the user's normal actions are dealt with by the normal application pool but the test instance also gets a copy of every request. This could cause all kinds of issues (for instance, both applications trying to write the same thing to the database at the same time), but it can also help you to test without hurting production traffic. We also mentioned earlier, in Chapter 5, *Testing and Releasing* shadow testing by copying and saving a record of the traffic pattern and replaying it against the server to test its load.

Once you have a single instance struggling under its load, you can compare its efforts with baseline instances. For example, if your single server struggles when it receives 100 requests per second, and pins itself at 100% CPU usage, then there is a possibility that 10 services can handle 1000 requests. That said, often these metrics are not linear, especially in the micro-service world. It is a reasonable way to figure out what your upper bound is but this is not a guarantee that your service can or cannot operate at that level. You can go more in depth by adding a second server and seeing how the load of the two machines reacts. If your server is fully loaded, if you double the capacity, does the load of the two machines cut in half? More often than not, the answer is no, because there is a baseline of load required by the system to operate, even if it has no traffic. You can also make a comparison to a larger set of servers. For example, if you were duplicating traffic, as mentioned above, once to a pool of 12 machines and once to a single server, you should in theory see one twelfth of the traffic and load on each of the machines in the pool.

$$x = 5000 * \frac{1}{12}$$

If your application is receiving 5000 requests per second across 12 machines, then x in this equation should also equal the amount of traffic a single machine can handle

Beyond the fact that some services have a base need for resources on a per machine basis (you can test this by spinning up a service and sending no traffic at it, and seeing that it isn't using zero resources), you may also find that the dependencies or architecture of the system are holding you back in terms of performance. Maybe your database is overloaded or maybe one service you talk to has concurrency issues and cannot handle more than one request a minute and you are sending it much more than that. When looking at these dependencies, note that some services do not scale well horizontally. Others do not scale well vertically. Both of these facts will negatively affect your predictions using the method above.

> Scaling horizontally is to increase the number of instances of a service. Scaling vertically is to increase the size of a single instance.

For example, databases scale very differently to traditional web frontends or other stateless services. Databases have very diverse patterns because of how they are used and because every database is different and optimized for different use cases. Each request can be dramatically different based on the query it sends. Some queries could be inserting or asking for millions of rows. Others could be asking for a single row but have a very complex query needed to find them or create them. Some databases are optimized for reading data out, while others are optimized for writing data in, and some are even optimized for developer happiness.

One example of database scaling at an organization I worked at involved a data warehouse. We were using a system called **Vertica**. Vertica is a closed source distributed database, but our usage was growing rapidly. Thankfully, it was easier to repartition than some more traditional relational databases, but it still required a lot of manual work to run a performant system. Repartitioning allowed us to scale from one machine to many more, by determining how much data was replicated and how many times it was replicated for each table, and having those tables distributed across the servers. One of our engineers realized that we were capacity planning this growth across machines for CPU usage, but users experienced their queries sat in queues for unreasonable amounts of time (hours). As he dug in, he discovered that actually what was limiting us was the amount of memory each node had available, because the majority of queries that our analytics team were running were memory intensive. While some user education on query creation and optimization was able to curb this a bit, it still seemed that memory was the systems-limiting metric. By changing this metric, our understanding of what our capacity was changed.

When are we going to run out of capacity?

Once you have metrics that define current capacity, the next step is to figure out when you are going to run out. You can do this in many ways, although the easiest way is to graph the data in either Microsoft Excel or code and then add a trend line to predict where your usage is going. Following, I have provided an example using Google's **JavaScript Chart Library**. There are lots of other options and some monitoring services, such as **Prometheus**, have functions built in to do this.

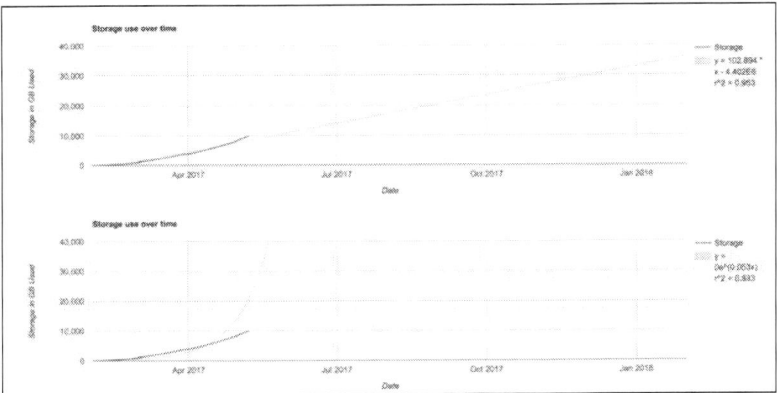

Figure 3: Trends of storage usage over time

These graphs show that with linear growth, we will run out of disk storage (our cluster has 30,000 gigabytes of space currently) in early December 2017. With exponential growth, we will run out much faster, in mid-May of 2017. Thankfully, 30,000 gigabytes is only three terabytes and you can buy hard drives much larger than that (when this book was being written, a 12 terabyte hard drive cost $400). Linear growth is defined as $y = c * x - d$, where c and d are constants. Exponential growth is $y = c * b^{x/d}$, where c, b, and d are all constants. Most tools for graphing data provide built-in methods for doing this math.

To generate these graphs, we just needed to write some JavaScript and HTML:

```
<html>
  <head>
```

```
    <script type="text/javascript" src="https:
//www.gstatic.com/charts/loader.js"></script>
    <script type="text/javascript">
      google.charts.load('current',
{'packages':['corechart']});
      google.charts.setOnLoadCallback(drawChart);
      function drawChart() {
        var data = new google.visualization.
DataTable();
        data.addColumn('date', 'Date');
        data.addColumn('number', 'Storage');
        data.addRows([
          [new Date(2017,01,01), 6.639196089],
          // Data truncated for simplicity
          [new Date(2017,04,08), 9993.884879]
        ]);

        var options = {
          title: "Storage use over time",
          vAxis: {title: 'Storage in GB Used',
minValue: 0, maxValue: 31000},
          hAxis: {title: 'Date', minValue: new
Date(2017,01,01), maxValue: new Date(2018,01,01)},
          trendlines: {
            0: {
              opacity: 0.2,
              showR2: true,
              visibleInLegend: true
            }
          }
        };

        var chartLinear = new google.visualization.
LineChart(document.getElementById('chartLinear'));
        chartLinear.draw(data, options);

        options.trendlines[0].type = 'exponential';

        var chartExponential = new google.
visualization.LineChart(document.getElementById
('chartExponential'));
        chartExponential.draw(data, options);
```

```
      }
    </script>
  </head>
  <body>
    <div id="chartLinear" style="height: 350px"></
div>
    <div id="chartExponential" style="height:
350px"></div>
  </body>
</html>
```

Google's library is doing all of the heavy lifting here. By building the `data` array, and setting the `trendlines` option, the library will generate a trend line for us. If we tell it to show in the legend, it will also show us the r^2 value, which tells us how closely the line fits the data that we gave it. The closer the number r^2 is to 1, the closer fit it has.

> Be careful of trying to find closely-fitting trend lines that use complex prediction models such as higher polynomials or filtering out outlying data. While this may increase your r^2, it can provide a false sense of security that your prediction is accurate. Another tool you can use is seasonal adjustment to see long-term data better. It's usually used on things such as labor markets and long-term economic studies. The idea of removing a consistent time period can help to make analysis easier but also hide important events.

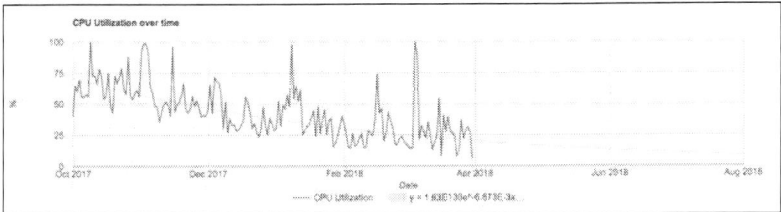

Figure 4: Graph of daily maximum CPU utilization over time for a cluster of servers

Note that the preceding graph, which has half a year of CPU utilization data, has a downward trend of utilization. While this exponential trend line has an r^2 of 0.495, which is not great, it also hides a key piece of information: the number of servers is not constant throughout this time. This graph is hiding the fact that our autoscaling function is increasing the amount of capacity that we are paying for. It is accurate because our capacity is in fact increasing, but it is dangerous because it also costs us more money. This is our entire cluster in aggregate, instead of a single server. Other changes were happening during this time, as this cluster is a development cluster that handles a diverse workflow (and only gets regular traffic on weekdays). Also, depending on our cloud provider, we could be changing the type of CPU we run on, which could create more confusion in our data.

It should also be noted that this graph was the daily maximum of CPU utilization for the cluster. We chose the max instead of the average because it is considered a bad idea to average percentages. This is because if each percentage has different numbers of data points, you are giving more weight to the percentages with less data behind them. The reason for this is that you are usually sampling the data behind metrics. Scientists often point out that if three separate systems monitor the same static item, they can have different data because of how they sample the data. It is often recommended that you get the raw metric instead of the percentage. For example, getting the CPU load, instead of the utilization.

You may ask, why bother making this prediction if we know that the performance of our service is going to change over time? We know that our system is not static and it will change with time. The answer to our question is to ignore the future. We can only know how our service performs now. We are not predicting how we will change our service or how we will become more or less efficient, but rather, given our current growth, where our service will be in time.

Given this data, hopefully, our goal will not be to improve performance, but rather to plan for growth. This is not to say that we should not use data to decide whether we should improve the performance of our system, but it is a bad idea to pin the hopes of performance improvements on our capacity plans. Some hypothetical examples of why this is a bad idea are:

♦ Your new system architecture makes performance worse

♦ New features dramatically change performance

♦ No one can figure out how to improve performance quickly

These outcomes are not guaranteed, but if you promise an improvement in overall performance, instead of planning for the future, you are setting yourself up for failure. Part of this failure could come from an initial failure, but also you are saying, "In the future, it is okay to base the performance of our team on the performance of the service." As such, in the future, you could be asked to dramatically improve performance, which may not be possible, and this could cost you your job, because any of the above could happen and make performance worse instead of better.

If it is not clear, this is also when you should be talking to other parts of the business. Find out whether the business has any large events coming up that will drastically change your traffic. Will we have a large presence at the Super Bowl? Are we the video streaming partner for Eurovision? Is there a presidential election coming up, which you think will drive more users to our service? These types of events can drastically affect your predictions and may require you to change your plans. Your sales team will probably have targets for the next month or quarter if they meet their goals, but can your infrastructure handle the change? What have the team done in the past? Do they usually double their goals? If so, it might be a good idea to be prepared for that.

It could also be the case that the sales team closes a deal and then there is a six-month integration period, in which case you do not need to plan for the increased usage immediately. All of this requires talking to people. When talking to folks, be clear that you do not need explicit answers about what a team is doing, but express that any plans or guesses about the future will help you to understand where the playing field may be going forward.

How should we change our capacity?

Now that we have a rough timeline for when our capacity will run out, we should come up with a plan to prevent this. This is hard to talk about because so much will differ between services, but we can talk about a few things that might help you to make your decision.

First off is how to scale. We mentioned briefly in the preceding section the idea of scaling horizontally and vertically. Neither of these scaling types are simple to pull off. If your code is not version controlled, it is difficult to make sure that multiple versions of your code are identical when running on many servers (let's say greater than five). If you do not have an automated way to deploy a new server or instance of your code, scaling will also be a lot more difficult. We talked about this a bit in *Chapter 5*, *Testing and Releasing*, but this is where it becomes essential. You should find a tool that can make a copy of an existing server (snapshotting) or a tool that can turn an empty server into a configured one (provisioning).

There are many technologies to create snapshots of your infrastructure and some filesystems even have it as a built-in feature. The simplest way is to snapshot the hard drive with a tool such as **dd** and apply it to a new machine. Most cloud services let you take a snapshot of a running hard drive. A much preferred way to do things, but something that requires more upfront work, is to provision new servers. You can use something such as **Chef**, **Puppet**, **Salt,** or **Ansible** to make sure the machine is set up properly and to create a template for the machine.

You can use **Docker** to create a self-contained version of your application inside of a Docker container image. All of these tools create ways to have identical versions of your infrastructure. If this seems like too much work, many organizations provide, sometimes for free, premade and preconfigured images of their applications for external developers to use. Identical versions of your infrastructure are important for scaling your service, so you can create new instances quickly without having to worry about the differences between machines.

One term for a service that you cannot scale is a snowflake. It means that the service is unique and there is only one. Often, this also means that the service is not backed up or the team has no way to recreate the service if it goes down, unless they build it by hand, which often no one remembers how to do. If you find a snowflake, make sure to kill it with fire. Automate its creation or back it up, so when there is an issue (there will be an issue), you can at least restore it to a point in time. Keep in mind that sometimes these servers keep state that you do not want to lose. Be sure if you do destroy the snowflake that others are aware before you destroy it.

For example, if you want to scale vertically, you are going to need to buy new hardware. This could be through a cloud provider or just by driving to your data center and plugging in a new machine. In some cases, you can plug more RAM into an existing machine, but that tends to be a rare scenario unless you already have spare capacity, so you can take existing capacity offline to increase its physical specifications. More often, you will have a blank piece of hardware and will need to make it look like another. This is especially true if you are scaling horizontally. To scale horizontally, you will either click a deployment button or physically install another machine, which will need to be similar to existing machines, at least regarding software. In this case, you will want to create many duplicates of a server or service.

State and concurrency

When creating many copies of a server, you need to be careful of a few things if you have never done it before. Running a single copy of an application is different from running multiple copies. If your application requires state to be on the local disk (for example, a session cache), and you spin up another copy of your application and then load balance requests across the two, there is a chance that a user might visit a server that does not have the state needed, which was there in the previous request. Another issue you might run across is dealing with concurrency. Take this example:

♦ User A deposits $1 into their account

♦ User B charges $1 to user A

♦ User A withdraws $1 from their account

Depending on the order and timing of those statements, if user A starts with a balance of $0, you could end up with a world where user A has a negative balance. User A, in general, should not be able to buy things with money that they do not have, so if the second two bullet points happen at the same time, because you have multiple instances of your application, you could get into financial trouble.

There are lots of tools and methodologies to improve how your system deals with state and concurrency. Some languages build concurrency at their core. Others provide powerful libraries or services for sharing state and filesystems between processes across many computers. These tend to be built on top of consensus protocols such as **Raft** and **Paxos**. There are also methodologies, such as the **Twelve Factor App**, which focuses on building applications for container-based environments, which help developers to think about a world where you are limited as to how you can interact with the machine that you are running on.

Is your service limited by another service?

If you are trying to grow a service, you may need to think about its dependencies. For instance, can your database handle an increase in the number of services that talk to it? Do your downstream dependencies know you are going to be sending more traffic to them? In some cases, you may need to reach out to external API providers to tell them that there is going to be a change in the traffic you are sending them. For example, if you are *Snapchat* and you know thanksgiving is going to be your busiest day traffic-wise by over two magnitudes of a normal day, you might want to let the third-party storage service that you use know that increased traffic is coming, so it can adjust its capacity planning. You might assume that the third-party provider is huge and does not need to know about your change in traffic, but these sorts of assumptions are how you have very visible outages.

Speaking of databases, many do not scale well horizontally, so your team's only option may be to scale vertically. Make sure to research how your database deals with growth. Some classical relational databases require excessive normalization or sophisticated sharding to grow to multiple machines.

In relational databases, normalization is the process of deduplicating data. The idea is that if you have a piece of data that is shared between many entries, instead of storing it with every row, you can move it to a separate table. Then, each row can reference its ID in the other table.

Denormalization is going in the opposite direction and explicitly duplicating data. Denormalization is common in NoSQL and key/value databases.

Database sharding is the act of partitioning a database into multiple shards. For example, machine A might have rows 1 through to 10 and machine B might have rows 11 through to 20. An easier-to-understand example is the idea of sharding by username. If you had 26 machines, you could split usernames alphabetically (assuming case-insensitive usernames).

Scaling for events

We mentioned the idea of planning for specific events earlier. This often involves having seen previous patterns and doing some pattern recognition. Maybe you are a corporate chat system that sees large spikes of traffic when a storm hits. Maybe you are a monthly book club that sees a magnitude of traffic difference between the first day of the month and every other day of the month. Alternatively, maybe you are an e-commerce site and make the majority of your money during four days in November. Preplanning for these events is difficult, as the less frequently they happen, the less data you have to plan for how much you should scale up. Most advice is pretty arbitrary and suggests taking the last time this happened, multiplying data by some random number, and using that to make your decision. I do not think this is a bad thing. It feels silly, but it is not a bad starting point.

Once you have a base starting place, talking to your business teams can help you to ascertain the importance of dealing with this event. If staying available for this event is the only way that your business will survive, you need to put more planning in for worst-case scenarios compared to if this spike happens once a month. The more urgent the scenario, the more effort and research you should put in.

Unpredictable growth–user-generated content

On the other end of the spectrum, the bane of planners everywhere is **user-generated content (UGC)**. UGC is problematic because users are unpredictable. You do not know whether someone will post a tweet that will get retweeted millions of times, nor do you know whether users will be excited about your new data API. To an extent, random content creation is a larger problem for smaller organizations, because they do not have the economies of scale to deal with it. One user doing many things in a short period has a much larger impact when you are smaller because you can see the impact. With a larger system, most times (unless the event is truly monumental), a single user's actions merge into the general traffic patterns and everything smooths out.

A bit of cultural history: it used to be that when a website was mentioned on *SlashDot*, an older popular technology news site, the website would stop working because of the massive increase in traffic. This happens rarely now, but every once in a while, sites such as *Hacker News*, *Product Hunt*, *HuffPost*, *BuzzFeed*, or larger news outlets such as The New York Times or The Washington Post take down smaller sites that weren't expecting the traffic. *SlashDot*, *Product Hunt*, and *Hacker News* are particularly known for this, because any user can submit a link, not just staff of the publication.

There are no good plans for predicting UGC (or traffic patterns on publicly accessible APIs for the same reasons), but you can often focus on *defense in depth*. This is a theory where you look at your entire system and find places where increased traffic will cause failures earlier than the rest of your system and change the architecture to prevent total failure. An example might be to prevent users from uploading videos but still allowing them to stream existing content. The idea being that if you can cause an outage for a portion of users, or a portion of use cases, you can protect a larger portion of your user base.

Preplanned versus autoscaling

This spectrum of known events to user-generated chaos is the spectrum of decision-making between preplanning and autoscaling. That is not to say that autoscaling or preplanning are the proper solutions to either, but the situations tend to dictate certain types of answers.

Preplanning is the act of scaling up capacity ahead of when you need it. Preplanning is necessary when dealing with physical hardware or physical space, or really anything that is not purely digital. This is because procurement times are long. So, if you need 10 new servers in your data center, you cannot just make them appear out of thin air. The same is true with people and physical space.

Autoscaling is automation that provisions capacity just as you need it. This works best for things that can be created with software. For example, new virtual machine instances, new container instances, new virtual load balancers, and so on. Autoscaling is also great because you only pay for what you use! The downside is it often has a time cost associated with it as well. Virtual machines usually take a few minutes to spin up, so if your traffic spike is very brief, then your extra capacity may not come up to a healthy state fast enough.

Choosing between the two is very dependent on your situation. Some organizations cannot deal with the unpredictable costs of autoscaling. Others prefer a more ephemeral infrastructure because they cannot spend the money upfront, so autoscaling matches their financial situation and they only grow when they have to. Whichever you choose, you will want to base it on your capacity metrics. If you are autoscaling, you can use multiple metrics to suggest whether you should increase or decrease capacity, but, in general, your primary capacity planning metric should get you the data you need.

One equation I have found useful deals with autoscaling container cluster instances. The following equation works if you are using a container scheduler that bin-packs your containers across multiple computers (`http://garbe.io/blog/2016/10/17/docker-on-ecs-scale-your-ecs-cluster-automatically/`):

$$\textit{Threshold} = \left(1 - \textit{max}(\textit{Container Reservation}) \,/\, \textit{Total Capacity of a Single Container Instance}\right) * 100$$

It says that you should take the max-reserved capacity of a container *max(Container Reservation)* and divide it by the total amount of that metric that the instance you are running on has *(Total Capacity of a Single Container Instance)*. The reservation is how much of a metric your container needs. For example, you could reserve 512 MB of RAM per container or one virtual CPU core. This part of the equation is saying approximately how many containers can fit on a machine.

If the max reservation is one and the total capacity is four, then you get 0.25, which is saying that the worst case is that one container is 25% of the machine. You then subtract from one and multiply by 100 to say that when you are *Threshold* percent full, you should create another instance. Otherwise, the next container that launches could fill up your instance. Continuing our example, *Threshold* would be 75%.

The point of all of this is that if we are running in the cloud on an **IaaS** provider (**Infrastructure as a Service**), we can just run a **cron** job, which checks our cluster metrics, and if they are ever 75% full, we can spin up a new instance with a single API call.

Delivering

The plan you actually want to deliver to people or share around can be all shapes and sizes. I try to have a plan that has three things:

◆ How much budget I need for the next year, broken down by quarter?

◆ What we are going to do with that budget?

◆ How long the money should last us?

By breaking things down by quarter or monthly, you can show how this plan will affect cash flow, as well as whether there is an upfront dump of money needed or whether this is a long-term thing. If we're integrating with a third-party service, we may need to pay a yearly fee to get the best deal. If we are just increasing the number of servers, it may be spread out.

Explaining what you are doing with the money falls into the same vein. Company executives and finance people want to know what they are spending money on and they usually prefer to get shown where the money will be going before it is spent and put in an expense report.

How long the money will last tells our finance partner how long it will be until we come back asking for more money. Some organizations require that people only request large sums quarterly or yearly. Others are incredibly flexible and as long as purchases made get expense reports the same year, it doesn't matter. Once we know how and when we want to scale and we've shared our plan, we should execute it.

Execute the plan

If your plan is solid and you have received approval for the money, then you can start following it. I like to put all of the steps for the plan as separate tickets in a ticket tracker and then add events on my calendar for each ticket, so I know what to do on each day if it is something that is spread out over time.

As you execute your plan, make sure to monitor your changes. An infrastructure change is like a code change: everything that goes wrong with committing code can go wrong with deploying infrastructure.

Along with general infrastructure and system health, you should also be making sure that your hypothesis is being validated. You made a plan based on facts at the time. It is very likely that between your initial plan and final execution the facts changed. Watch your bills and invoices. Watch your overall performance. Do you have the spare capacity that you expected? Is it filling at the rate you expected? If not, is it time to start over, given the new state of the world?

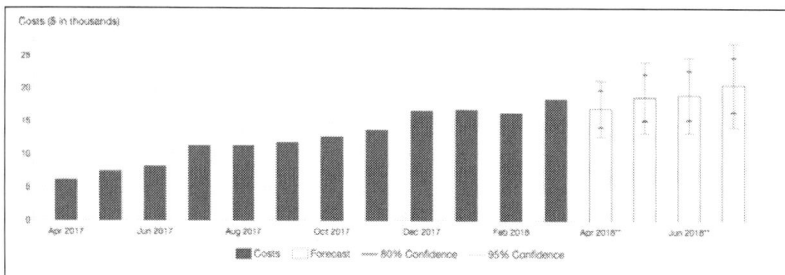

Figure 5: AWS graph of a monthly bill over time, with four months of predicted costs

Architecture–where performance changes come from

One of the most consistent reasons for dramatic performance changes is changes in infrastructure. You can dive into the code and find bugs or do deep research on tuning, but more often than not, putting a cache in the right place or removing a dependency will change performance with orders of magnitude. A quick example would be taking a simple web application and adding a **Content Distribution Network** (**CDN**) in front of it. This allows for a global cache of content, reducing the load on your actual applications, assuming the content can actually be cached.

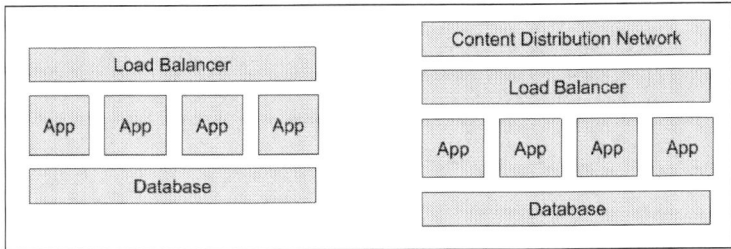

Figure 6: An architecture of a simple web app,
before (left) and after adding a CDN (right)

Now, because of this significant change in performance, architecture decisions can also have a dramatic effect on capacity planning. It is highly recommended that you try and get involved in the planning stages for architecture changes. The reasons for this are twofold:

1. You have deep knowledge of how the infrastructure works and how code runs on it. So, because of this knowledge, you can often see things from a fresh perspective in the planning process.

2. Decisions made could and probably will affect how many resources are available to other systems. Some architecture decisions could dramatically hurt other systems or increase the cost of your infrastructure beyond levels that you can afford.

An example of this is a rough approximation of three **CMS (content management systems)** we had when I was working for *Hillary for America*:

1. A static generated website made from markdown files. It was generated by a script run on someone's desktop.

2. A pipeline system where a dynamic website wrote content to a database and then a cron job read from the database and wrote out static files to **S3**.

3. A dynamic system that generated pages every time there was a new request.

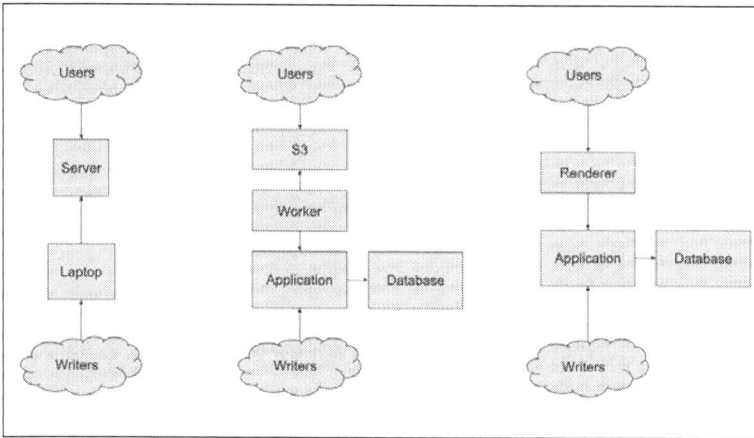

Figure 7: From left to right, systems #1, #2, and #3

System #3 was the fastest at getting new content to the consumers, but system #1 had the highest performance and lowest cost. System #2 had the best uptime. System #2 could also be easily modified to have better performance and had a faster publish time compared to system #3, by adding a cache and an automated cache clearing system. In the end, we scrapped systems #1 and #2 and created system #3, which ended up increasing our costs by a multiple of 10. We solved the content creator's need to have content out faster, but by not working through the full implications of the design early on by bringing SRE, developer, and product teams together, we lost a lot of time building the new solution and lost money operating the newly created system #3.

Another classic example is adding **Varnish** (an HTTP cache system) in front of a web server and telling Varnish to `Vary` on the `Accept-Language` header without normalizing it. The `Vary` header determines how many versions of a cache Varnish stores. You want a small number, so that every request to Varnish is a cache hit. However, because browsers send languages in many different ways, you can end up with many cache misses if you aren't normalizing the `Accept-Language` header before caching in Varnish. For example, if user A sends `en-uk`, `en-us`, user B sends `en-us`, `en-uk`, and user C sends `en-uk`, you might expect to send them all the same version of your website. However, because you are not normalizing the header, Varnish will store three separate caches of the content, instead of just one, and so all three users will get uncached content.

Tech as a profit center and procurement

As mentioned earlier, depending on your company, tech can be thought of as a profit center or a cost center. Usually, if technology is the product you are selling, your team is a profit center, and if technology is helping your company succeed, you are instead a cost center. If this is rubbed in your team's face too much, it can feel like an insult. Engineers are builders and creative types, and some may feel unmotivated or depressed to be thought of as not an integral part of the company's success. This is utter nonsense, but it happens. One way to remove it from your team's mind is to fight harder for a larger budget. Often, engineers only notice the difference if they find that they cannot do things they want to because *things are not in the budget*. The team's manager probably needs to do a better job of helping their manager or executive team to understand the value their team is providing and how investment in them improves the company overall.

This often comes up when evaluating new technology, when figuring out how much a piece of tech is going to cost, what it is going to take in terms of people hours to implement and become useful, and how it will improve the company. Helping people to understand the cost/benefit ratio of a decision will often involve using the terminology mentioned at the beginning of the chapter. Some decisions might seem obvious to you, like paying $20 per month per server for improved monitoring. However, if you do not bring up the fact that it will help prevent outages, which cost the company $10,000 in 2016, or that it is needed to do capacity planning for time periods longer than a month, you may never get the money you need for your project. Moreover, maybe, just maybe, the company will falter due to lack of capacity.

Summary

In this chapter, we talked about the basics of business finance. We mentioned a bunch of finance jargon that is useful to know. We explained why we need a plan. We also walked through the four steps of creating and executing a capacity plan. Finally, we talked about how engineering and finance decisions can affect each other and cause ripples throughout the company.

This is all important to SRE, because a lack of capacity causes service downtime. By working with your coworkers, you can improve your long-term reliability by having a plan to deal with future outages. Remember to first define what your current capacity is, see how it's changing over time, and then get access to the budget to make sure you can handle the predicted growth.

In the next chapter, we will be talking about building tools to improve reliability!

7

BUILDING TOOLS

Writing software is the reason I got into tech in the first place. I love how you can create something, with very few resources, that can touch millions of people. Software can often feel like the pure act of creation for the masses. With just a text editor and an interpreter or compiler, you can create something new. Something you make can often improve the lives of many or, more commonly, just make your own life easier. Often, as engineers, we are tool builders. Building tools for others and yourself can be incredibly rewarding, but tools are often also overlooked. Good tooling can be essential to making developers happy and keeping team speed high. Building tools can also be the momentum that helps you to keep evolving as an engineer.

Despite being birthed from a software engineering role, some days **SRE (Site Reliability Engineering)** can feel very far from writing software. You spend a lot of time tracking down other people's mistakes, helping people to work together, documenting things, and just adjusting graphs. Hopefully, as you work through the hierarchy, you will get past that and start to write software. As mentioned in *Chapter 1, Introduction*, SRE was founded because a software engineer approached operations. As such, you should still engineer software in the job. The goal is to have 50% of your time devoted to writing code, 30% of your time devoted to dealing with people, and 20% responding to emergencies.

Priority number one is to write code to remove yourself, and others, from the equation. A great SRE once said to me that "I'll do it once, I'll even do it twice, but if you make me do it a third time, I'll burn it all down." I'm roughly quoting here, but she was referring to responding to a certain type of incident in which she could do nothing, but her greater point was that humans are temperamental, imperfect, and not machines. If we do not need humans to do a task, then write code so that humans do not need to be involved.

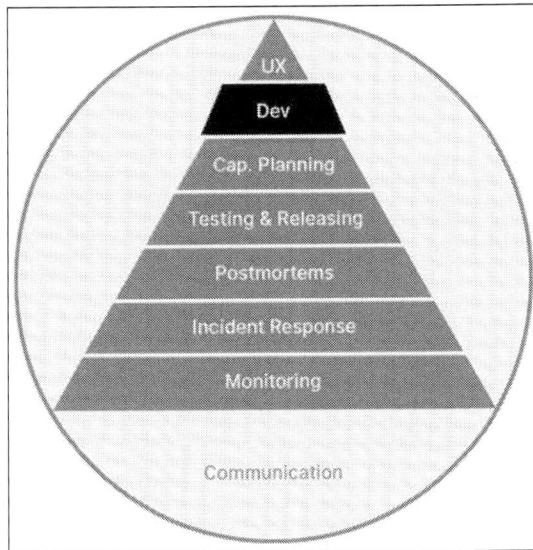

Figure 1: Development is near the top of the hierarchy. It requires a lot of work to be in place to be effective, and like all of the previous layers of the hierarchy, requires communication to be successful. It is not to say that development cannot happen earlier in the hierarchy, but it is most effective and useful when the other layers have been approached.

In this chapter, now that we are much further up in the hierarchy, we will talk about writing software to improve our day-to-day life. We will discuss how to make it easier for others to move up the hierarchy, even if we have to drag them kicking and screaming. Software lets us build the means to help people without them even knowing it. As such, let us talk about building tools that help others and let us stop thinking about stuff, so we can move on to other problems.

This chapter will cover the six main things you need to think about when you want to write code or start a larger software project:

♦ Finding projects

♦ Defining projects

♦ Planning projects

♦ Building projects

♦ Documenting projects

♦ Maintaining projects

Finding projects

If you join an existing team or are a junior engineer, your first projects may be dictated to you. Often, an organization will hire someone because they have a need that their current team isn't meeting. As you complete the task you were hired for, you'll probably want to start finding projects you want to fix or improve. This chapter will generally focus on starting new projects, but do not underestimate the value of helping out with someone else's work. A great way to learn and grow is to write software with others. By being part of a group trying to implement a piece of software, you often learn about their processes and needs. For example, I found out about a project's broken testing environment because I offered to pick up a small bug that needed fixing. The tests had been broken for months and either no one noticed or no one mentioned it.

All of that aside, if you're looking to start a new project, instead of joining an existing one, you will need to find a problem that you think needs fixing. This inspiration can come from all sorts of places. My project inspiration tends to come from a few different places:

♦ **Fixing something that annoys me**: This is more of a form of self-care than anything else. If I complain about stuff, I should fix it. An example is that I dislike that some of our services at *First Look Media* are not end-to-end encrypted, so I plan on implementing a generic **SSL (Secure Sockets Layer)** truncation proxy for our apps on each server. There are probably also things that do not annoy you that need cleaning up, which we'll come to later on in this list.

♦ **Preventing people from hurting themselves**: This is all about preventing future outages or unintended consequences. An example might be to add tools that test configuration changes before they are deployed or to prevent a user from running commands that will hurt production.

♦ **Cleaning up things**: Often this is just working to remove technical debt. The first implementation of a software will take the shortest route possible, focusing on delivery instead of long-term maintainability. Taking the time to transform a hack into something more stable and long lasting is important work. Work may include refactoring sections of code to be up to date with modern standards, updating dependencies, rewriting something to make it more performant, or removing unused code.

♦ **Automating tasks someone has been doing by hand**: This is one of the most classic SRE tasks. By automating something, you can free up time for yourself and others to work on other things. This is a huge category but could include taking any human process or checklist and automating it into code.

♦ **Improving a dependency to make it more resilient**: Analyzing dependencies and parts of your infrastructure to look for possible failures is valuable because often people will be fine with the state of a service until it fails.

Analyzing and fixing a solution like this can be thankless but will save you lots of pain in the future. This could be done by making it run with multiple copies of itself, having backups, or improving the failover or deployment process.

Things can always be better, so coming up with a project is usually about finding something that interests you. Sometimes that may just be a gut feeling. Outside of observations and gut feelings, though, it is useful to be reading about what is currently going on in software engineering and other fields, so that you can learn about how others approach problems and the types of problems they are seeing. Reading about large companies' new open source projects, watching talks from conferences, and just reading technical blog posts are all ways to do this. You may see someone who has made similar design choices to those made at your company but is much further down the road in terms of scale. They may have valuable insights.

It is also useful to talk to coworkers about their problems. Maybe you have a lot of different environments and a coworker is complaining that they can never figure out which version of code is on which environment. Depending on your setup, you could write a command-line tool, build a dashboard, design a chatbot, or even create a browser extension that tells someone which version they are currently looking at. You can build lots of tools that solve a fellow employee's problem, and also provide a solution that does not require much change in their workflow.

The key is to listen and observe. Are there things that many people are worried about, that could cause an outage, that software could protect you from if you invested in it? A trick to get people to talk to you about this is to go on walks or coffee breaks with coworkers. I try and do this twice a week at 3 PM in the afternoon. It forces me to talk to people and also learn about the issues people have. If you are remote, you could schedule one-on-one video chats with people to keep up with them and see how they are doing.

Some people are hesitant to spend time on this during the work day but because software requires people to work together for it to get created, it's useful to know the people who are writing software that integrates with yours, in order to understand them. Some cultures have this built into their day, for example, the idea of afternoon tea in England or fika in Sweden. A coffee break can be very good for fostering community in an office and also for letting coworkers share concerns, weekend plans, and just general chat over a non-alcoholic drink.

Another great way to find a project is to find a piece of software that no one has looked at recently. Every team has some feature, service or other piece of code that works fine but no one has touched in six months or longer. These pieces of software are often unknown to you, so the act of exploring them for bugs and possible improvements will also improve your skills in reverse engineering, which are very important to have. Being able to be given a piece of software and figure out how it works is invaluable because often no one else knows how it works either.

One last thought: your goal is to automate yourself out of a job. If you are doing the same thing (or type of thing) six months from now, you will find yourself frustrated and unhappy. Write software to remove the unpleasant, boring, and tedious work from your day-to-day life.

Once you have an idea for some problem or task that you would like to approach, it is a good idea to define the impetus for your work and how you will approach it.

Defining projects

Once you have your task or problem, you need to figure out how you are going to approach it. Personally, I start by writing down the problem in a notebook and start taking notes about what I do not know, what I do know, and how I might try and solve it. This research phase often involves searching online to figure out how other people have solved the problem, if there are any open source tools that people have already released that are in the problem space, or if no one else has this problem, why that is.

Evaluating other people's solutions teaches you about how this problem surfaces in different environments. It's also useful to figure out if a piece of open source software could solve your problem or nearly solve it. Every situation is different, but often you can find a software project that does 90% of what you want and you can either expand it or work with the maintainer to see if the software would work for your situation. All of this research will help to save you work and make sure that you know what you are getting yourself into. Do not let your research discourage you though! If you find a problem that no one else has solved yet, it does not mean it is too hard: it just means that there are more unknowns going into the project.

Once you have done your research, it is time to figure out the scale of the project. Is this something small that you can do in a few hours or days? If yes, I usually follow what is called **Readme Driven Development** or **RDD**. If it is going to be larger, you should probably write a design document. The reason for this is that the larger the project (in terms of scope, people or time), the more planning you should be doing, so there are less surprises along the way. If people you do not know are going to be using the software or if you will be working with others to make it, I also suggest writing a design document, so that they can understand what you are doing and how you would like it to be done.

RDD

I first heard about RDD from Tom Preston-Werner, one of the founders of GitHub. The general premise is that every project should have a README.md file in the root, which describes the project. This should be the first thing you write, and it should describe the basic requirements of the project and how it is going to work. The idea is that if anyone stumbles across the project, they should be able to get a deep understanding of what problem you are trying to solve, how you are trying to solve it, and other things you were thinking of.

> `.md` is a typical extension for a **Markdown** file. Markdown is just a plain-text markup language. The readme could easily be in any markup language you want, but markdown is just very simple and nice.

RDD is the casual version of the design document, which we will describe next. It does not need to be too formal, but it should be easy to understand. Focus on succinct statements, along with details that you find important. Bullet points, links to external resources, and drawings are all useful. I enjoy writing, so it is possible that you are rolling your eyes right now, but hear me out. Describing what you are going to do is good for you because it forces your brain to work through the problem in a space that is not code. This is important as we need to communicate with others because, at the end of the day, our code does not exist in a vacuum: it affects all of those around us. The document also leaves a record for the future, which we've already talked about being useful in *Chapter 4*, *Postmortems*. It will help someone in the future who has to reverse engineer your project when there is an outage involving it and you, or others involved, are not around to help.

Example

The following is a fictitious example. It involves a project that I have wanted to exist for a long time but have never built. Feel free to build it if you are looking for a side project. This document is written in markdown, so it can easily be turned into a PDF or HTML.

```
# enki.garden

Enki Garden is a personal internet archive. Its goal
is to create a searchable index of websites and
documents a user likes and can be hosted on their
laptop or cheaply on a personal server.

## Background

I love the Internet Archive. It is an archive of
```

digital culture. Everything from old video games
to old websites and books is stored in its vaunted
public archives online at archive.org. I think its
hoarder approach to the Internet is the only way we
can preserve history for the future. We are already
getting to the point where there are programs we
cannot run, art we cannot see and machines we cannot
fix. We need to preserve all of this so that our
children's children can understand how we got to
where we are today.

Due to copyright laws, non-disclosure agreements
(NDAs) and other general privacy concerns, you
cannot upload everything to the Internet Archive,
nor do you want everyone to have access to it.
For example, I want my tax documents searchable,
but I do not want them on the Internet Archive for
everyone to see. Also, the Internet Archive respects
'robots.txt', so it will stop sharing archives for
URLs someone puts in robots.txt, even if they want
to archive it.

> robots.txt is a file served by a website that
defines which robot spiders (also known as web-
crawlers, indexers or scrapers) can index its pages.
It is a blacklist of pages and a list of bots that
should not access those pages.

Minimum Viable Product

While the eventual goal would be to search all files
across all of my computers and every website I have
ever visited, I believe a good starting place is to
be able to give a starting URL, scrape its contents,
take a screenshot, and then scrape every page it
links to.

Every day, I would like to re-scrape and screenshot
every page I have stored but not the pages it
linked to.

I want to store everything on a cloud service
because I have a few different computers and I
think it'd be a good start to solving the problem.

```
## Alternatives

- https://archive.org/
- https://archive.is/
- https://webrecorder.io/
- https://github.com/marvelm/erised
- https://github.com/rahiel/archiveror

## Inspiration

- https://www.gwern.net/Archiving-URLs
- https://www.archiveteam.org/

## Implementation

There are three main functions:

- Users submitting URLs and scanning for linked
pages
- Scraping and screenshotting each URL
- Browsing historical archives

There will be a relational database that has two
tables: one for URLs and one for scrape history.

We will store all scraped assets in a cloud object
store and provide a link to them in the scrape
history.

There will be four processes. The first is the web
UI for browsing and adding new URLs. The second
will screenshot URLs. The third will capture
HTML and related assets and compress them into
an archive. The fourth will scan user-submitted
URLs for links and add those to the database.
```

You could expand this example over time by adding details on how to run the application, descriptions of important files, links to code documentation, or screenshots of the UI.

Note that the level of detail isn't too deep. The goal is to just provide broad strokes, while still providing direction. Notice that I suggested four separate pieces of work, which gives a bit of structure to how someone could contribute.

This is good for a smaller project or a personal project, but what about something larger?

Design documents

There is often a fear of design documents in smaller organizations. They taste like a formal requirements document, which is the fear of all software developers everywhere, due to a fear of the waterfall development process. In the past, a requirements document was written and software could not deviate from it. Teams on this path, two years after starting a project, sometimes delivered a piece of software which did not actually do what you wanted. However, because it matched the initial requirements document, you could say it was a success. This type of situation is often why people complain that government software contracts in the United States were broken before the creation of **18F** and **USDS** (**United States Digital Service**) because to even put out a contract, you needed a full requirements document.

The software world has moved past strict requirements documents into a world of constant iteration. That being said, defining a starting point is still a good idea. Like I said above, by creating an initial description of the work you will be doing, you can circulate the document to find possible concerns and existing alternatives and introduce slight modifications to improve your design.

When writing a more formal design document, that a lot of people might see, I try to follow the below structure. It is not a hard and fast outline, but it at least gives me a starting point:

- **Summary**: This is the executive summary, which is a paragraph that describes what this document is describing.

- **Background**: This is the problem we are trying to solve and includes past attempts to solve the problem and other details about the problem.

- **Overview**: A high-level, one-to-two paragraph description of our solution.

♦ **Detailed design**: The in-depth dive on how to solve the problem. It starts with architecture and then has subsections of things other people might be concerned with. The goal of this is to be as descriptive as possible. It includes architecture diagrams and pseudocode of possibly complicated sections. Some subsections might include the following:

  ○ Testing

  ○ Migration

  ○ Security

  ○ Dependencies

  ○ Privacy

  ○ Billing

  ○ Logging

  ○ Monitoring

♦ **Alternatives considered**: This is a list of alternatives and descriptions of why you aren't using them.

♦ **Implementation plan**: This is a rough timeline of how you will build this, which is important if you view the project as having many phases.

♦ **Production impact**: This is a section to describe the things people should be worried about when this goes to production. Could this triple the number of requests to the database? Does it encrypt a subset of internal network traffic? These are questions that people might want answers to.

As you might see, with all of these sections, this could be a very long document. When writing, remember the goal is not to explain everything you might do but rather to raise possible issues to others. The more explicit you are, the more reviewers' questions will be detailed, but the more specific you are, the less flexibility you may feel that you have later. Just remember that this isn't the end.

You will need to constantly evaluate if the project you are working on solves the problem you are trying to solve (and if the problem is still the same). Also, this document is not a contract: it is more of a directional statement.

Planning projects

Once you have a rough idea of what it is you are going to build and you have documented it at some level, you will need to starting working on the project: planning work and moving forward.

Earlier we mentioned **Agile**. There are lots of definitions of Agile and lots of similar philosophies (including Scrum and extreme programming), but the rough idea is a period of iteration, where after each period, the team regroups, adjusts priorities and plans based on feedback, then gets back to work. As with everything in tech, there are zealots out there who will tell you the right and wrong ways to do Agile. Just remember, if it works for you and your team then ignore the zealots because they cannot tell you what to do. For example, some teams use pair programming exclusively, while other teams cannot because their team is not all in the same time zone or there are people who have to work different schedules because of family obligations. The point isn't to ignore people but rather to evaluate what they are saying and try to figure out if that'll work for your team.

Lots of modern teams use Agile as a way to keep the team organized and to make sure a single team member doesn't get too lost in the weeds. By checking in at a regular interval (once a day, week, or fortnight), you can keep an eye on progress and help coworkers to understand what you're working on and what's blocking you.

When trying to decide on what to work on and how to approach a large project, it is best to break the project into small pieces. Instead of thinking about how you can implement everything, think about which features you want to exist. Then pick a feature and make a list of functions or pieces that you will need to implement to make the feature work.

Then slowly work down the list. By breaking things up, you provide yourself with a to-do list, as well as the ability to see progress in your project as you complete tasks. There are few things more demoralizing than looking at a project and feeling like it's too big for you to be able to complete. By breaking things up, you prove to yourself that you can succeed and that you are making progress.

Some people like following **test-driven development** (**TDD**), which takes the idea one step further. You break the project into a series of tests and then work on slowly getting the tests to pass. As each test passes, you get a green check mark showing your improvements. If you graph a history of passing tests, you will be able to visualize your progress. If you want to learn more about TDD, there is a lot of good documentation about the topic. I personally love Kent Beck's *Test-Driven Development: By Example*. Just be careful, as there are many TDD zealots out there. Remember that these are all tools for you to use, and each situation requires deciding what tool is best for the job.

I prefer to-do lists to tests, just because that's how my brain works. That is not to say that I do not test: I just do not use them as the framework for organizing my future work. Finding a way to break apart projects that works for you is the key because everyone's brain works differently. Along with this, don't be afraid to refactor or admit failure. If you finish a piece of the project and realize that you will have to change it because of things that the next part needs, that is not a failure of planning: instead it is just an opportunity to improve old code. Your ability to plan grows as you learn how best to break apart projects.

Example

To provide an example, I'm going to show how I would break up tasks for building a board game. This isn't a traditional SRE piece of software, but it is something that is transitioning from physical to digital. Professor David Janzen, from California Polytechnic State University, once called it *atoms to bits*. These sorts of projects often help people to visualize how to break things apart.

We are going to build a **Tak** server. Tak is a board game that is like chess or checkers. It has a notation for tracking play, which shows how the board's state changes over time. Each line in the notation is a move played by a player. The main difference from chess or checkers is that you start with an empty board and can place a piece each turn or move an existing piece. Pieces are flat colored squares and the goal is to build a road of your colored pieces from one side of the five-by-five board to the other. You can place pieces on top of each other and you can unstack stacks of pieces.

If we think about a normal board game, we can probably come up with the most basic of features. We need to store the current board state. We need to modify the state as someone plays the game. Finally, we will need to provide an external API, so that clients can interact with the server.

Initial features are as follows:

♦ Game state storage

♦ Game play

♦ Web API

For the first feature, we are going to want to create a game state data structure. We are going to need something that returns the history of the state as well. We also are going to need some marker of whose turn it is, and we need to somehow decide if the game is over.

Next, for gameplay, we will need methods to change the state. We will need logic to validate moves, so that clients cannot modify the state illegally, where an illegal state modification is equivalent to an illegal board game move (such as robbing the bank in Monopoly, moving another person's pieces in checkers, or moving a pawn four spaces in chess).

These two features will cover the basics of gameplay. They will be easy enough to test because we can list most of the valid inputs and thankfully there are a lot of game notations on Reddit that we can download and test with, although we need to write a notation parser to be able to do that.

Our rough to-do list is as follows:

- Game storage
  - Game state storage
  - Board
  - Pieces
  - Players
  - Game state history
  - Current state
  - Moves made

- Gameplay
  - Game move input
  - Game move validation
  - Game completion checking
  - Game notation parsing

- Tests using real game notations

Once that is all done, we can move on to the next feature: a REST API using JSON for playing. This will add the idea of user and game identifiers because clients will have to say which player is making a move in which game. We will need to make sure that the players don't change during a game and provide reasonable errors to users if they make illegal moves. When a game is finished, we will want to return the game history, so that people can keep it for their records.

The following is a possible to-do list for the JSON API. Notice that we include routes that we want to define:

- JSON API
  - GET /game/$id
  - Returns a game of ID $id with the most recent state
  - GET /game/$id/$move

- ° Returns a game of ID $id after move $move
- ° POST /game/$id/move
- ° Client sends a move for a game of $id. The request must include a valid player ID and a valid move
- ° POST /game/new
- ° Creates a new game and returns a game ID. This must provide player IDs

After we have this done, maybe we will add some sort of authentication as the next feature. Then a follow-up feature could be some matchmaking to pair two random people together. Other features that I would want to break down include the following:

♦ Scoring

♦ Authentication

♦ Player ranking

♦ Sharing of game histories between friends

♦ A gallery of well-played games

♦ A simple AI to play against if no one else is around

Building a board game at a high level could seem scary, but by breaking down the project, we can come up with a reasonable plan. It might not work fully, and we may find pieces that we need to add or break up into smaller parts, but at least we have a plan to move forward.

Retrospectives and standups

Two aspects that we haven't talked about from Agile, that I really enjoy, are retrospectives and standups. A standup is a daily meeting for everyone on your team to mention what they worked on yesterday, what they are doing today, and what they are blocked on. This is a great way to keep people updated on a project and informed of any changes. Even if everyone is working on different stuff, it allows people to stay in the loop. It can be held over chat, email, or in person, whatever works for your team.

Retrospectives are a way to continue looking back on the plans from the previous week or month or fortnight or whatever. They are regular meetings where people share what has gone well, gone poorly, and gone just okay. The most successful of these meetings I have been part of were held at four in the afternoon on a Friday, with a whiteboard with three headings: *Yay! Meh! Blargh!* Each team member would go and put post-it notes in the columns to match their moods about things. It was a good way to rant and to express feelings about projects that were ongoing.

Another tool for retrospectives is the **4L**s. Like the above idea, you create a board with four categories: **Liked**, **Learned**, **Lacked,** and **Longed For**. Then members of the team put post-it notes in each category. Afterwards, the post-it notes are grouped by topic and discussed. Similar is the **Glad Mad Sad** framework for retrospectives. Users put post-it notes in each of the three categories. The interesting thing that this framework proposes is giving each team member a number of points that they can vote with on post-it notes. This means that they can show support for a post-it, saying that they agree with the sentiment expressed.

These are just tools, so you do not have to use them and there are many more frameworks you can look at, but they can be useful in organizing thoughts and removing problems when working. It should be mentioned that standups and retrospectives are not only important for looking at work but also for evaluating the mood of the team and possible issues inside the team's dynamic.

Allocation

We should also talk about allocating this work. There is a danger in software, which outside of engineering is rare and due to physical limitations does not exist in many other fields of engineering. This danger is the fact that a single engineer can, if they want to, develop the entire system by themselves. A single developer has all of the tools to complete the same amount of work as a larger team, just on a different timescale.

This is dangerous for a variety of reasons. The first is that humans are fallible, as we have been saying time and time again through this book. So, because humans make mistakes, there is a higher chance of introducing bugs or creating errors in code when a person works alone. The second danger is if a person leaves the organization. When someone leaves, often they take all of their knowledge with them. If a software project is poorly documented, as most projects owned by a single person are, then when a bug appears in the software that the person who left maintained, someone on your team will have to dig deep to figure out how it worked. This will take far more time than if you had two people working on the software.

Having only one person know something is often called having a bus factor of one. Bus factor describes how many employees can be hit by a bus before the project falls apart.

One solution to this is to have one person dedicated to code reviewing a project that a single person is working on. This way, every line of code that is committed to a project is reviewed by the same person, and two people can discuss the project and bounce ideas off each other. Another solution is to just have multiple people working on the project. Divide the work up between the developers, then have them collaborate and code review each other's work. However, once the work is allocated, make sure not to overcommit an individual.

Try to figure out how much work a person can handle per time period, and make sure that they feel like they can complete the amount of work assigned. Talk to your team members and understand their feelings around their workload. The goal is not to burn people out, the chance of which is very high because SREs are often involved in some sort of on-call rotation. As mentioned in earlier chapters, on-call rotations can cause people to be overwhelmed and tired. Switching from a reactionary role like that to long-term creative work, such as designing and writing code, can be jarring and exacerbate those feelings.

On top of those feelings, people may feel overcommitted. You run into the possibility that people will start feeling ineffective in their job because they constantly will not be able to finish the work assigned. This ineffectual feeling, plus feelings of physical and emotional exhaustion, are signs of chronic stress and burnout, which can have a negative impact on an employee's wellbeing and may lead them to quit.

Building projects

Once work is planned and assigned, you can sit down and start coding. As the developer, you need to remember all of the previous levels of the hierarchy as you introduce new code into your infrastructure. Often, as an SRE, your work will be looked to as a model for what the rest of your developer teams should be doing. If you skimp on a level, you may find the teams and developers you work with also skimping on it because of your example and hypocrisy.

A simple checklist for new software that you are writing based on our hierarchy framework is as follows:

◆ **Monitoring**: Do you have basic metrics coming from the code that you are writing? Are they being collected and stored?

◆ **Incident response**: Are you writing documentation on how to operate your service? Are there alerts that if they get fired, anyone who receives them will know what to do?

◆ **Postmortems**: When your code has an outage, are you treating it like other code having an outage and writing a postmortem?

◆ **Testing and releasing**: Are you writing unit and integration tests for your code? Are you documenting both the release process and the rollback process?

◆ **Capacity planning**: Are you documenting how this will affect the performance of your system?

Services built by SREs are no different than services built by any other engineer. Making sure you and your team follow the same standards you suggest for others is important.

Advice for writing code

When I originally outlined this chapter, I wanted to provide tips and best practices on building systems, but most advices that came to mind tended to be too domain specific or hyper specific to certain types of patterns that can appear in code. As I thought about it, I came up with four pieces of advice which can be applied to executing and delivering any project:

♦ **Use version control**: This is the *use sunscreen* of computer programming. There is no project too small that you should not use version control. Humans make mistakes and version control lets you easily revert mistakes or see when a mistake was introduced.

♦ **Always do code reviews**: As a developer, you only know so much, so having another set of eyes read over your work helps you to find bugs and remove assumptions that you may have made. Your code deserves at least one editor to help you limit the number of errors.

♦ **All projects should have a designated owner**: At some point, all projects will raise questions from external parties. All projects should have a designated owner so there is someone who can answer those questions. It is also important for when you are deciding on priorities. Having an owner means there is one person who can make the final decision on what is most important.

♦ **The problem is always people**: As you may have picked up from the previous three suggestions, humans are often the problem. Working with code and knowing that it will be consumed by humans is very important.

This could be by making sure processes are in place to deal with the fact that humans will need to work on the code or by changing how you program to assume that all inputs to your software will come from humans (either directly or indirectly) and thus need to be resilient. Humans will often change requirements, miscommunicate needs, or just cause chaos. Always be ready to be empathetic towards others and your own failures. A willingness to show others kindness and understand their feelings will improve people's moods and probably increase the possibility that they will help you when you fail. Remember that failures will happen, so smile and move forward.

Separation of concerns

One aspect of software to think about during the design and building phases is the separation of concerns. The idea is that all of the code for dealing with certain types of data should be located together and provide an API, then any other software that wants to work with that data does so through the API. This means that your data is not touched by other code or services. In some cases, this is easy, but more often than not, making data more separated by an API can cause data duplication or poor performance. This is because distributed state management is difficult.

If four pieces of software need to know how much money a user has in their bank account, for example, querying the database may seem easier, but in the long term, calling a well-defined API will make your life easier. An example is changing the schema of how your data is stored. If you keep the API consistent, you can change how the data is stored underneath, without having to update client applications. If you do want to make performance improvements, you can achieve significant gains by just updating the API interface, instead of having to improve every client that talks to your database.

If you do this separation well, then in theory, when needed, you can rip out a part and replace it with a service. A common example of this is authentication. Often teams start with authentication inside their application, but as other services start to need to do authentication, they replace the code in the app with a call to an external service, which presents a similar API.

> An **API** (or **application programming interface**) is the signature of a program. It defines how you communicate with a library or service. I like to think of it as if a piece of software is a gigantic box and the API is holes in the box that let you put specific shaped objects into it.

A somewhat similar idea is the Unix philosophy. This philosophy has a few tenets, but the two that I like to focus on are writing software that does one thing and writing software that works together. You can see this in most common Linux command-line programs. For example, you can take the output of cat and sort it with the sort command. cat file{1,2,3}. txt | sort > sorted.txt takes three files (file1.txt, file2.txt and file3.txt), merges their output into a single stream and then sends that stream to sort, which sorts all of the incoming data, then is written to sorted.txt. The point is that cat, sort, and many other programs use standard input as their text input and standard output as their text output. Normally, a shell writes standard out to the screen, but by adding a pipe (|), your shell points the standard output of the first program into the standard input of the second program.

Note that separation of concerns and the Unix philosophy are often used as reasoning for moving to a service-oriented architecture or microservices. Both of these terms are the idea of separating your code into lots of smaller services or pieces. There are problems with such an infrastructure (more pieces to monitor, possibly more expensive and a higher possibility of a network failure), but usually separation of concerns is not a great argument if it is the sole argument to move. You can separate concerns inside your code if you want, just using separate classes or other organizational techniques.

Long-term work

Another factor that we should probably talk about in regard to development is long-term planning and thinking. So much of modern development is focused around fast iteration, that often people do not remember to look at where they have gone and where they are going. I like to do a quarterly retrospective and plan for myself to solve this. Some businesses have this built into their planning process, but you can also do it for yourself.

A common framework that some businesses use, I also use for my personal planning. It is called **objectives and key results** (**OKRs**). The idea behind OKRs is that you take a list of things that you want to achieve, which are objectives, and then create measurable checkpoints as your key results. Then, at the end of the quarter, you look at your OKRs and look at what you planned on doing, before comparing them to what you completed. In a larger, more formal organization, you may score your progress based on the OKRs you completed, but for yourself, it is just a benchmark. Look at what you thought you were going to do and ask: what prevented you from completing some projects? What other things did you do that you didn't plan for? Did you want to do those things? If not, can you make goals for the next quarter to remove them by building a tool to make them easier, automating them, removing the need for them, and so on. Then, looking forward, create new or adjusted OKRs based on the next quarter. Often, I will create year-long goals. Some are work related, such as unifying how all of our services do job scheduling, while some are life related, such as losing 40 pounds of weight. In my current role, my OKRs are completely disconnected from my management structure. So even though my boss is horrible at doing performance reviews, I can still do self-reflection and track progress for both my work and personal life.

Example OKRs

The following example is inspired by Niket Desai, a friend and former co-worker. He writes a lot about product management and planning. It's a rough set of scored OKRs that a more formal business might have. This is what you might see at the end of a quarter.

In the table below, we see objectives for a quarter, with their completion percentage at the middle of the quarter, as well as their final score. Then, at the bottom, there is a total average for the whole quarter. The first place I used OKRs regularly was at Google. There, it was suggested that you want to get between 70% and 100% of your objectives. If you hit 100% every quarter, then you aren't aiming high enough.

Objective	Mid	Score
Increase user base	0.4	0.60
Improve deploy speed	0.5	0.66
Investigate A/B testing	0.4	0.75
Total	0.43	0.67

Objective: Increase user base

Owner: Melissa

Key results:

♦ Increase per-day views to 1,000

♦ Increase total monthly unique visitors by 45,000

Objective: Improve deploy speed and reliability

Owner: June

Key results:

♦ Paralyze test builds

♦ Implement canary rollouts

♦ Add build asset caching

Objective: Investigate A/B testing

Owner: Xander

Key results:

♦ Investigate top five A/B testing frameworks

♦ Implement proof of concept with one framework

♦ Write design document

♦ Pitch chosen platform to product team

Another example is much more casual and not scored at all. These are a subset of my goals for 2017. Note that they still have measurable key results and higher-level objectives.

♦ Improve physical health

  ○ Stretch every morning

  ○ Successfully complete a 5K

  ○ Successfully complete a half marathon

  ○ Cook eight meals a week (out of the 21 possible)

  ○ Record all eating

  ○ Join some sort of sports team

♦ Put out content to improve the internet

  ○ Take in revenue from one side project

  ○ Write 200 posts in 2016

  ○ Maintain a four-post-per-week average on https://writing.natwelch.com

  ○ Give five talks to groups larger than 10

♦ Grow your brain

  ○ Read 70 books.

  ○ Go to four art exhibits, live shows, or movies a month.

  ○ Read one non-fiction book a month. Note that I checked out these objectives every quarter to see how I was doing and if I needed to add or remove any goals. This quarterly reflection shows me how much I've progressed in three months, reminds me of things I did and reminds me of things I want to be doing.

Notebooks

Sometimes looking for future ideas can be difficult. I keep a notebook where I write random things in throughout the day. Sometimes I put down ideas that I want to build in the future. Some are one sentence, while others are bullet lists of features and some are very rough infrastructure and architecture sketches or wireframes of user interfaces.

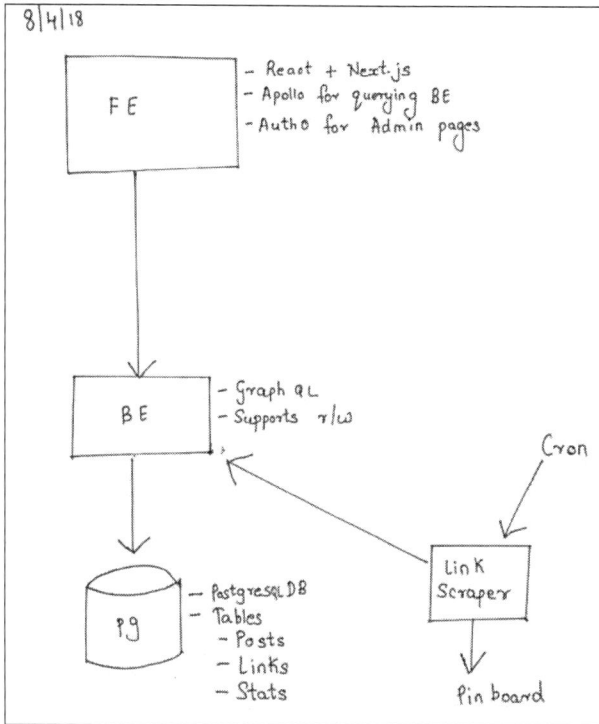

Figure 2: In this photograph, I have sketched out the rough design for a blog. The frontend, or FE, is built in JavaScript using React and Next.js for rendering content. Apollo is used to query the backend (or BE). The backend is a Go app with one path, /graphql, which controls the data. It sits on top of a PostgreSQL database for storing state. There is also a cron job that gets data from an external service, Pinboard, and makes queries to the GraphQL endpoint.

Notebooks are also great places to record how you are feeling, things you want to do, and things you want to get off your chest. A classic tool is to write a letter to a person you are angry with and then never do anything with it. I used to write these in emails, often in an inebriated state and still ended up sending a few, which often got me into trouble or hurt a relationship with someone when I didn't need to do that. By writing it on paper, that never happens! There's no way that I can accidentally send an email when it's on paper.

Documenting and maintaining projects

A last but very important detail is the documentation and maintenance of the code that you produce. Hopefully, your code will last as long as it is needed. Setting good standards early on for documentation promotes others to write documents in the future. One way to promote this is to tie documentation changes to code reviews, so your reviewer can see not only the internals changing but also the messaging to users changing.

Another thing that you can do is to publish a change log. A change log is a document showing what has changed since the release. If you release often, you will probably want to automate this in some way. More often than not, this document will be for other developers or product people if it is automated. Many organizations I have worked for keep an internal change log for each release and then the product team will translate that into a simpler document for external consumption by executives and customers.

Figuring out the right documentation for your code, though, is something that you and your team will need to work on. You probably do not want to end up on either side of the documentation spectrum:

♦ The code documents itself!

♦ Every little thing must be documented!

On the one hand, you are lying to yourself. Some code may document itself, but I have seen enough outages to know that there is always code that someone misunderstands. On the other hand, you have a demand that takes too much time and effort to maintain. If every line and function is documented, more often than not it ends up being out of date. Finding a happy medium is important. My general policy is that every function that someone else could use needs at least two sentences of documentation. This is incredibly abstract and more of an idea of what a middle ground might look like. I have lots of code that does not follow this advice and lots of code that does. Writing documentation is like writing code: your team will have a style and the goal should be accuracy and consistency, not perfection because perfection is impossible.

The owner can also be responsible for tracking down weird bugs or test failures. They do not have to do all of the work, but they can be the person to receive alerts if tests stop passing or a library that the project depends on has a security vulnerability.

Summary

This chapter was all about building tools. We talked about finding and defining projects, then figuring out what you want to build and how to describe it to others. We discussed actually planning and doing the work. Finally, we explored some tips for the long-term maintenance of code.

There is a danger in some SRE relationships of becoming the person or team that just does configuration management or just does incident response. Making time for software development helps your team to avoid this fate. It is high in the pyramid, but as a team, you should not forget its importance.

In the next chapter, we will discuss the final level of the hierarchy: user experience.

8

USER EXPERIENCE

User experience (UX) focuses on defining, changing, and improving how people interact with an object. This could be anything from decreasing the number of steps it takes to get a user to buy a product, to making a building easier to navigate, or improving the boarding speed of an airplane. This relates to SRE in two ways. First, we need to support the UX of the systems we support. For example, making sure the application is responsive and available, so users have a consistent experience. Secondly, our tools need to provide a good experience. Do we know how people will use our tools? Can they interact with other tools we have built? A good experience means that users of the services we build and support will enjoy using them, and be able to do what they need to without getting frustrated. A good experience is also one that respects the user's privacy and security. If a user gives us a credit card number to buy a pair of pants, they want to be charged the right amount of money and also receive the pants. They also want to know that our organization won't sell off their personal information or be easily compromised and have the user's credit card information stolen.

UX sits at the top of the hierarchy; not because it is unimportant (or the most important), but because it requires other fundamentals to be in place before it is useful. For instance, later on, we will talk about how measuring user flows can help you to determine how users use your service. If you have no way to collect that data, or if you aren't developing tools or publishing postmortems, UX has less impact. UX also sits on top of the hierarchy because software needs to be developed before you can improve its UX. That's not to say that UX should be ignored when creating software, but if most of your time is still spent responding to incidents instead of writing software, you probably should not be focusing on UX.

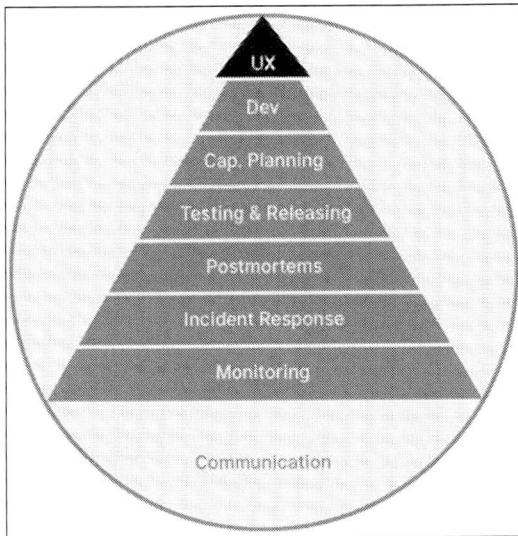

Figure 1: Our current position in the hierarchy.
UX is at the very top, building on what we have learned so far.

The study of graphic design and UX focuses on improving user productivity, user happiness, and user engagement. Some aspects of graphic design, such as those related to designing advertisements, prioritize getting people to focus on things. For example, persuading people to smoke cigarettes less, to donate to a political candidate, or to buy a certain type of jeans.

This relates to SRE because, as a profession, we are often fighting to get people to focus on our priorities, or tools, or system health. As an SRE, you could be making sure developers pay attention to the alerts you send, making features you build in tools easy to find and use, or presenting work in such a way that other people understand what to complete and how. Even if you do not see an immediate connection to graphic design, designers have done great research into how much information the human brain can absorb at a glance and how to best organize important data on a page to make it visibly important.

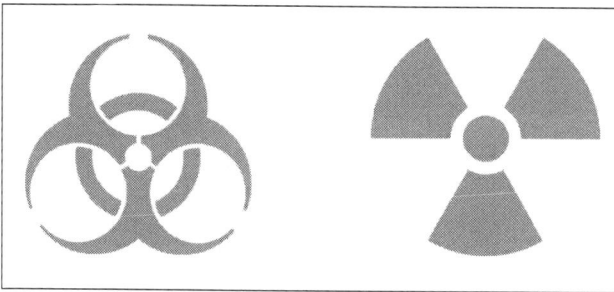

Figure 2: On the left is the biohazard symbol,
while on the right is the international radiation symbol

One of my favorite examples of this is the biohazard symbol. This symbol was designed by Dow Chemical Company to make sure people stayed away from biohazard storage signs. The company had six design criteria for making sure people stayed safe (https://99percentinvisible.org/article/beyond-biohazard-danger-symbols-cant-last-forever/):

1. **Visually striking**: If you see it, it needs to be very noticeable.

2. **Unique and unambiguous**: It should not be reused. The example Dow chemical company gave was the Jolly Roger, or skull and crossbones. While it was used to specify poison, it also specified pirate treasure. You don't want people digging for biohazard waste!

3. **Easily recalled and recognizable**: This stops people from using common shapes or using color as the specifier.

4. **Easy to stencil**: It should be easy to create and apply to all sorts of surfaces.

5. **Rotationally symmetric**: That way, no matter how it is displayed, you can tell what it is.

6. **Acceptable to people from all backgrounds**: It should not be offensive or confusing, no matter where in the world you are or who the viewer is.

These requirements are very similar to what you might expect for a piece of software. By that, I mean they are easy to understand and, with the right tests, measurable and testable. Design systems, which are a collection of rules around a set of designs, are similar to systems for a piece of software. You use them to determine whether a design meets the project's requirements. Some design systems are much more specific, such as brand guidelines (use this color, this logo, this wording, and so on), while others require more testing to determine whether the design meets the requirements of the system, just as some pieces of software can be verified with simple unit tests, and others require more detailed integration tests.

There was also follow-up research to Dow Chemical Company's initial designs, by the US Department of Energy, to figure out how to make sure no one stumbled onto waste for 10,000 years (the length of time that much of this waste is dangerous to humans for). Some of the suggestions focused on creating intimidating architecture or creating religions that revered glowing animals to create a place that was noticeable and well-known, but that no one wanted to approach. The researchers didn't come up with a good answer but lots of ideas were sent around. This is interesting, because often, as SREs, we are working on much shorter timelines, but we have to think about how people we don't know will interact with our tools. It is very possible that an alert you write will fire and someone will react to it who does not know you because you have moved on, or the team responsible for the service has changed.

An even more apt design system, very close to the SRE world, is the design of airports, especially post-9/11 (`https://99percentinvisible.org/episode/episode-32-design-for-airports/transcript`). Large airports support people coming through them, usually in the worst possible moods, all day, everyday. Post-9/11, especially in the US, people spend more time between security and their gate, and less time outside of security. Airports are realizing that and increasing the number of places to sit, eat, and relax before flights. John F. Kennedy International Airport (JFK) saw 60 million travelers pass through its gates in 2015. Many of those people had never been to JFK before and, considering over half of those travelers were on international flights, there was a high possibility that millions of people came through who did not speak English well. On top of all of that, JFK suffers from weather shutdowns a few times a year due to heavy snow or strong winds.

This is not a set of problems just for JFK, though. Consider San Francisco International Airport (SFO), which is the cause of many flight delays. Like complex distributed systems, cascading failures are common in the airport world. For example, if there is heavy fog at SFO, flights back up because SFO operates with limited runways when there is poor visibility. Airlines then delay flights because they know that there will be a delay to landings, which then delays the return flights as well, which causes the airport to have to shift its timetable. Creating design systems to calm travelers, improve movement between flights, help people find their way, and help travelers to survive when their flights are canceled or delayed are all very important and require focusing on both the experience of the people using the airport, and the experience of the people maintaining the airport.

A cascading failure is a type of outage when one service going down causes another service to go down, which then causes other services to go down. Cascading failures can happen because of load spikes or a change in behavior. You can imagine five servers that traffic is load balanced between. One crashes and the others cannot handle the load, and so others start to fail. The system then begins to auto-scale to handle the load, but every new server that comes up dies as well from the load. The solution to this specific problem is to shed the load, by stopping all, or a large amount of, traffic from hitting the servers. However, in general, cascading failures are scary because many things are failing and you often don't know the root cause.

Figure 3: JFK's Terminal 4 baggage claim at four in the morning, January 6th, 2018. 12 hours after this photo was taken, this area flooded, soaking thousands of bags. As this area was full of people, Delta gave people free bag delivery to their homes or hotels, so people would go home and free up space for more incoming customers.

In this chapter, we will talk about some very high-level fundamentals of design and UX, so you can easily work with your design team and apply methodology to the software you build. We will also talk about common ways to improve your application's experience and discuss some ethics around tools and software.

An introduction to design and UX

Design is a very large field, with a long history and many diverse sub-fields and adjacent fields. When software developers talk about design, they are usually referring to one of two things; the first being software architecture design, which we talked about in *Chapter 7, Building Tools*. The other is the design of how people interact with software. The part of software that people interact with is usually called the **user interface** (**UI**).

As mentioned in the introduction, the idea of studying how users interact with the UI is called UX. In the SRE world, that often shows up as defining a **command-line interface** (**CLI**), but sometimes UX is designing a website interface. Other times, it is a **graphical user interface** (**GUI**), and sometimes it is a lever or button in real life.

Pronunciation point: people often pronounce GUI as gooey. When I first heard this, I did not understand, so here is a note in case you run into it as well. CLI is often just pronounced "C. L. I." A web UI is just a website.

```
● ● ●                    1. nat@Tokyo: ~/Projects

[ Wed Aug 29 21:17:46 ]
[ nat@Tokyo ~/Projects ]$ terraform --help
Usage: terraform [-version] [-help] <command> [args]

The available commands for execution are listed below.
The most common, useful commands are shown first, followed by
less common or more advanced commands. If you're just getting
started with Terraform, stick with the common commands. For the
other commands, please read the help and docs before usage.

Common commands:
    apply              Builds or changes infrastructure
    console            Interactive console for Terraform interpolations
    destroy            Destroy Terraform-managed infrastructure
    env                Workspace management
    fmt                Rewrites config files to canonical format
    get                Download and install modules for the configuration
    graph              Create a visual graph of Terraform resources
    import             Import existing infrastructure into Terraform
    init               Initialize a Terraform working directory
    output             Read an output from a state file
    plan               Generate and show an execution plan
    providers          Prints a tree of the providers used in the configuration
    push               Upload this Terraform module to Atlas to run
    refresh            Update local state file against real resources
    show               Inspect Terraform state or plan
    taint              Manually mark a resource for recreation
    untaint            Manually unmark a resource as tainted
    validate           Validates the Terraform files
    version            Prints the Terraform version
    workspace          Workspace management

All other commands:
    debug              Debug output management (experimental)
    force-unlock       Manually unlock the terraform state
    state              Advanced state management
```

Following is the execution of terraform --help
command

Here, we have the output of terraform --help. It is a common interface paradigm to make either -h, -? or --help return an output as shown in the preceding code block, so you can know the basics of how to call a program. The first line of the output, terraform [--version] [--help] <command> [args], says that the terraform command can be run with three optional arguments (optional is usually designated by square brackets). Then, you specify a command to run. If you run with the --help flag, as shown in the preceding example, it gives all possible commands you could provide. If you want to find out about the plan command, you could run it with the -help flag as well: terraform plan -help. If you were to run this command, you would see lots of output.

We can see that there are a bunch of options. Terraform, at least at the time of publishing, follows a common pattern in CLI design, where it includes each option's default value. If you do not add a flag to this command, the default values are used. You could run terraform plan -parallelism=6 and run with six parallel workers, instead of the default 10. I do not know why Terraform's default parallelism is 10, but another common design decision is sane defaults. The first time someone interacts with your software, you do not want them to hurt themselves. For example, Terraform modifies infrastructure and it could easily have defaults that would delete all of their infrastructure. This is not a good default, because rarely do users expect bad things to happen when they run a command. Now, because software is often immaterial, I know some people have trouble attributing design to it. How can a system be beautiful? In the next section, we will talk about places that you can find interaction design and UX in the real world, so that you can try to find some parallels.

Real-world interaction design

If you are having trouble thinking about UX, think about entering a restaurant. How do you know what to do after you walk in the door?

Figure 4: A bar in Brooklyn, New York

Sometimes there is a counter with a cash register, while other times there is a sign asking you to "please wait to be seated." Other times, you just walk in and stand awkwardly. Visual cues are just one way to design a system to show people how to interact with it. Another example is a siren on an ambulance or a police car. When we hear a loud, piercing sound, we know to get out of the way. Every society has a different siren sound, but they all consistently signal that we should pay attention and get out of the way.

A lot of design is learning to interpret what you are seeing, discovering why something is made a certain way, and thinking about how to improve it. You can start developing an eye for this by reading about how designers tear things apart. I have provided a few examples in the *References* section, but the key is to start thinking about why you do things.

Which signs at the airport tell you what the flow is from the moment you get out of your car or get off a train? Try thinking about how you would get around a new airport if you did not speak the language. Could you make it from the airport curb to boarding the plane without being able to hear? What visual signs exist for people who can't hear? What audible cues exist for people who can't read or see well?

Figure 5: A McDonald's in Brooklyn, New York

Places like McDonald's are very good at this. You can usually see a large menu from the moment you enter and often signs that point to where to order are right by the front door. Employees are very explicit in making sure you don't forget to add things such as extra food or drinks to your order.

Another place optimized for UX, but with different design goals, is IKEA. IKEA is masterful at getting you to look at everything before you actually buy anything. The stores take you on a path that shows you 10 options for what every room in a house could look like. After wandering through IKEA once, the next time, go in and try and return an item. Knowing the entrance and where the stairs lead, see how your different goal changes your path and which signs stand out. Often, the returns desk is near the exit. Notice how, if you miss some signs, you will end up going through the whole store again.

Even in the digital world, you see people optimizing their design in different ways. For example, if you click a button, think about what led you to click it. If the button was in another place, would the button have been easier to find? One of my favorite examples is **multi-factor authentication** (also known as **MFA** or **2FA**) code forms.

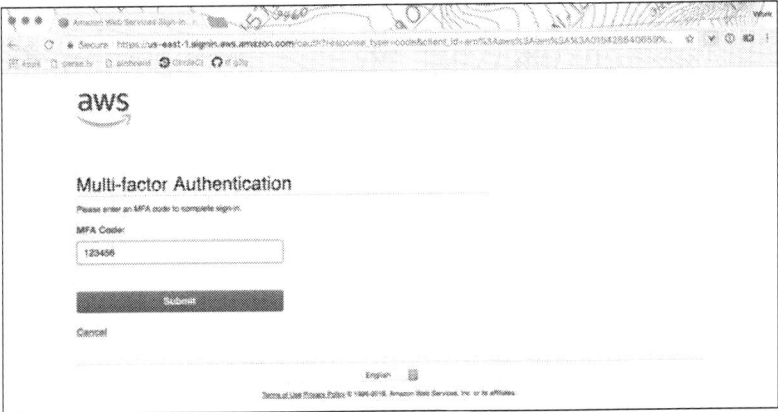

Figure 6: Amazon Web Service's MFA entry form web page in 2018

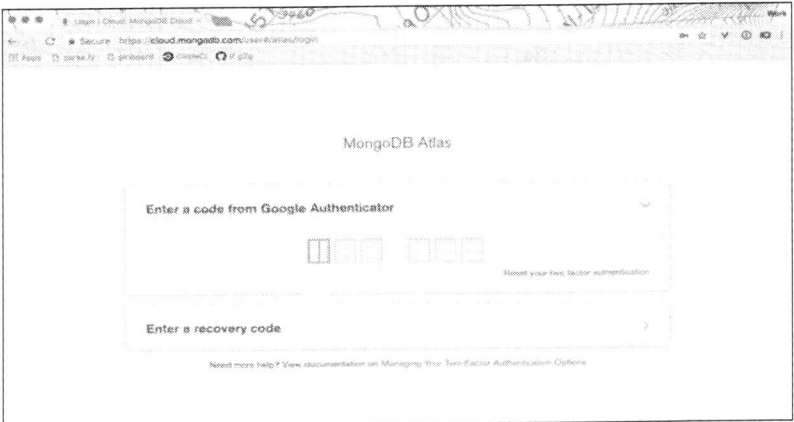

Figure 7: MongoDB Atlas's MFA entry form web page in 2018

Above, we have two web pages. One is the **Amazon Web Services (AWS)** page for entering an MFA. For Amazon, you type in the code and then press the *Enter* key or click the **Submit** button. The other is the MongoDB Cloud login page. On this page, once you type in your six-digit MFA code, it auto-submits the form and logs you in. It saves you having to click any buttons or touch your mouse. It is a small change, but it feels much smoother when logging in and decreases the time it takes me to get to my metrics during an outage, which is always appreciated.

Once you start training your eye to understand that design is in everything, you can begin testing designs for the things you build.

User testing

User testing is the act of working with users to determine whether certain experiences are optimal (or at least good) and if they are what the user actually wants to do. These are often called user interviews. The idea is that you ask a user questions to see how they do, or would, interact with a piece of software. To create a user test, you need to come up with an experience that you want to investigate, come up with questions and tests, and find people to test.

In most of my examples, I am talking about software that is already built. Just remember throughout this chapter that you can do user testing with paper diagrams or frontends that have buttons that don't do anything, or even using a slide deck. The more ephemeral the thing your users are interacting with, though, the more you need to set up the test to explain what is going on.

You can use these tests to design user stories. User stories are a description of a type of action a user will take. They often combine three pieces of information: user type, user goal, and user reason. A user type describes a group of users. A user goal is something someone from that group might want to do. A user reason is the reason why someone from that group would want to achieve that goal. Each one of these stories is an experience you might want to test during user testing.

Picking an experience

There are lots of experiences in your service you could test and you can test very broad things, as well as very specific interactions. If you want to test an entire tool, come up with user flows you want to test. An example flow might be the rollback flow. Given a service, how does the user rollback that service? Another flow might be launching an application locally. You could also test more traditional flows, such as the checkout flow: how does a user with something in their cart actually buy it?

Before you start talking to users, you can also instrument the flows using tracing or user tracking tools. Products such as *Google Analytics* and *New Relic* can show you how a user goes from one page to another by giving you a graph of user flows. You could also collect metrics about how mobile applications are used or CLIs. This will let you see how users may branch out and give you specific paths that you want to test or compare.

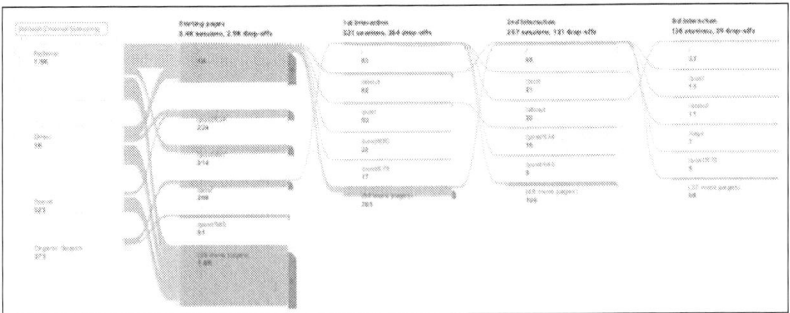

Figure 8: An example user flow graph for a website using Google Analytics

While deciding on flows to compare, try to come up with the goals of the test. Do you want to know what users notice while using the tool? Do you want to know what users find confusing?

Designing the test

Once you have a flow, or set of flows, you would like to test, put together some questions to ask people. Usually, a user test works by sitting a user in front of a computer with the preconditions set up as you would expect the user to see the service. You then ask them to perform an action, and record what they do. After they are done, you ask them questions about their experience and record the answers. This is then repeated for multiple users.

The goal is to let users do most of the talking and not try to force them down paths or toward certain answers. You also want to avoid open-ended questions, as they tend to be harder to compare between users.

Some example questions:

♦ You are here to answer an alert requesting that you roll back the service, so how would you do that?

♦ What button would you click to silence the alert?

♦ On a scale of one to five, where one is trivial and five is very complicated, how did you find that experience?

♦ Did you feel that you completed the rollback successfully?

♦ You need to write a monitoring config that stores the 95th percentile of request latency. How would you begin doing that?

You should record all answers and compare them between users who take the test.

Finding people to test

The best users to test are people who actually use the software. Often, you can get a few people to go through a test just by asking. If you have lots of people using your software, you can use tools that do heat map tracking on your pages to see where people actually click, so you don't even need to collect people.

If you are testing people, make sure to record data about them before the test, such as their experience with the tool, their role, and time in that role.

There are also organizations that will put together pools of people to be part of a test if your product is something used outside of your organization. If it's an internal tool with lots of users, you could send out an email and offer something like cool merchandise in exchange for people participating in a user study. Currently, the trend is free socks with logos, but I have received cups, t-shirts, sweatshirts, hats, USB drives, and even flashlights in exchange for helping people with internal projects.

Don't forget to thank people for their time. It is also useful to share your findings with the folks who take the test, so that they feel their time was well spent and helped the project.

After testing out user flows, it is important to focus on the developer's experience of working on your tools.

Developer experience

I would like to talk about two personal pet peeves that pop up in the world of writing software and relate to developer experience. They are code quality and **not invented here syndrome** (**NIHS**). Focusing on the developer experience is like focusing on the experience of people who work in airports. They aren't the core customer but improving their quality of life will improve your customer's experience and the quality of work they deliver. Airports do this by providing expedited paths through security, designated parking, or discounted meals. You can help the people who work on your product to improve their experience when building tools.

When I say code quality, I'm referring to the style in which people write code together. If you can, I highly recommend defining a team style guide for each language you write in. This lets you set a base line so that people can develop in the same style. In the journalism world, there is a *house style*, which is a style guide published by the organization that determines how staff deal with common things, such as how they refer to people throughout an article or how they deal with stories about mental illness. For coding, a code style guide describes how the team deals with unusual language features. It often describes what type of whitespace is used, how loops and conditionals are dealt with, and answers to common questions about style. The benefit of this is that, when people move between projects, they do not have to get used to a new style if using the same language. It also means that people who often jump between code bases, such as SREs, feel comfortable writing code, and it fits in with the rest of the code in a file or directory.

NIHS is when people want to only use software that was written by people at their organization and have a lack of trust of anything built by software developers who do not work there. This is incredibly dangerous, because it can lead to you writing more software than your organization can afford to maintain. The classic advice is that the software you should build is the thing that is your core competency and you should have other people build things that are not your number one priority. For example, if you are a media company, it makes a lot of sense to write your own **content management system** (**CMS**) so that you can be very specific about how you create and serve your content, which is the core job of your business. On the other hand, you probably do not need to invent a new monitoring service or load balancer, because there are many out there. If you can't find something that meets your exact needs, try looking into adding the functionality to an existing project and then merging it upstream, so you are giving back to the world, and also not making your team the new sole maintainer of something that is important to you but not your number one priority.

NIHS is also dangerous because it can cause a sense of elitism within your development team. This can often lead down a road to the team thinking that no one else can build as well as they can and that they are invincible. This is a toxic culture and will prevent other people from joining your team, and will also often cause burnout, as team members will try to perform at the level of their inflated egos.

This is not to say that you shouldn't build software; just make sure that you evaluate everything available before deciding to take on building and maintaining another piece of software.

Experience of tools

There are lots of things you can do to improve your tools. Often, they are found just by treating your tools like products. This means not treating them like throwaway scripts and not just hacking on them as needed. Instead, they need to be invested in, loved, and maintained.

One way this often comes out is by having what is referred to as *opinionated tools*. This means tools that do not support every single possible workflow. Instead, they focus on the right and wrong way to do things. The downside of this is that tools can be unable to support new workflows when they grow within the organization. As an upside, though, you as the maintainer know exactly what workflows exist and how they work, and can research improving them to make the experience better.

That does not mean that tools should not be configurable. I, personally, love configuring tools through configuration files and environment variables. Configuration files are great when you need to keep all of your configuration in code and bake settings into a build. On the other hand, environment variables let you build software independent of configuration and then change how it works on each run.

Figuring out what is best is up to you: it all depends on your service and how it is used. You can define that, but make sure it works for your users and continues to work over the lifetime of the tool.

Performance budgets

Another way you can improve the UX of a service is by defining a performance budget. We talked about performance budgets very briefly in *Chapter 5, Testing and Releasing*. The concept is that for every code change, you measure its effect on system performance. If performance changes enough to take the service out of valid bounds, you need to stop working on features until you modify the application to get performance back to normal levels.

In *Chapter 6, Capacity Planning*, we said that tying goals to performance is dangerous. We said that this is because making changes and knowing the performance impact is hard. Instead, by measuring performance constantly and seeing how changes made for features affect system-wide performance, your team can make a cost-benefit analysis to determine how much effort is needed to meet your performance goals.

Performance budgets were first introduced to me by Lara Hogan. Lara is a very distinguished engineering manager, the author of *Designing for Performance* and also a prolific public speaker. The idea is that you define a maximum allowed page load speed under certain conditions, such as *WebPagetest* using Dulles location in Chrome on 3G. This defines how speed is measured (WebPagetest is an online service for evaluating page loads) and under what conditions the test is run. If you're thinking that this sounds like an SLO, you are right! It is a metric we can evaluate and use to inform our decisions. Lara even suggests that you add the SLO check to your tests, so that if you break the requirement, you cannot deploy.

The reason that page speed is so important in web UX is multifaceted. First off, many search engines, including Google, use page speed as one metric to evaluate a page's ranking. The slower the page is, the lower the ranking. Secondly, users hate slow pages (https://perspectives.mvdirona.com/2009/10/the-cost-of-latency/). In 2006, Marissa Mayer, the former Google and Yahoo executive, when talking about Google, said, "Half a second delay caused a 20% drop in traffic." (https://glinden.blogspot.com/2006/11/marissa-mayer-at-web-20.html)

Users will often also abandon shopping carts that take too long to load or checkout screens that process their credit cards too slowly. Amazon found that 100ms extra delay caused a 1% drop in sales (http://highscalability.com/blog/2009/7/25/latency-is-everywhere-and-it-costs-you-sales-how-to-crush-it.html). Google redid its test in 2009 and when it added 400ms of extra time to page results, it saw upwards of 0.5% less searches (https://ai.googleblog.com/2009/06/speed-matters.html).

You do not have to be running a website for performance to matter, though. You could define the performance of a car with an electric paddle shifter as requiring the paddle press to gear shift delay to be less than 800ms.

In the US, there is the **Transportation Security Administration** (**TSA**), which controls access to the nation's airports. The TSA will occasionally measure the time it takes for random passengers to get through airport security lines, to measure the performance of its current processes and system load. If the time gets too high, it can open additional lines, so that people do not miss their flights.

As software has grown as an industry, another important factor has become part of the UX of a service, which relates closely to the SRE world: security.

Security

Security is essential to gaining the trust of users. In our modern age, data breaches are very common and information security is very important. Users are starting to select products based on their security and privacy. Security is a huge field on its own, with many companies having their own security engineers and entire companies devoted to working as consultants to examine other companies' security practices. Security is the responsibility of everyone, just like monitoring, incident response, or UX. You should have experts on your staff to direct you, but you must not be ignorant about the topic and defer to your experts for everything.

When building software, or auditing technology for security matters, try thinking about the three following aspects of a piece of technology:

♦ **Authentication**: How do you give a user a token saying they can interact with things? For example, a user logging in with a username and password.

♦ **Authorization**: How do you determine whether a user can access something? For example, a user with a token can change a post on a blog. Another example is that anyone on your network subnet can connect to the human resources help pages.

♦ **Risk profile**: The idea of a risk profile is what type of information you have, who would be interested in obtaining that information, and their technical capability. For example, a news organization might not have much customer information, but it would seek to protect information about sources and ongoing article research. That being said, a news organization that took donations or sold a print publication could have credit card numbers and shipping information. Credit cards and personal information tend to attract a wide number of attackers, while journalistic sources are of more interest to large crime organizations or state actors (people connected to governments).

By being on the internet, you are at risk of being attacked. The internet lets anyone connect and send traffic to anyone else. The chance of something being insecure is high, so often people are scanning the internet looking for IP addresses with open ports and vulnerable services. Following are some tips for addressing common issues, and in the *References* section, you can find more external sources to read and watch to continue your learning.

	Incidents				Breaches			
	Large	Small	Unknown	Total	Large	Small	Unknown	Total
Accommodation (72)	40	296	32	368	31	292	15	338
Administrative (56)	7	15	11	33	5	12	1	18
Agriculture (11)	1	0	4	5	0	0	0	0
Construction (23)	2	11	10	23	0	5	5	10
Education (61)	42	26	224	292	30	15	56	101
Entertainment (71)	6	19	7,163	7,188	5	17	11	33
Financial (52)	74	74	450	598	39	52	55	146
Healthcare (62)	165	152	433	750	99	112	325	536
Information (51)	54	76	910	1,040	29	50	30	109
Management (55)	1	0	1	2	0	0	0	0
Manufacturing (31-33)	375	21	140	536	28	15	28	71
Mining (21)	3	3	20	26	3	3	0	6
Other Services (81)	5	11	46	62	2	7	26	35
Professional (54)	158	59	323	540	24	39	69	132
Public (92)	22,429	51	308	22,788	111	31	162	304
Real Estate (53)	2	5	24	31	2	4	14	20
Retail (44-45)	56	111	150	317	38	86	45	169
Trade (42)	13	5	13	31	6	4	2	12
Transportation (48-49)	15	9	35	59	7	6	5	18
Utilities (22)	14	8	24	46	4	3	11	18
Unknown	1,043	9	17,521	18,573	82	3	55	140
Total	24,505	961	27,842	53,308	545	756	915	2,216

Table 1.   Security incidents and breaches by victim industry and organization size

Figure 9: From page 25 of the 2018 Verizon Breach Report (https://www. verizonenterprise.com/resources/reports/rp_DBIR_2018_Report_en_xg.pdf). This shows just one year of attacks that Verizon knew about, categorized by victim industry and organization size. An incident is where an organization is compromised, with the possibility of its information being taken or made unavailable. A breach is an incident where data is explicitly disclosed by a third-party source. Note this table does not show the severity of the incidents.

Authentication

The following are some basic suggestions for writing code that deals with authentication:

♦ Always verify contact information. If your user puts in a phone number or email, make sure they actually own it by sending a verification message.

♦ Do not put a maximum on password length or restrict which characters can be in a password.

♦ Always store passwords with a one-way hash such as bcrypt. If someone else gets access to your datastore, they should not have access to a user's password.

♦ For sensitive accounts, support multi-factor authentication. This usually requires a user to have an ID, a password, and some sort of device, such as a cell phone.

♦ If possible, remove passwords from your authentication flow. `Haveibeenpwned.com` tracks data breaches and has around five billion passwords at the time of writing. Given that there aren't that many more people on the planet, it's highly possible that a password you use is in there.

♦ Send notifications when users authenticate with unusual circumstances, such as after changing a password, or from a new location and browser combination.

♦ Expire authentication after a time, requiring users to re-authenticate, instead of letting users only log in once.

Note that these measures will not guarantee that people will not find a way to get into your system, but they are a good start.

Authorization

Authorization, as mentioned in the preceding section, is determining whether a user has permission to do what they want to do. Always use authorization with authentication if you can. Just because a user is on your network, or has access to your corporate email system, this does not mean that they should be able to access something. For example, if I walk into an office and plug a computer into a wall socket, or connect to your Wi-Fi from the street, I should not be able to access everything about your organization without also logging in as a user. Also, make sure people are not sharing logins. If the same authentication token means multiple users, you don't actually have authentication because you can't audit which users are doing what. It should be mentioned that adding authorization logging is very useful for knowing which users ask for permission to do which things, and which things you give them permission for.

Risk profile

Determining your risk profile is not a science, but it's something you can think about to determine how paranoid you should be. First, think about an individual person. They have stuff that other people want, such as data or money. Then think about the level of effort an attacker would have to go through to take it from them. If the individual doesn't use two-factor authentication on their bank account, and reuses passwords (or reuses similar passwords), then the possibility that another human could get access to their bank account increases. So, the more valuable a person and their stuff is, the more the risk increases because external actors will target them. Also, the worse a person's security practices are, the more the risk increases because of the chance of automated attacks, and the more the effort required to compromise them decreases.

For example, if I use the same password everywhere for the same email address (for instance `email@example.com` and `qwerty1234256` are my logins for Gmail, Netflix, and my bank) if any one of those companies is compromised and my email and password are leaked, then future attackers can add that combo to their automated scripts. These scripts can just look at every popular website online and start trying every leaked password and email combo ever. Since my username and password is the same, the chance of me being compromised is higher. If I'm a public figure, such as US political consultant John Podesta, for example, and people know my email address, attackers will try targeting my email with phishing scams (described in the next section) and brute forcing my password with scripts, hoping that they can get into an account of mine and gain valuable information.

A service is just like a person: a service belongs to an organization, which has value. Apple, for example, has trillions of US dollars to its name. Most countries have databases on all of their citizens for tax purposes. Apple is more technically advanced than smaller companies, so its risk decreases, as it has the resources to invest in security. Comparably, Wells Fargo bank has high assets, but it is also technically competent. A credit union, on the other hand, might have a decent amount of money, but not have anyone competent taking care of security.

Phishing

Phishing is one of the most dangerous and common attack vectors in computer security today. It is the act of taking an email that someone might normally interact with and modifying it to have the user who clicks on it be taken to a fake page, where they type in their credentials for a real site (such as their email password). As an operator, phishing is particularly dangerous, because SREs, DevOps engineers, and system administrators are all common targets for phishing, as they often have credentials for many sensitive systems.

In 2014, Edward Snowden, who famously leaked classified information from the US, revealed that sysadmins were some of the National Security Agency's top targets (`https:// theintercept.com/2014/03/20/inside-nsa-secret-efforts-hunt-hack-system-administrators/`). Whether or not that is true anymore, the point remains that people who might target systems might target both your personal and work life to gain access to a system.

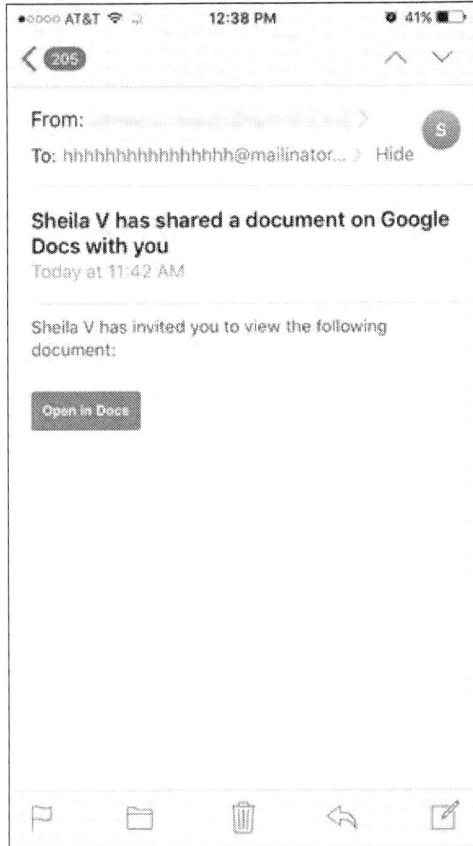

Figure 10: An example phishing email from Wired magazine after a large-scale Google Docs scam in 2017 (https://www.wired.com /2017/05/dont-open-google-doc-unless-youre-positive-legit/)

These attacks might come as something as innocuous as an email asking you to renew your Netflix subscription or to change your password for your Gmail. They often work because many people use the same password on many accounts. This is why it is often recommended to use a different password on every website and account. It is also why we recommend using MFA where possible, so that even if someone gets your username and password, they will still need your phone or some other device to get access to the account.

ACM code of ethics

The final topic of our hierarchy is ethics. I am just going to touch on this briefly, but it is a very large topic like security or design, so please go and read about it. The Association for Computing Machinery has a code of ethics for software developers. It contains 24 rules for ethical software creation and working as a software developer.

There are many very interesting and important morals throughout the document, but my two favorites are near the front:

♦ Avoid harm to others

♦ Contribute to society and human well-being

These two rules are actually about UX. If you follow this code of ethics, you are saying that you will not write software that harms users and that your software will improve society. Design is often the aspect that determines whether a service meets these two needs. A good example comes from architecture, which also has a code of ethics. In their code, architects cannot design a structure with the purpose of harming people. To that end, there is a belief that architects who design maximum security prisons are breaking their code because research has shown that the solitary isolation chambers in maximum security prisons in the US physically and mentally hurt those who live in them.

If your software causes someone mental distress, or if you allow features to exist that leave the user able to harm themselves or others, then you could be writing unethical software. For example, if you have an administrative tool that lets someone easily delete company assets without checks, or if you ignore operating your service in a reliable way, which causes pain to an individual, are you acting ethically?

These are philosophical decisions for you to think about, but I hope that you build systems that are easy to use, reliable, secure, and ethical.

Summary

We have reached the top of Dickerson's Hierarchy! Our climb up this pyramid has been long, but fruitful. In this final hierarchy chapter, we discussed the field of design and UX, and talked about how to evaluate systems for their usability. We focused on user testing, user stories, and how to improve the experience of the services you manage.

We also explained the importance of performance, measuring performance, and how performance impacts UX. We covered security and the dangers of always being online. We also briefly talked about ethics and how they relate to the UX of your software.

In the next chapter, we leave the hierarchy behind and begin talking about networking fundamentals.

References

1. *ACM Code of Ethics and Professional Conduct.* Association for Computing Machinery, `https://www.acm.org/code-of-ethics`.

2. Alvarez, Cindy. *Lean Customer Development: Building Products Your Customers Will Buy.* Oreilly Media, 2017.

3. *Design Lessons for Everyone, Curated by Top Designers.* Edited by Alex Baldwin, Hack Design, 13 June 2018, `hackdesign.org/`.

4. Gellman, Barton, and Ashkan Soltani. *NSA Infiltrates Links to Yahoo, Google Data Centers Worldwide, Snowden Documents Say.* The Washington Post, WP Company, 30 Oct. 2013, `www.washingtonpost.com/world/national-security/nsa-infiltrates-links-to-yahoo-google-data-centers-worldwide-snowden-documents-say/2013/10/30/e51d661e-4166-11e3-8b74-d89d714ca4dd_story.html`.

5. Hogan, Lara Callender. *Designing for Performance: Weighing Aesthetics and Speed.* O'Reilly, 2015.

6. Newman, Lily Hay. *Don't Open That Google Doc Unless You're Positive It's Legit.* Wired, Conde Nast, 3 June 2017, `www.wired.com/2017/05/dont-open-google-doc-unless-youre-positive-legit/`.

7. Rankin, Kyle. *Linux Hardening in Hostile Networks Server Security from TLS to TOR.* Pearson Education, Inc., 2018.

8. Smith, Yvette. *NASA Graphics Standards Manual.* NASA, 8 Sept. 2015, `www.nasa.gov/image-feature/nasa-graphics-standards-manual/`.

9. Ulwick, Anthony W. *Jobs to Be Done: Theory to Practice.* Idea Bite Press, 2016.

9

NETWORKING FOUNDATIONS

When I started as an SRE, one of the topics that I found most daunting, and incredibly hard to find good writing on, was networking. Networking is one of the most integral parts of our industry, though, because it is how communication happens between services. Without networking, we would not have distributed systems or the internet. I personally wouldn't be able to save copies of this book into Dropbox, while flying between New York and San Francisco, nor would I be able to work regularly with my editors in the United Kingdom and India. However, despite modern networking being wonderful, it also needs to be resilient to deal with physical problems that constantly occur, such as cables getting cut, weather interfering with wireless, and sharks destroying oceanic cables.

As we have highlighted throughout the book, communication between people is very important. We're moving toward a world of more distributed systems, which means that consistent and reliable communication between services is more and more important. As we'll discuss later, networks are very finicky. In this chapter, I will show you how fragile the internet is and how impressive it is that it works at all. The chapter will also discuss how to debug and understand issues that might arise between two services.

The other goal of this chapter (and *Chapter 10, Linux and Cloud Foundations*) is to help you to pass an SRE interview. Often, employers ask system debugging questions or want to know how fundamental parts of a system might work. If you're coming from a more traditional programming role, you might not know any of these things or only have rough ideas. I hope to flesh that out or at least provide you with a direction for future research.

The internet

The internet is a constantly evolving system. When I say internet, I mean the global network of cables, **Internet Service Providers (ISPs)**, routers, switches, and computers that let all of us communicate. There are cables on poles, underground, underwater, hanging between buildings, inside buildings, and really anywhere you can shove a cable.

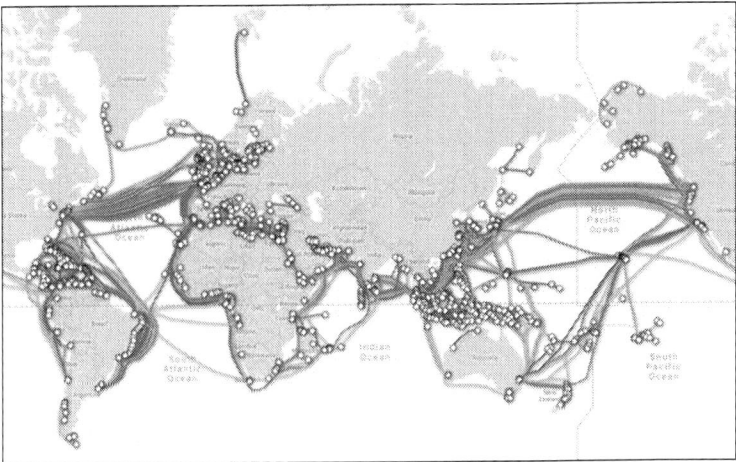

Figure 1: A map of all submarine cables from submarinecablemap.com in 2018

Some countries have one ISP, while others have hundreds. In some countries, the government owns the cables, while in others they are owned by private businesses. Many places do not have any cables and receive all of their internet via wireless from long-distance towers or from satellites.

Often, when people try to draw a graph to describe the internet, they draw something looking like a complete bipartite graph, where every node connects to every other node. Instead, it's more like a city sewer system—lots of trees and graphs connecting to large pipes that connect to other large pipes. These pipes are all of varying lengths and at each intersection there is a computer deciding which pipes you should go down next.

This is all fraught, because each node just knows how to tell you to get to the next node. Most nodes do not know the health of other nodes or even whether the tunnels you will go down are intact. To deal with this, most networking software adds some overhead to verify that messages are received in full. The starting node adds a way for the final node to verify that each message is fully intact and whether there are any more messages after this one.

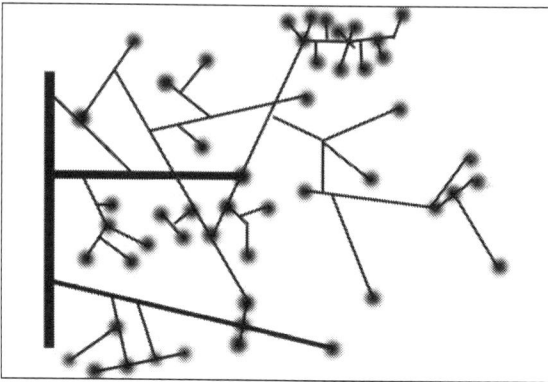

Figure 2: Here, we have a chaotic piece of lines and dots. Each dot is connected to other dots via lines and they often have to go through other dots. This image is purely random, but by viewing dots as computers and lines as cables, you have a very rough representation of a network.

This chaotic mesh of nodes is constantly changing and evolving. Things are removed, added, and changed every second, and the scale is such that it is often quite surprising that anything works. There is no true master architect, just a lot of people saying, "Okay, we'll all do it this way," and then people mostly following the rules.

I hope this gives you a sense of the chaos existing in a network. The rest of the chapter will cover technologies used to deal with this chaos and how to understand what is going on when two computers talk.

Sending an HTTP request

One of my favorite interview questions, which seems to be used by just about everyone, is to ask the interviewee to describe all of the steps of an HTTP request. There are lots of ways you could dig into this. I once had someone explain to me how the computer interprets keyboard presses. While that is fascinating, for now we will walk through the networking side of things.

Let's say you type `natwelch.com/resume` into your browser. We will go through all of the steps that happen for that to deliver content for your browser to render.

DNS

DNS (domain name system): Computers talk to each other using IP addresses and DNS translates a domain into an IP address. Technically, DNS does a little more than that, but let's start by describing domain names and go from there. In our example, `natwelch.com` is the domain and `/resume` is the path.

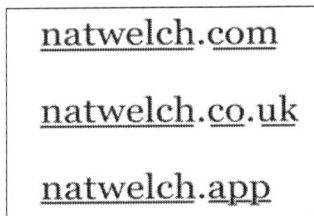

natwelch.com

natwelch.co.uk

natwelch.app

Figure 3: In all three of the above domains, `natwelch` on the left is the domain. In the first example, `com` is the TLD. In the second, `uk` is the TLD, and `co` is the SLD. In the third example, `app` is the TLD.

A domain name is made up of a few parts:

♦ **Top Level Domain (TLD)**: This is the last part of the domain, such as com, net, org, app, horse, and so on.

♦ **Dots**: These are periods and the separators in domain names. Also, all domains technically end in a dot. This is because a dot at the end means a domain is absolute, while one without a dot is relative. Most people imply the end dot, such as in the preceding image, but technically it is required to imply the absolute end of the domain.

♦ **Second Level Domain (SLD)**: The part to the left of the rightmost dot. This is actually controversial. In some cases, people only call the co in .co.uk the SLD. Others say that natwelch in natwelch. com is a SLD. There seems to be no real consensus.

♦ **Subdomain**: This is the piece of text to the left of the domain. If we have www.natwelch.com, www is the subdomain.

Domain names are actually parsed recursively like a tree.

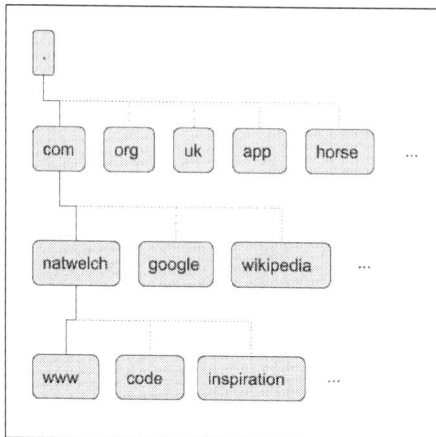

Figure 4: In the preceding example, you can see a very rough idea of how data is controlled in the DNS tree. The root servers control the root dot. There is a name server for each TLD. Then, each domain has name servers for its subdomains and records.

DNS requests ask for data recursively via a tree. Usually the flow is like so:

♦ You ask a local cache (either on your machine or on the network) if it knows where `natwelch.com` is.

♦ If the local cache doesn't know where, then you ask the DNS server if it knows where `natwelch.com` is.

♦ If the DNS server doesn't know, then you ask the "root" servers (aka "dot" servers). They won't know where `natwelch.com` is, but they will know where the `.com` servers are.

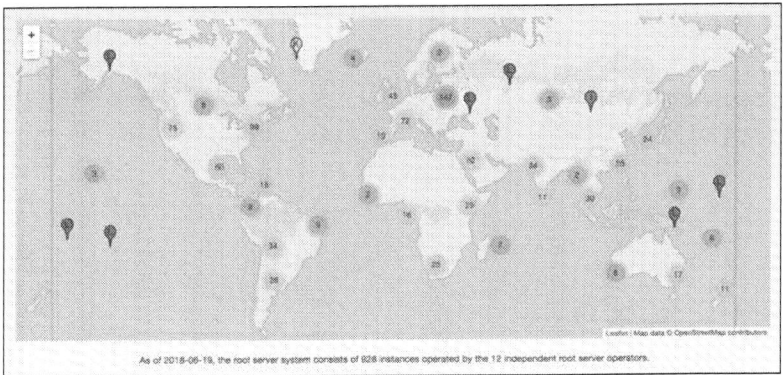

Figure 5: `root-servers.org` is the definitive page for each of the 13 root server organizations. It provides a map of where all root server machines are hosted and who maintains them. It also provides statistics about how the root servers are used and how to connect to them.

♦ The `.com` servers won't know where natwelch.com's servers are, but they will know the name servers that do know. This is known as an NS record and it points to the name servers for a domain.

♦ The name servers will then return whatever record was requested.

When you are configuring DNS, you will often write out zone records, so your name server will know where to point things. Following are some common record types:

A	An array of IPv4 addresses where this domain is located.
CNAME	This domain is an alias for this other domain.
AAAA	An array of IPv6 addresses where this domain is located.
MX	Used for mail delivery.
NS	Where this domain's name servers are.
TXT	Text strings for descriptions.
ANAME or ALIAS	Non-standard record types for putting a CNAME on the root of a domain. By default, CNAME records can only be on subdomains.
SOA	A Start of Authority record. It contains a bunch of information about who is the administrator for a DNS zone. It also describes the current state of the zone to help other DNS servers properly cache the data about the zone.

There are lots of other possible DNS records, but the preceding are the most common.

dig

To make DNS requests from the command line, you can use the dig tool, which is very powerful for exploring DNS. The most basic usage is to run dig with a domain name:

```
; <<>> DiG 9.10.6 <<>> natwelch.com
;; global options: +cmd
;; Got answer:
;; ->>HEADER<<- opcode: QUERY, status: NOERROR, id: 5354
;; flags: qr rd ra; QUERY: 1, ANSWER: 1, AUTHORITY: 0,
ADDITIONAL: 1

;; OPT PSEUDOSECTION:
; EDNS: version: 0, flags:; udp: 1280
;; QUESTION SECTION:
;natwelch.com.                    IN      A
```

```
;; ANSWER SECTION:
natwelch.com.          180    IN    A      35.190.39.138


;; Query time: 55 msec
;; SERVER: 2604:2000:1281:f9:2e30:33ff:fe5f:55af#53
(2604:2000:1281:f9:2e30:33ff:fe5f:55af)
;; WHEN: Tue Jun 19 01:45:59 UTC 2018
;; MSG SIZE  rcvd: 57
```

The only real line that matters is:

```
natwelch.com. 180 IN A 35.190.39.138
```

The line says that this natwelch.com. record has 180 seconds until it is no longer valid. It returned a single A record, with the IP 35.190.39.138. If there were multiple A records, there would be multiple lines.

dig also lets you specify a DNS server that you wish to query.

```
$ dig www.natwelch.com @8.8.8.8 +nocomment


; <<>> DiG 9.10.6 <<>> www.natwelch.com @8.8.8.8
+nocomment
;; global options: +cmd
;www.natwelch.com.          IN    A
www.natwelch.com.    183    IN    CNAME  natwelch.com.
natwelch.com.        183    IN    A      35.190.39.138
;; Query time: 45 msec
;; SERVER: 8.8.8.8#53(8.8.8.8)
;; WHEN: Tue Jun 19 01:58:39 UTC 2018
;; MSG SIZE  rcvd: 75
```

@8.8.8.8 specifies that we want to use Google's DNS server at 8.8.8.8 to provide us with an answer. Also, notice here that I requested a domain with a CNAME instead of an A record, and the DNS server also responded with the appropriate A record, saving me a round trip. DNS don't have to do this, but many do.

The preceding +nocomment simplifies the output a bit. If you wanted very short output, you can use +short:

```
$ dig google.com @8.8.8.8 +short
172.217.12.206
```

You can also add a record type that you would like to query. In the following example, we ask gmail.com for its MX records:

```
$ dig gmail.com MX +nocomment

; <<>> DiG 9.10.6 <<>> gmail.com MX +nocomment
;; global options: +cmd
;gmail.com.                    IN     MX
gmail.com.           1330    IN     MX      5 gmail-smtp-
in.1.google.com.
gmail.com.           1330    IN     MX      10 alt1.gmail-
smtp-in.1.google.com.
gmail.com.           1330    IN     MX      20 alt2.gmail-
smtp-in.1.google.com.
gmail.com.           1330    IN     MX      30 alt3.gmail-
smtp-in.1.google.com.
gmail.com.           1330    IN     MX      40 alt4.gmail-
smtp-in.1.google.com.
;; Query time: 47 msec
;; SERVER: 2604:2000:1281:f9:2e30:33ff:fe5f:55af#53(2604
:2000:1281:f9:2e30:33ff:fe5f:55af)
;; WHEN: Tue Jun 19 02:01:28 UTC 2018
;; MSG SIZE   rcvd: 161
```

You can do lots more with dig, so run man dig and find out about all of its cool uses.

Ethernet and TCP/IP

Now that we've talked about translating a domain name into an IP, how do you connect two IPs? The most common way for thinking about networking is the **Open Systems Interconnection** (**OSI**) model. The OSI model describes networking as layers:

- **Layer 1**: Physical layer
- **Layer 2**: Data link layer
- **Layer 3**: Network layer
- **Layer 4**: Transport layer
- **Layer 5**: Session layer
- **Layer 6**: Presentation layer
- **Layer 7**: Application layer

In our example of an HTTP request, layer 1 is the physical connection and layer 2 contains Wi-Fi, Ethernet, and other protocols used for controlling a physical connection. Layer 3 is for the IP, which is how things are routed. Layer 4 is for TCP and UDP. Layers 5 and 6 are rarely talked about, but they are where things such as SSL encapsulation and other networking wrappers happen. Finally, layer 7 is where HTTP and other user-level messages are sitting.

Layers are often useful for describing features of networking tools. For example, **Amazon Web Services** (**AWS**) sells two separate **load balancers** (**LB**). Its classic Elastic LB is a layer 4 LB. It can only do routing based on what IP and port a request comes in on. Amazon's newer application Elastic LB is a layer 7 LB because it can route based on details inside the HTTP request, such as headers and the request path.

Ethernet

The physical and data link layers of networking are often generalized as "Ethernet." Technically, a lot more is going on here, but the important information to know is that every networking device has a MAC address. **MAC (media access control)**, but in modern-day networking, MACs are just a way of specifying a network connection, such as an Ethernet port, Wi-Fi adapter, Bluetooth connection, or cell phone antenna. Most networking devices come with a default MAC address burned into them, although you can usually change it if needed, because every device on a network needs a unique MAC address.

A MAC address is six octets long, which means it contains 48 bits of data. That means there are 2^{48} possible MAC addresses. MAC addresses are usually shared as 12 hex digits. For example, `da:99:9c:e1:a5:f3`.

IP

IP is the protocol for routing packets around the internet. There are three common packets floating around on the internet: TCP, UDP, and ICMP. There are others as well and you can send arbitrary data, but IP is what tells routers how to route your packets and provides a wrapper around them.

A packet is a bunch of bytes sent over the network. It is grouped by bytes and the first few are headers that store data about the connection. Each protocol over the network has extra data. IP starts with the connection data, then inside of it are the higher layers. So, layer 2 wraps layer 3, which wraps layer 4, which wraps layer 5, and so on.

IP promises absolutely nothing, so there is no guarantee that your data will ever make it to a host, and if you don't control that host, there is no central monitoring to see how the data gets there.

Each packet that traverses IP has a source IP address and destination IP address. It can contain other metadata as well.

I won't go into detail here, but reading about **Address Resolution Protocol (ARP)**, **Interior Gateway Protocol (IGP)**, and **Border Gateway Protocol (BGP)** will explain the complicated mess of how each router that receives a packet determines where to send the packet next on its way through the mesh of the internet toward the packet's final destination IP address.

Some books that go into detail on these topics include:

♦ *Computer Networks* by *Andrew S. Tanenbaum*

♦ *TCP/IP Illustrated*, Volume 1 by *W. Richard Stevens*

CIDR notation

Classless Inter-Domain Routing (CIDR) notation is a compact way to describe a range of IP addresses. CIDR notation contains an IP address, a slash, and an integer. For example, 10.0.0.0/8. This example is often read as "ten dot zero dot zero dot zero, slash 8."

To know how many IP addresses a slash (also known as a prefix) contains, you need to know powers of two, or at least how to use a calculator. $2^{address\ length\ -\ slash\ number}$ tells you how many addresses. IPv4 contains 32 bits. So, for our earlier example, $2^{32\ -\ 8} = 2^{24} = 16,777,216$ addresses, a slash eight is the largest continuous block of IP addresses that were given out in the early days of IPv4. Organizations such as Apple, the US Postal Service, and AT&T all have /8s. The United States Department of Defense has 13 /8, which is the most any one organization owns: 218,103,808 addresses.

For IPv6, there are 128 bits in an address. So, while a /32 in IPv4 is one address, in IPv6 it is $2^{128\ -\ 32} = 2^{96}$, which roughly equals 79 billion billion billion addresses.

ICMP

The **Internet Control Message Protocol** (**ICMP**) is used for testing IP. ICMP is often blocked by modern network configurations because it can leak lots of information about infrastructure topology. That being said, ICMP is often used to debug things. The tools most commonly used are `ping` and `traceroute`. Both use ICMP packets, which are small packets with just IP data and control messages. Control messages tell receiving networking hardware what to do with the packet. ICMP packets can also be sent by hardware to tell you that you cannot connect to what you are trying to connect to.

If you want to see ICMP packets fly by, you can use `tcpdump`. In one window, we run `sudo tcpdump -i any -v icmp`. We use `sudo` because `tcpdump` needs root permissions to access all of our networking interfaces. In another window, we run `ping google.com -c 1`, which sends a single ICMP packet to *google.com* and times how long it takes to get it back:

```
$ ping google.com -c 1
PING google.com (172.217.10.110): 56 data bytes
64 bytes from 172.217.10.110: icmp_seq=0 ttl=55
time=213.133 ms

--- google.com ping statistics ---
1 packets transmitted, 1 packets received, 0.0%
packet loss
round-trip min/avg/max/stddev =
213.133/213.133/213.133/0.000 ms

$ sudo tcpdump -i any -v icmp
tcpdump: data link type PKTAP
tcpdump: listening on any, link-type PKTAP
(Apple DLT_PKTAP), capture size 262144 bytes
02:59:58.459604 IP (tos 0x0, ttl 64, id 56927,
offset 0, flags [none], proto ICMP (1), length 84)
    192.168.1.17 > lga34s15-in-f14.1e100.net: ICMP
echo request, id 28065, seq 0, length 64
02:59:58.672657 IP (tos 0x0, ttl 55, id 0, offset 0,
flags [none], proto ICMP (1), length 84)
```

```
    lga34s15-in-f14.1e100.net > 192.168.1.17: ICMP
echo reply, id 28065, seq 0, length 64
```

If you want to see all of the routers in between you and a website, you can use traceroute or mtr. traceroute just does the trace once, while mtr runs it many times. Both are great—they show a bunch of data about all of the hops you pass through:

```
$ traceroute google.com
traceroute to google.com (172.217.10.110), 30 hops max,
60 byte packets
 1  gateway (207.251.90.49)  0.206 ms  0.209 ms  0.198 ms
 2  206.252.215.173 (206.252.215.173)  1.147 ms  1.174
ms  1.308 ms
 3  ae-12.a00.nycmny13.us.bb.gin.ntt.net (128.241.0.233)
9.558 ms  9.580 ms  9.571 ms
 4  ae-4.r07.nycmny01.us.bb.gin.ntt.net (129.250.6.66)
1.046 ms ae-4.r08.nycmny01.us.bb.gin.ntt.net
(129.250.6.74)  1.038 ms  1.053 ms
 5  ae-0.a01.nycmny01.us.bb.gin.ntt.net (129.250.3.214)
3.042 ms ae-1.a01.nycmny01.us.bb.gin.ntt.net
(129.250.6.69)  3.057 ms  3.013 ms
 6  ae-0.tata-communications.nycmny01.us.bb.gin.ntt.net
(129.250.9.114)  5.005 ms  0.740 ms  0.774 ms
 7  72.14.195.232 (72.14.195.232)  1.200 ms  1.147 ms
1.139 ms
 8  108.170.248.33 (108.170.248.33)  2.116 ms  2.147 ms
2.305 ms
 9  216.239.62.157 (216.239.62.157)  1.119 ms  1.269 ms
216.239.62.159 (216.239.62.159)  1.232 ms
10  lga34s15-in-f14.1e100.net (172.217.10.110)  1.193 ms
1.208 ms  1.206 ms
```

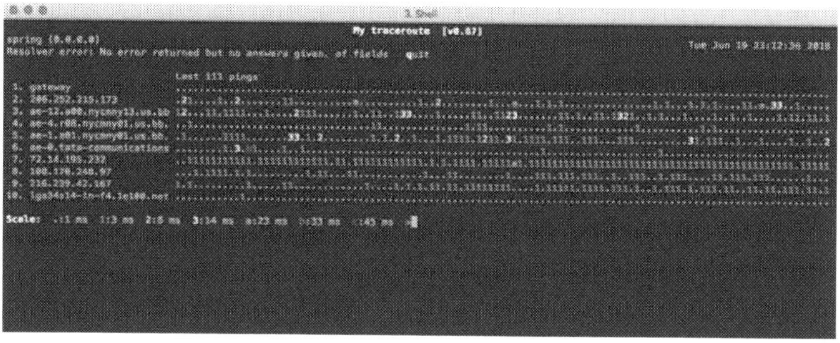

Figure 6: mtr provides the same information as the traceroute above, but instead of preforming it once, it constantly runs the traceroute and records how it changes over time.

mtr is a curses application, which means it uses the curses library to draw constantly updating graphics in the Terminal. So, while the preceding is a screenshot, if you run mtr google.com in your Terminal, you will see data constantly updating. You can press ? to see all of the options, d to change the display, and q to quit.

UDP

Byte Offset	0	1	2	3
0	Source Port		Destination Port	
4	Length		Checksum	
8	Data			

Figure 7: A picture of a UDP packet header

The **User Datagram Protocol** (**UDP**) is a layer 4 protocol for sending data on the network. On top of the basics of IP, UDP adds destination and source ports. It also adds length, which specifies how much data follows the headers. There is a checksum in the header, although it is optional. It lets you verify the data you receive. The first 8 octets or bytes contain header information, and the next length bytes (with a max of 65,507 bytes) contain data.

UDP is fire and forget—UDP packets do not retry if they don't get delivered or if they get delivered corrupt.

TCP

The **Transmission Control Protocol** (**TCP**) is the main way people connect to websites. Whenever you use your browser, your browser opens hundreds of TCP connections in the background to download data.

Byte Offset	0	1	2	3
0	Source Port		Destination Port	
4	Sequence Number			
8	Acknowledgement Number			
12	Metadata			
16	Checksum		Urgent pointer	
20	Options + Padding			
...	Data			

Figure 8: A picture of a TCP packet header

TCP is different from UDP in that the services try to verify that all data gets there and it is in order and not corrupt. Before data is sent, there is first a handshake, which agrees on the parameters of the transfer. Most of the data needed for the handshake is included in the metadata field in the packet's headers. You never really need to know about the packet headers, but it's something that people seem to love asking in interviews. The more useful point to remember is how the TCP handshake works. This is useful because TCP does have an overhead compared to UDP. UDP just starts sending data and hopes that it gets there. TCP makes sure the server is there and tells the server how much data it is getting.

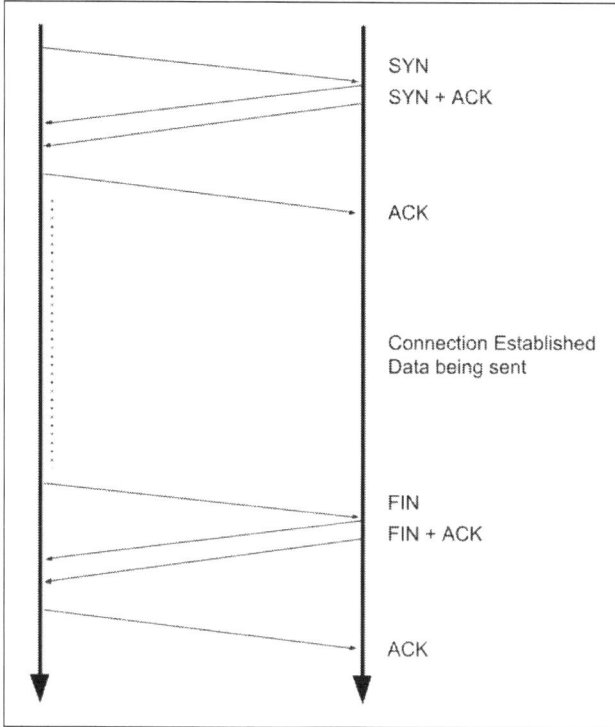

Figure 9: Here, the source client on the left is initiating a connection with a target. It starts by doing a three-way handshake. Then, the connection is established and the client starts sending the target data. When the client is done, it initiates a graceful shutdown of the open connection with a three-way handshake again. When someone says **SYN**, **SYN/ACK**, **ACK**, or **FIN** in regards to TCP, they are referring to flags set in the TCP packet headers during the handshake process.

HTTP

Okay, now we know how packets get to a server, so let's start sending HTTP requests to a server. **HTTP (Hypertext Transfer Protocol)**, is a plain text protocol. You send plain text requests to a server and the server sends back plain text responses.

A standard HTTP request looks like the following:

```
Method Path Version
Header: value (0 or more rows)
empty line
Message body (optional)
```

Headers are always case insensitive and header names cannot have spaces. They are traditionally just ASCII characters and dashes. The simplest request looks like the following:

```
GET / HTTP/1.1
```

This request says, "Give me the content at / (commonly referred to as root). I'm using HTTP version 1.1." The problem with this in modern systems is that a single IP may be hosting hundreds of domains. This is why you should always specify a host header with your request. This is not required, but many services will react differently, or not respond at all, if you do not include a host header.

```
GET / HTTP/1.1
Host: google.com
```

If you want to build and send an HTTP request by hand, you can use `telnet`. HTTP servers traditionally run on port 80 (and HTTPS servers are traditionally on 443), so to build a request to `google.com`, we would type the following:

```
$ telnet google.com 80
Trying 2607:f8b0:4006:803::200e...
Connected to google.com.
Escape character is '^]'.
GET / HTTP/1.1
HOST: google.com
Connection: close


HTTP/1.1 301 Moved Permanently
Location: http://www.google.com/
Content-Type: text/html; charset=UTF-8
Date: Sun, 17 Jun 2018 21:19:15 GMT
Expires: Tue, 17 Jul 2018 21:19:15 GMT
Cache-Control: public, max-age=2592000
Server: gws
Content-Length: 219
X-XSS-Protection: 1; mode=block
```

```
X-Frame-Options: SAMEORIGIN
Connection: close


<HTML><HEAD><meta http-equiv="content-type"
content="text/html;charset=utf-8">
<TITLE>301 Moved</TITLE></HEAD><BODY>
<H1>301 Moved</H1>
The document has moved
<A HREF="http://www.google.com/">here</A>.
</BODY></HTML>
Note all we typed above was:
GET / HTTP/1.1
Host: google.com
Connection: close
```

The `Connection:  close` bit is because we are telling the server that we will not be sending another request after we get the full response. It's not necessary but it makes working with `telnet` easier. Everything else in the output is from either the `telnet` program or a response from Google. Let us walk line by line through Google's response to understand what it is sending us:

```
HTTP/1.1 301 Moved Permanently
```

Google is responding with HTTP version 1.1. The response has a status code of `301` and a status message of `Moved Permanently`. Status messages are mostly ignored in this day and age. This is mainly because status codes have become relatively standardized and humans rarely look at the response messages from servers. There are common messages tied with status codes, but as a server operator, you can basically return anything in the status message, as they are for humans, not for software.

Status codes are categorized by their first digit and are always three digits long. The last two digits provide more information, but status codes are almost always grouped by their first digit:

- **1xx**: Messages are usually telling the client to continue and sometimes asking to change version

- **2xx**: Success!

- **3xx**: Redirection to somewhere (see the headers)

- **4xx**: Bad request, client error, or user error

- **5xx**: Server error

Now let us look through the headers:

```
Location: http://www.google.com/
```

The location header tells us, in the case of a 3xx response, where to make a follow-up request to get the correct content. In this specific case, it is because we included a `Host` header with a domain without a www prefix.

```
Content-Type: text/html; charset=UTF-8
```

This header is telling us the content of the response body is HTML and is encoded to `UTF-8`.

> UTF-8 is text encoding that is controlled by the Unicode consortium. Unicode and text encodings are very important but probably too complicated for this book. Instead, I suggest you do some research on Unicode and encodings. Stealing from Joel Spolsky (https://www.joelonsoftware.com/2003/10/08/the-absolute-minimum-every-software-developer-absolutely-positively-must-know-about-unicode-and-character-sets-no-excuses/), though, I will say that there is no such thing as plain text, and assuming the encoding of something you receive as ASCII or any other encoding almost always ends in a bad user experience.

```
Date: Sun, 17 Jun 2018 21:19:15 GMT
```

This header tells us when the response was sent.

```
Expires: Tue, 17 Jul 2018 21:19:15 GMT
Cache-Control: public, max-age=2592000
```

The expires and cache-control headers are used to tell the client how long it can cache the response for. expires says that at Tue, 17 Jul 2018 21:19:15 GMT this content will no longer be good. The cache-control header gives two pieces of information. public means anyone can cache this response (a user, a CDN, and so on). max-age=2592000 means that whoever caches this can cache it for 30 days or 2592000 seconds.

Server: gws

The server header is purely vanity. You can put whatever you want in there to tell clients which application served this response. In this case, Google is responding with the string gws:

Content-Length: 219

The content-length header tells us that we should receive 219 bytes of data in the body of our response. Technically, this is the count of octets, not bytes, but in most modern systems, 8 bits = 1 octet = 1 byte.

X-XSS-Protection: 1; mode=block

X-Frame-Options: SAMEORIGIN

These two headers are more modern security headers and they tell browsers how to deal with the content:

Connection: close

This final header is agreeing with our request that the connection will close after the body is received. The response ends with an empty line and then a blob of HTML.

> We are not going to talk about HTTPS in detail in this book, but HTTPS is HTTP with **Transport Layer Security** (**TLS**). The goal of this is to prevent anyone between the client and the server reading the contents of the HTTP request. It does not prevent someone from seeing which host the request is going to, however. In modern situations, it is recommended that HTTPS is used everywhere to promote a baseline of security for users.

curl and wget

Two of the most popular tools for building HTTP requests from the command line are `curl` and `wget`. `wget` has some sane defaults and by default downloads request responses to a file. `curl` sends response data to standard output by default. In general, I prefer `curl`. Both tools can do the same things, but I just tend to remember the `curl` command-line flags better, so that's what I use.

The most common thing I do with `curl` is to request a page, throw the content away, and look at the headers:

```
$ curl -svL google.com > /dev/null
* Rebuilt URL to: google.com/
*   Trying 172.217.4.206...
* TCP_NODELAY set
* Connected to google.com (172.217.4.206) port 80 (#0)
> GET / HTTP/1.1
> Host: google.com
> User-Agent: curl/7.54.0
> Accept: */*
>
< HTTP/1.1 301 Moved Permanently
< Location: http://www.google.com/
< Content-Type: text/html; charset=UTF-8
< Date: Sat, 23 Jun 2018 17:20:42 GMT
< Expires: Mon, 23 Jul 2018 17:20:42 GMT
< Cache-Control: public, max-age=2592000
< Server: gws
< Content-Length: 219
< X-XSS-Protection: 1; mode=block
< X-Frame-Options: SAMEORIGIN
<
* Ignoring the response-body
{ [219 bytes data]
* Connection #0 to host google.com left intact
```

```
* Issue another request to this URL:
'http://www.google.com/'
*   Trying 216.58.194.100...
* TCP_NODELAY set
* Connected to www.google.com (216.58.194.100)
port 80 (#1)
> GET / HTTP/1.1
> Host: www.google.com
> User-Agent: curl/7.54.0
> Accept: */*
>
< HTTP/1.1 200 OK
< Date: Sat, 23 Jun 2018 17:20:42 GMT
< Expires: -1
< Cache-Control: private, max-age=0
< Content-Type: text/html; charset=ISO-8859-1
< P3P: CP="This is not a P3P policy! See g.co/p3phelp
for more info."
< Server: gws
< X-XSS-Protection: 1; mode=block
< X-Frame-Options: SAMEORIGIN
< Set-Cookie: 1P_JAR=2018-06-23-17; expires=Mon,
23-Jul-2018 17:20:42 GMT; path=/; domain=.google.com
< Set-Cookie: NID=133=QXSN94wGKlX7EAQRKXcaaadBdvjh5zlr
RRBBpLYbIbOIn4lINCGUD53jO2DAJyvT-y0Q8-nWKuYqUpplb5H3L
eztzGD5CB2taBaq98gjkX_WZu0eJIT_omJznNIDi; expires=Sun,
23-Dec-2018 17:20:42 GMT; path=/; domain=.google.com;
HttpOnly
< Accept-Ranges: none
< Vary: Accept-Encoding
< Transfer-Encoding: chunked
<
{ [2143 bytes data]
* Connection #1 to host www.google.com left intact
```

In this example, I am passing three flags to `curl`:

♦ `-s` removes a progress bar that would normally appear

♦ `-v` prints the headers of your request

♦ `-L` follows redirects

The `>` `/dev/null` at the end redirects the output to `/dev/null`, which is a device in Unix and Linux that discards the information written to it. This is useful because you can inspect both the full request and the full response you get from the servers you talk to. By default, `curl` makes a GET request. With the `-I` header, `curl` makes a HEAD request instead and prints out the response headers. You can also send any method you want to a server with the `-X` header:

```
$ curl -sv -X TEST www.google.com/ > /dev/null
*   Trying 216.58.194.100...
* TCP_NODELAY set
* Connected to www.google.com (216.58.194.100)
port 80 (#0)
> TEST / HTTP/1.1
> Host: www.google.com
> User-Agent: curl/7.54.0
> Accept: */*
>
< HTTP/1.1 405 Method Not Allowed
< Content-Type: text/html; charset=UTF-8
< Referrer-Policy: no-referrer
< Content-Length: 1589
< Date: Sat, 23 Jun 2018 17:37:46 GMT
<
{ [1589 bytes data]
* Connection #0 to host www.google.com left intact
```

Here, we're sending a random method called TEST because HTTP methods are actually just arbitrary strings. If we wanted to, we could also send data with our request. Both the previous and next request fail because these aren't things I would expect to work, but they are repeatable tests:

```
$ curl -sv -X DELETE -d '' www.google.com/ > /dev/null
*    Trying 216.58.194.100...
* TCP_NODELAY set
*    Trying 2607:f8b0:4000:813::2004...
* TCP_NODELAY set
* Connected to www.google.com (216.58.194.100)
port 80 (#0)
> DELETE / HTTP/1.1
> Host: www.google.com
> User-Agent: curl/7.54.0
> Accept: */*
> Content-Length: 0
> Content-Type: application/x-www-form-urlencoded
>
< HTTP/1.1 405 Method Not Allowed
< Allow: GET, HEAD
< Date: Sat, 23 Jun 2018 17:41:29 GMT
< Content-Type: text/html; charset=UTF-8
< Server: gws
< Content-Length: 1591
< X-XSS-Protection: 1; mode=block
< X-Frame-Options: SAMEORIGIN
<
{ [1589 bytes data]
* Connection #0 to host www.google.com left intact
```

Here, the -d flag lets you specify the request body. By default, curl will make any request you send a POST request when you specify that flag. The above example is overriding that default with -X to send a different method. Instead of an empty string, you could send JSON or form data, or just random bytes, whatever you need. If you start your argument to -d with an @ symbol, you can load data from a file. If your argument is @-, you can read from standard in. In the following example, we take a file, look for the google string, sort and remove duplicates, and then post to google. com, which then ignores what we sent because we are sending way too much data:

```
$ cat urls.txt | grep google | sort -u | curl -d @- -sv
google.com/ > /dev/null
*    Trying 216.58.216.206...
* TCP_NODELAY set
* Connected to google.com (216.58.216.206) port 80 (#0)
> POST / HTTP/1.1
> Host: google.com
> User-Agent: curl/7.54.0
> Accept: */*
> Content-Length: 1677433
> Content-Type: application/x-www-form-urlencoded
> Expect: 100-continue
>
< HTTP/1.1 413 Request Entity Too Large
< Content-Type: text/html; charset=UTF-8
< Referrer-Policy: no-referrer
< Content-Length: 2398
< Date: Sat, 23 Jun 2018 18:00:20 GMT
< Connection: close
<
{ [2398 bytes data]
* Closing connection 0
```

curl is incredibly powerful, as is wget. Both tools can be used to explore how a service works by sending requests and data and seeing how the server responds. They can also be used to interact with services that publish REST APIs. One of my favorite things to do is to open Google Chrome Developer tools, click on the networking tab, and right-click on a request. Chrome lets you copy a request as a curl command, with all of the proper flags to repeat your request many times from the command line.

Tools for watching the network

Now that you know some basics of how networking works, let's run through some quick introductions to some tools. Many of these tools are very powerful and have lots of options. Make sure to read their documentation to understand everything they can do. I will mainly be talking about one action you can use each tool for and will not provide an exhaustive list of their capabilities or possible uses.

netstat

netstat is a tool for evaluating the state of open connections on a Linux box. The tool can do a lot, but the main thing I use it for is to see which services are using which ports. I would suggest reading the man page for netstat by running man netstat. netstat can also list active outgoing connections and all sorts of cool stuff about your computer's active networking. Like every other tool in this book, though, read the documentation to find out lots of cool ways to use it.

The following example shows which ports are open on one of my computers. The mnemonic I use to remember these flags is "Tuna Plz!":

```
$ sudo netstat -tunapl | head
Active Internet connections (servers and established)
Proto Recv-Q Send-Q Local Address          Foreign
Address           State        PID/Program name
```

```
tcp        0     0 0.0.0.0:2222           0.0.0.0:*
LISTEN     28938/VBoxHeadless

tcp        0     0 0.0.0.0:35695          0.0.0.0:*
LISTEN     -

tcp        0     0 0.0.0.0:111            0.0.0.0:*
LISTEN     1095/rpcbind

tcp        0     0 207.251.90.53:9009     0.0.0.0:*
LISTEN     10330/julia

tcp        0     0 0.0.0.0:43473          0.0.0.0:*
LISTEN     1156/rpc.mountd

tcp        0     0 207.251.90.53:9010     0.0.0.0:*
LISTEN     10374/julia

tcp        0     0 0.0.0.0:1234           0.0.0.0:*
LISTEN     5487/python

tcp        0     0 207.251.90.53:9011     0.0.0.0:*
LISTEN     10423/Julia
```

nc

nc or Netcat is a tool for sending requests. It's basically a version of `telnet` that is easier to script. For example, if we wanted to send a GET request to Google, with the same request we did with `telnet` in the previous section, we would create the request and pipe it into nc:

```
$ printf "GET / HTTP/1.1\r\nHost: google.com\r\
nConnection: close\r\n\r\n" \
 | nc google.com 80
HTTP/1.1 301 Moved Permanently
Location: http://www.google.com/
Content-Type: text/html; charset=UTF-8
Date: Mon, 25 Jun 2018 01:37:04 GMT
Expires: Wed, 25 Jul 2018 01:37:04 GMT
Cache-Control: public, max-age=2592000
Server: gws
Content-Length: 219
X-XSS-Protection: 1; mode=block
X-Frame-Options: SAMEORIGIN
```

```
Connection: close


<HTML><HEAD><meta http-equiv="content-type"
content="text/html;charset=utf-8">

<TITLE>301 Moved</TITLE></HEAD><BODY>

<H1>301 Moved</H1>

The document has moved

<A HREF="http://www.google.com/">here</A>.

</BODY></HTML>
```

The first command, printf, is like echo command, but it allows for more diverse formatting options. The above printf command outputs four lines to form our request. Those are then piped into nc, which sends them, in order, to the IP resolved at google.com, on port 80.

The other point I want to show about nc is using it to test client software. If you run nc with -l, it will create a listener port on the port of your choice. You can then point your client code at it and see exactly what you are sending. For example, I can create a server and then use curl to send a request to it:

```
$ nc -l 8080
GET / HTTP/1.1
Host: localhost:8080
User-Agent: curl/7.54.0
Accept: */*
```

The preceding is the server that has started and has received an HTTP request. It will reply with any text you type or you can type *Ctrl* + *D* to end the connection. The following is what curl saw:

```
$ curl -svL localhost:8080
* Rebuilt URL to: localhost:8080/
*   Trying ::1...
* TCP_NODELAY set
* Connection failed
* connect to ::1 port 8080 failed: Connection refused
```

```
*    Trying 127.0.0.1...
* TCP_NODELAY set
* Connected to localhost (127.0.0.1) port 8080 (#0)
> GET / HTTP/1.1
> Host: localhost:8080
> User-Agent: curl/7.54.0
> Accept: */*
>
* Empty reply from server
* Connection #0 to host localhost left intact
```

nc is insanely powerful and there is no way I can do it justice. I highly recommend you look around the internet for things you can do with it, such as using it to tunnel network traffic, scan ports on the network, transfer files, and much more.

tcpdump

I've been showing examples all through this chapter using tcpdump. It is an incredibly useful tool for watching packets coming and going from your machine. It can listen to any port or interface and listen to packets. You can apply filters to only get a subset of packets and you can write the output to pcap files to be used in programs such as Wireshark that provide tools for digging through lots of packets.

There are many cheat sheets on the internet that provide good tips on using the tool, so as a learning suggestion, try the following:

♦ Listen to all DNS traffic on UDP

```
tcpdump -i any -n -p udp port 53
```

♦ Get all traffic to and from one IP

```
tcpdump host 8.8.8.8
```

♦ Write all traffic to a PCAP file

```
tcpdump -i any -w output.txt
```

♦ Read all traffic from a PCAP file

```
tcpdump -r output.txt
```

Summary

In this chapter, we talked about the networking basics and explored lots of tools for interacting with the network. Earlier in the chapter, we mentioned an interview question, which was "how does the browser make a request to google.com?" After reading this chapter, you should be able to explain the OSI layer model, explain how DNS works, explain the parts of an HTTP request, and use tools to examine each part of the request.

Next, we'll talk about the Linux operating system and the cloud!

References

1. *Computer Networks* by *Andrew S. Tanenbaum*
2. *TCP/IP Illustrated, Volume 1* by *W. Richard Stevens*

$\sim 10 \sim$

LINUX
AND CLOUD
FOUNDATIONS

In *Chapter 9, Networking Foundations*, we talked about networking fundamentals. If you think of chapter 9 as to how applications talk to each other, in this chapter, we will talk about how applications operate both on servers and as groups in the cloud.

Many people are coming to SRE without much operational experience. In a world with tools like Heroku and Serverless, many developers have not had much experience running servers or even in using Linux or common cloud software. The hope is that after this chapter, any fear of Linux or the cloud will be dissipated or you will at least have a base lexicon to do more research.

Many of the pieces introduced in this chapter will help you with an SRE interview where you need to troubleshoot issues on a Linux machine or design architecture for a larger application. After we close out Linux and cloud fundamentals, we will walk through an example architecture question and how you could possibly answer it.

Linux fundamentals

Linux is a group of operating systems. Originally released in 1991 by Linus Torvalds, Linux has grown to be the de facto operating system of servers. The Linux foundation claims that Linux servers were almost 80% of all servers running in 2014 (`https://www.zdnet.com/article/linux-foundation-finds-enterprise-linux-growing-at-windows-expense/`). Linux also goes by the name GNU/Linux, because the GNU project created a lot of the utilities bundled with the Linux kernel in most Linux operating system distributions. This is all just dogma though. The key is that the Linux kernel has a few basic tenants and is pretty consistent between distributions. Whether you use Fedora, Centos, Debian, Ubuntu, Arch, or something else, the following section should introduce you to the basics of your operating system.

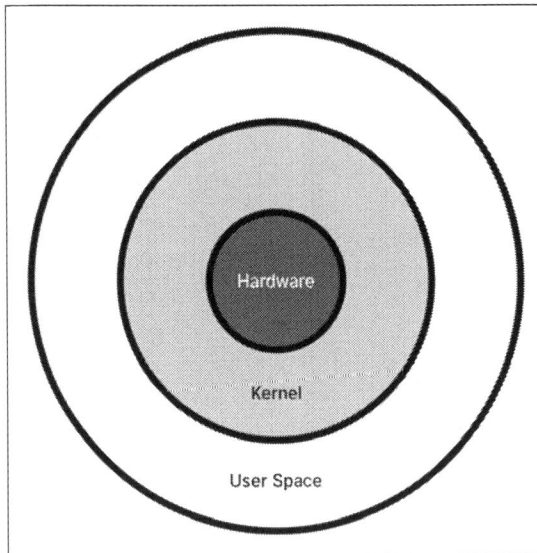

Figure 1: A kernel is the core part of an operating system. It tends to provide
the base interface to all hardware of a computer, especially in terms of managing
CPU time and memory allocation. The user space is the place where all applications
and non-kernel code runs. The kernel provides boundaries between user space
applications, as well as common interfaces for those applications to talk to each other.

The **Free Software Foundation** (**FSF**) is a non-profit organization focused on maintaining and promoting open-source software. The FSF is the maintainer of a popular open source license, the GNU **General Public License** (**GPL**). It also holds the copyrights on a lot of GNU and organizes contributions to parts of the GNU project. GNU stands for GNU is not Unix.

Everything is a file

One of the greatest parts of Linux is that everything is a file. It is one of the core philosophies of the kernel and makes for a lot of interesting uses, as you can write to things such as devices, settings, sockets, and other things as if they were a normal file. An example of this was shown in *Chapter 9, Networking Foundations*, where we wrote output to /dev/null, which is a device that acts as a black hole. In the following section we will give examples of different parts of Linux that act like files and how you can manipulate them.

Files, directories, and inodes

The first thing that is a file, is a file! A basic file in Linux is just a selection of bytes. How Linux actually makes files usable is using what are called **inodes**. Inodes are a data structure that store all of the metadata about a file (https://www.tldp.org/LDP/tlk/ds/ds.html and http://pubs.opengroup.org/onlinepubs/009695399/basedefs/sys/stat.h.html):

♦ **Two device identifiers**: One is the filesystem on which this inode is located, while the other only exists if this is a special device and points to the physical hardware identifier.

♦ A unique file serial number.

♦ File mode defining access permissions.

♦ A count of how many hard links point to the inode (if zero, the file is ready to be deleted).

♦ The user and group identifiers of the file's owner.

♦ Timestamps:
  ○ ctime, inode change time
  ○ mtime, file modification time
  ○ atime, file last access time

♦ The size of the file in bytes

Each file on a disk has an inode and to see a file's inode, you can run the command stat. The stat command lets you read all inodes. When you run ls to output all files in a directory, you are reading an inode table, which is all that a directory is. Each inode table has two special files, . and ... The . file is the inode for the current directory and .. is the inode for the parent directory.

The entire Linux filesystem is a tree, where every node in the tree is an inode. Multiple entries in an inode table can link to a single file, which is why an inode includes a link count. When the link count reaches 0, the file is deleted.

Permissions

As mentioned in the preceding section, each file has permission bits. Two fields are the owner and group, which are specified by an integer ID. They can be changed with the chown command. Three bytes (also known as octal numbers) specify who can read, write, and execute a file. The first byte is for the user who owns the file, the second byte is for the group that owns the file, and the third byte is for others. Each byte is a number of 0 to 7:

♦ The read permission adds 4
♦ The write permission adds 2
♦ The execute permission adds 1

So, a file that everyone can read, write, and execute has the permissions of 0777. This is often also displayed as -rwxrwxrwx. Another common permission is 0640. This is -rw-r-----, which means the user can read and write, the group can read, and others cannot access it at all.

On most Linux operating systems, the front bit is for the sticky bit, which lets executables and directories control who can change their links in the inode table and if a file can change the permissions of the user running the file. You'll notice the zero at the front of these three numbers. This is the `setuid` bit. This octal is used for files that when executed will run as if they are the owner of the file instead of the user running them. If the octal equals four, the process gets the permissions of the user. If two, the process gets the group permissions. If six, the process gets both. This is useful but incredibly dangerous. If a file has the `setuid` octal set, and is owned by root, no matter who executes it, the process is run as if root was running it. You can also set the bit to one on directories, which prevents people from moving or removing files in the directory that they do not own. This is called the **sticky bit**.

Sockets

Sockets are also files. Sockets are network connections that you can read from and write to as if they are a normal file. When created, they specify a network protocol and a destination. Sockets are given socket numbers, but that number can only be referenced on the same machine. On most systems, that number is randomly generated by the kernel.

A socket is often viewed in a similar way to a pipe in a shell. In your Terminal, you can, for instance, write `cat file.txt | sort`. This will take the contents of `file.txt` and write them to standard out. The pipe (`|`) will then connect the standard out of the first program (`cat`) to the second program's standard in (`sort`). The content finally written to the Terminal, from standard out, will be the standard out from sort. In the networking world, a socket is just that: it receives input, deals with the network connections, and then on the other side of the connection, the receiver can read out of a different socket to get the data.

For the simplest of examples, you can read from a socket in your command line. If you use Bash, it will automatically dynamically create sockets on the following path: /dev/ {protocol}/{host}/{port}. If you use any other shell, you will need to use nc (which we discussed in *Chapter 9, Networking Foundations*) to open a socket. The United States Government operates the simplest server to show this: the **National Institute of Standards and Technology (NIST)** Internet Time Service. This service, when a connection is made to it on port 13 at time.nist.gov, will return the current time:

```
$ cat < /dev/tcp/time.nist.gov/13
58298 18-06-29 04:09:39 50 0 0 689.3 UTC(NIST) *


$ echo "" | nc -4 time.nist.gov 13
58350 18-08-20 00:55:38 50 0 0 643.1 UTC(NIST) *
```

You can also send an HTTP request by opening a socket with an HTTP server on port 80:

```
#!/bin/bash
exec 100<>/dev/tcp/hello.natwelch.com/80
echo -e "GET / HTTP/1.1\r\nHost: hello.natwelch.com\r\
nConnection: close\r\n\r\n" >&100
cat <&100
```

In the preceding script, exec 100<>/dev/tcp/hello. natwelch.com/80 is assigning file descriptor 100 as a read and write socket to port 80 on hello.natwelch.com. >&100, is taking the output from the echo command and writing it to file descriptor 100, instead of standard out (file descriptor 1). Then the cat command is reading the content off file descriptor 100 with <&100. When we run this script, we get a response from the server printed to standard out:

```
$ ./hello.sh
HTTP/1.1 200 OK
Content-Security-Policy: default-src 'self'
Content-Type: application/json
Referrer-Policy: same-origin
```

```
X-Content-Type-Options: nosniff
X-Frame-Options: DENY
X-Xss-Protection: 1; mode=block
Date: Fri, 29 Jun 2018 04:20:52 GMT
Content-Length: 35
Via: 1.1 google
Connection: close


{"status":"ok","msg":"Hello World"}
```

If we wanted to implement something similar to the NIST time server, we could do so in Go. We could write this in any language, but Go makes it pretty easy to read.

```go
package main

import (
    "log"
    "net"
    "time"
)

func main() {
    // We could run on any port. Here we are running
on 13 to
match the DAYTIME
    // standard as described in RFC 867.
    port := ":13"
    tcpAddr, err := net.ResolveTCPAddr("tcp", port)
    if err != nil {
        log.Fatalf("resolve addr: %+v", err)
    }

    listener, err := net.ListenTCP("tcp", tcpAddr)
    if err != nil {
        log.Fatalf("listen: %+v", err)
    }

    for {
        conn, err := listener.Accept()
```

```
        if err != nil {
            log.Printf("connection open: %+v", err)
            continue
        }

        go Handle(conn)
    }
}

// Handle does two things, log when it receives
a connection, and writes the
// current time to the connection and closes it.
func Handle(conn net.Conn) {
    now, err := time.Now().MarshalText()
    if err != nil {
        log.Printf("get time: %+v", err)
    }

    conn.Write(now)
    conn.Close()
}
```

The preceding code is broken into two functions. The main() function is the beginning of the program and it opens a listener on port 13. It then starts an infinite loop waiting for connections on port 13. For every connection, it creates a new thread (with go) and runs the function Handle(conn net. Conn) in it. Handle doesn't bother to read the connection: it just writes the current time to the connection and closes the connection.

If in one Terminal you run $ sudo go run timeServer. go with the preceding code, and then access it as we did the NIST server, you get the current time. We have to run the code with sudo because only the super user (also known as root) can create services on ports 1 to 1024. An example of querying our server, first with Bash and then with nc:

```
$ cat < /dev/tcp/127.0.0.1/13
2018-06-29T04:47:00.398289971Z
$ nc 127.0.0.1 13
2018-06-29T04:48.357276832Z
```

Devices

As we've mentioned a few times, /dev is a directory on most Linux systems, with files for each device connected to the machine. Each hard drive and hard drive partition has a file. All sorts of things exist in here and each one is special and unique.

Devices are often dependent on the Linux distribution (which can name things differently) and also on what physical devices are attached.

Kernel modules are pieces of software that can be added to a kernel both when it is compiled as well as during runtime with the modprobe command. Modules are like Window's device drivers and change how the operating system interacts with physical hardware or creates virtual devices for the operating system to use.

When you enable a module, it may add support for a new webcam, add a new filesystem, or add a new backdoor into your operating system. Now, because all modules are part of the kernel, they can often do dangerous things. A classic experiment is writing a module that creates a device where if you write a process id into it, the module will change what user is running that process. This could be incredibly dangerous because it would let a user turn their shell into a root shell, which would have permissions to do just about everything. So, because of this danger, many files in /dev are only writable or readable by the root user.

/proc

The **proc filesystem** (**procfs**) is a virtual filesystem that presents itself as a series of files that live in the /proc folder. Each process running in the operating system has a directory. For example, earlier when I was running the time server, I ran ps aux | grep go to find the running process (I could have also run pgrep go) and get its process ID. That ID was 9170. There is a folder at /proc/9170/ which contains all the information the operating system knows about the process.

Proc also contains things like /proc/cpuinfo, which provides information about every CPU core in a machine. /proc/uptime, /proc/diskstats and many others exist to provide system-level information to users and applications. Some even let you write settings into them. /proc/sys has all sorts of settings you can change. An old Thinkpad laptop I had even let you control the fans by writing integers into /proc/acpi/ibm/fan.

Not all systems have a procfs. OS X infamously does not have /proc. It also isn't Linux, but rather based on BSD, another Unix. Most Linux systems do, as they are based on versions of Unix that had them.

Filesystem layout

Okay, this is going to be really quick, but this is the classic Linux filesystem layout:

♦ /bin holds the executables everyone can use

♦ /boot holds files related to starting the computer

♦ /dev holds all of the devices

♦ /etc holds global configuration files

♦ /home holds the user directories that often include a user's personal files

♦ /lib holds libraries

♦ /mnt is a common place for mounting file systems

♦ /proc is system information from procfs

♦ /root is the home directory for the root user

♦ /sbin contains executables for the root user

♦ /sys is also system information but using sysfs

♦ /tmp is temporary files, usually mounted on a ram disk

♦ /usr is user libraries and binaries

♦ /var is runtime files, including logs, caches and other things

Other folders may be in the root of your filesystem (/), but the preceding are the common ones. There is a common standard, the Filesystem Hierarchy Standard, but it's not always followed closely.

What is a process?

A process is a human inside of the Matrix. Jokes aside, a process is a running program on a computer. Put another way, it is an instance of a running program loaded in memory. Every process has an ID greater than one because in Linux, every process knows what process started it. The first process that starts when the computer boots is init. Then init spawns children processes, which can then also create children, creating a gigantic tree of processes. To create a child, a process must first run fork(), a system call that creates an identical process belonging to the caller (note that fork() is actually a wrapper around clone() in Linux, but it serves the same purpose). Processes then often call exec() (or one of its many variants) to run a separate process in place of themselves.

Every Linux process has information about who started it, its file descriptors, its current state, its current working directory, and other metadata.

Zombies

A zombie process is a process in Linux that is common but rarely seen. It is a process which is no longer running, but its state information has not been cleaned up. This is usually because the parent process did not wait for the process to collect its state information. Its state is halted or dead, and yet it still shows up as existing in the operating system. It is rare that you will see one of these processes exist for a long time because they will often be cleaned up (or reaped) by init or the parent process.

Orphans

As all processes have parents, when a parent process dies, and does not stop its children processes, its children processes become orphans. Orphans are automatically reparented to init. Even though after this reparenting happens all processes have a parent of ID one, they are still called orphans because they had to be reparented.

What is nice?

nice is a command and piece of metadata that tells the Linux scheduler how important a task is. Note this only applies to tasks and processes in user space. Nice values will not affect kernel space. All programs by default have a nice value of zero and everything at the zero level is treated equally. The higher the nice value, the less important the process. Nice values range from -20 to 19.

When two equal priority CPU-bound processes are running at the same time on a single-core Linux machine, the ratio of each one's share of the CPU time will be $(20 - niceA)$ / $(20 - niceB)$. So, a process run with nice value of 15 will receive 25% of the CPU time compared to a process with nice value of 0: $(20 - 15)$ / $(20 - 0) = 0.25$.

syscalls

There are a lot of system calls on an operating system and you can view a list of all of them by running man 2 syscalls:

```
● ● ●                                    1. Shell

   System call              Kernel      Notes

   _llseek(2)               1.2
   _newselect(2)            2.0
   _sysctl(2)               2.0
   accept(2)                2.0         See notes on socketcall(2)
   accept4(2)               2.6.28
   access(2)                1.0

   acct(2)                  1.0
   add_key(2)               2.6.10
   adjtimex(2)              1.0
   alarm(2)                 1.0
   alloc_hugepages(2)       2.5.36      Removed in 2.5.44
   bdflush(2)               1.2         Deprecated (does nothing)
                                        since 2.6
   bind(2)                  2.0         See notes on socketcall(2)
   bpf(2)                   3.18
   brk(2)                   1.0
   cacheflush(2)            1.2         Not on x86
   capget(2)                2.2
   capset(2)                2.2
   chdir(2)                 1.0
   chmod(2)                 1.0
   chown(2)                 2.2         See chown(2) for
                                        version details
   chown32(2)               2.4
   chroot(2)                1.0
   clock_adjtime(2)         2.6.39
   clock_getres(2)          2.6
   clock_gettime(2)         2.6
   clock_nanosleep(2)       2.6
   clock_settime(2)         2.6
   clone(2)                 1.0
   close(2)                 1.0
   connect(2)               2.0         See notes on socketcall(2)
   copy_file_range(2)       4.5
   creat(2)                 1.0
   create_module(2)         1.0         Removed in 2.6
   delete_module(2)         1.0
   dup(2)                   1.0
   dup2(2)                  1.0
   dup3(2)                  2.6.27
   epoll_create(2)          2.6
   epoll_create1(2)         2.6.27
   epoll_ctl(2)             2.6
   epoll_pwait(2)           2.6.19
   epoll_wait(2)            2.6
   eventfd(2)               2.6.22
   eventfd2(2)              2.6.27
   execve(2)                1.0
   execveat(2)              3.19
   exit(2)                  1.0
   exit_group(2)            2.6
   faccessat(2)             2.6.16
   fadvise64(2)             2.6
   fadvise64_64(2)          2.6
   fallocate(2)             2.6.23
   fanotify_init(2)         2.6.37
   fanotify_mark(2)         2.6.37
   fchdir(2)                1.0
   fchmod(2)                1.0
   fchmodat(2)              2.6.16
Manual page syscalls(2) line 54 (press h for help or q to quit)
```

Figure 2: A snapshot of the syscalls man page. Each row specifies a syscall, what man section it is documented in, and what Linux kernel version it was introduced in.

A system call is a low-level function in the kernel which you can call to signal the kernel to modify the system in some way. The classic ones are `fork`, `read`, `write`, `exec`, `open`, and `exit`.

As I mentioned, the `man` command can give you access to the manual pages. Section 2 of the `man` pages provides documentation for `syscalls`. Not only does it provide a list of syscalls, it also describes how to call each one from the programming language C, which the Linux kernel is written in.

How to trace

`strace` is a tool that lets you see all of the syscalls being made when you run software. There is also `dtrace`, which is more powerful, but not as common on Linux. You can do lots with `strace` to see how things are operating. The most basic action is to just run `strace ls`, which will run ls to list all of the current files in a directory. I won't paste the output because ls actually does a lot of system calls, but with the `-e` flag you can limit the output to only a subset of syscalls. For example, `fstat` is how programs find out about files on a filesystem. With this, we can just show the `fstat` calls `ls` makes.

```
$ strace -e fstat ls -l /tmp
fstat(3, {st_mode=S_IFREG|0644, st_size=58176, ...}) = 0
fstat(3, {st_mode=S_IFREG|0644, st_size=154832, ...}) =
0
fstat(3, {st_mode=S_IFREG|0755, st_size=2030544, ...})
= 0
fstat(3, {st_mode=S_IFREG|0644, st_size=464824, ...}) =
0
fstat(3, {st_mode=S_IFREG|0644, st_size=14560, ...}) = 0
fstat(3, {st_mode=S_IFREG|0755, st_size=144976, ...}) =
0
fstat(3, {st_mode=S_IFREG|0444, st_size=0, ...}) = 0
```

```
fstat(3, {st_mode=S_IFREG|0644, st_size=3004224, ...})
= 0
fstat(3, {st_mode=S_IFREG|0644, st_size=2995, ...}) = 0
fstat(3, {st_mode=S_IFREG|0644, st_size=26376, ...}) = 0
fstat(3, {st_mode=S_IFDIR|S_ISVTX|0777, st_size=4096,
...}) = 0
fstat(4, {st_mode=S_IFREG|0644, st_size=545, ...}) = 0
fstat(4, {st_mode=S_IFREG|0644, st_size=58176, ...}) = 0
fstat(4, {st_mode=S_IFREG|0644, st_size=39744, ...}) = 0
fstat(4, {st_mode=S_IFREG|0644, st_size=58176, ...}) = 0
fstat(4, {st_mode=S_IFREG|0644, st_size=47576, ...}) = 0
fstat(4, {st_mode=S_IFREG|0644, st_size=97176, ...}) = 0
fstat(4, {st_mode=S_IFREG|0644, st_size=47568, ...}) = 0
fstat(4, {st_mode=S_IFREG|0644, st_size=1964, ...}) = 0
fstat(4, {st_mode=S_IFREG|0644, st_size=925, ...}) = 0
fstat(3, {st_mode=S_IFREG|0644, st_size=578, ...}) = 0
fstat(1, {st_mode=S_IFCHR|0620, st_rdev=makedev(136, 2),
...}) = 0
total 12
fstat(3, {st_mode=S_IFREG|0644, st_size=3545, ...}) = 0
fstat(3, {st_mode=S_IFREG|0644, st_size=3545, ...}) = 0
drwx------ 3 root root 4096 Jun 25 15:48 systemd-
private-49929b2b26cc4098a09b442d3eb837be-redis-server.
service-7r6j1E
drwx------ 3 root root 4096 Jun 25 15:48 systemd-
private-49929b2b26cc4098a09b442d3eb837be-systemd-
resolved.service-UzIJL3
drwx------ 3 root root 4096 Jun 25 15:48 systemd-
private-49929b2b26cc4098a09b442d3eb837be-systemd-
timesyncd.service-eBayRt
+++ exited with 0 +++
```

Here we can see ls calling fstat for every folder in /tmp, and all of the links they have.

Next, we can have strace record all syscalls made by a running process. In the following example, -c tells strace to summarize all syscalls it saw. -p 5765 tells strace to attach to the process and record syscalls made. When we run this command, strace runs with no output until we hit *Ctrl* + *C*, which is the classic terminate keyboard command. strace then prints the output. In this case, process ID (pid) 5765 is rsync downloading some files from another server, so most of the calls are to write.

```
$ sudo strace -c -p 5765
strace: Process 5765 attached
^Cstrace: Process 5765 detached
```

% time	seconds	usecs/call	calls	errors	syscall
34.58	0.004667	203	23		write
33.80	0.004562	15	300		select
31.41	0.004240	14	300		read
0.21	0.000028	7	4		ioctl
100.00	0.013497		627		total

Watching processes

Two common tools for seeing what is running on your computer are top and ps. top is a real-time dashboard of everything running on the processor right now. ps is a snapshot of all currently running processes.

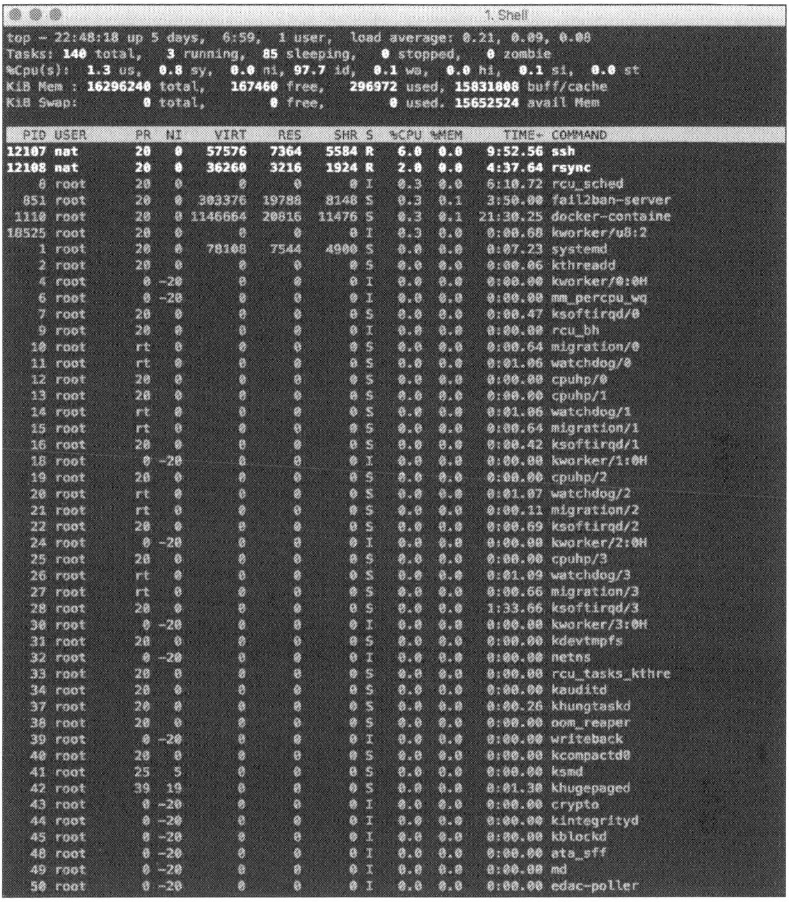

Figure 3: A screenshot of top running on a Linux server

top has a lot of information in it, including uptime, load averages, user counts, process CPU usage, memory usage, process nice values, and lots of other things.

I often run ps with the argument aux. Interestingly, I've always just viewed those flags as what's needed to see every running process. I recently found out (from reading the man pages), that arguments without a flag on ps are from the older BSD version of the command. BSD is another Unix-based operating system (similar to Linux but often very different).

According to the man page, a and x show all processes. a shows all processes with a TTY attached and x shows all processes that do not have a TTY attached. u changes the output format to be easier to read. To get a similar output, you can also run ps -ef which is the new format of arguments for Linux.

Load averages

I mentioned load averages in the preceding section. You can see these in top or just run the uptime command.

```
$ uptime
 23:16:07 up 5 days,  7:27,  1 user,  load average:
0.04, 0.09, 0.07
```

From left to right, we have the following:

♦ The current time

♦ An uptime of five days, seven hours and 27 minutes

♦ One user currently connected

♦ Three load averages: 1 minute, 5 minutes, and 15 minutes

These three load averages are the Linux system load averages. They are the average system load over a given period of time. You can also see these in /proc/loadavg:

```
$ cat /proc/loadavg
0.10 0.11 0.09 1/230 23457
```

The number is how many processes were using how many CPU cores during that time period. This is actually an over simplification (http://www.brendangregg.com/blog/2017-08-08/linux-load-averages.html). Instead, on Linux, the system load average is a five second sliding window over a time period of running tasks and uninterruptable tasks. These uninterruptable tasks could be writing to disk, memory modification, changing swap, scheduler calls, and all sorts of other system calls.

Running tasks are just normal running processes, but, for the sake of simplifying how we think of it, if the one-minute load average is 1.0 on a single core CPU, we can roughly assume no programs were waiting for CPU resources. If there were two cores, 1.0 would mean that one core was sitting idle for the minute. You can find out how many cores there are available by running nproc, lscpu, or cat /proc/cpuinfo.

So, if you have a load average output of 1.00, 10.09, 100.00 on a four-core machine, it would mean you are just coming off a massive spike of load. Over the last minute, three cores were sitting idle on average. Over the last five minutes, though, the system was overloaded by 609%. Six cores of work were waiting to be done on average. Over the last fifteen minutes, things were really bad: the system was 9600% overloaded or there was, on average, 96 cores worth of work waiting.

Build your own

There is a lot more we could talk about with Linux fundamentals, but there are many books you could read and also lots of experimentation you could do. I suggest you check out the following programs by reading their man pages and exploring how they work:

♦ df

♦ grep

♦ sort and shuf

♦ du

♦ mount

♦ tail & head

♦ su

♦ rsync

♦ stat

♦ time

♦ date

All of these tools, plus the ones we mentioned earlier throughout the chapter, are simple. They do one or two things and do them well. This is part of the Unix philosophy. The Unix philosophy, as defined by Doug McIlroy (an early engineer at Bell Labs) in 1978 [3] is as follows:

♦ Make each program do one thing well. To do a new job, build afresh rather than complicate old programs by adding new features.

♦ Expect the output of every program to become the input to another, as yet unknown, program. Don't clutter output with extraneous information. Avoid stringently columnar or binary input formats. Don't insist on interactive input.

♦ Design and build software, even operating systems, to be tried early, ideally within weeks. Don't hesitate to throw away the clumsy parts and rebuild them.

♦ Use tools in preference to unskilled help to lighten a programming task, even if you have to detour to build the tools and expect to throw some of them out after you've finished using them.

With these four mentalities, you can think about how to possibly write software. With the base knowledge so far in this chapter, plus other research, I recommend that you try reimplementing some of this software in the language of your choice. One of the best ways, in my experience, to learn something, is to try to imitate it. Some example things you might try are as follows:

♦ Try building a very simple shell that can just take in commands and execute them. Then try adding pipes to send output from one command to another.

♦ Try building a load average calculator.

♦ Try building a very simple replica of ps that just displays your users currently running commands.

♦ Write your own version of ping.

♦ Write your own version of du.

All of these tasks are doable by one person. It may take time to figure out the right system calls and get the edge cases correct, but you'll learn a lot in the process. Linux was originally created by someone who just wanted to try building an operating system and you can totally carve off a task, and try to replicate a piece.

Cloud fundamentals

After talking about Linux, we need to talk about running many computers, not just one. I have spent most of my professional career dealing with IaaS products. In August of 2006, Amazon launched EC2, which is a **virtual machines (VMs)** as a service product. This was a change from what most people were used to, as most companies had servers running in data centers and had to buy physical hardware to run their product. Now, with a click of a button, you could get servers running and make them do whatever you wanted.

This was the beginning of the cloud and the basic features **Amazon Web Services (AWS)** offered became common for many future IaaS to offer. Often, these pieces are considered the building blocks for most services. For example, you can often build most cloud products by adding orchestration on top of these basic cloud products: VMs, **load balancers (LB)**, and storage.

The second half of the 2000s were the beginning of boom time for services. Along with IaaS, there were **Platforms as a Service (PaaS)** and **Software as a Service (SaaS)**. Examples of PaaS are *Google App Engine* (launched in 2008) and *Heroku* (launched in 2007). Both of these platforms provided one layer on top of IaaS. You would give both services your code and they would make sure it just ran. SaaS, on the other hand, are just hosted software. Salesforce (launched in 1999) is often referenced as one of the earlier pioneers of SaaS, but most web software built for and sold to enterprises using a subscription model is usually considered SaaS. Most PaaS and IaaS make money by charging users for what they use, and users agree to a subscription saying they will pay the bill at the end of the month.

VMs

VMs are great—affordable computers at a click of a button or after a quick API call. The general things you need to know before setting up a VM depend on the cloud provider, but they usually shake down to the following:

♦ A base operating system image
♦ A VM size
♦ Networking configuration
♦ Extra metadata

The base image can be built by yourself, either by starting from scratch, or by starting from one provided by your cloud provider. Most cloud providers provide images with common configurations for running popular Linux distributions, popular databases, or other common tools.

The VM's size also depends on a cloud provider. Some provide names for certain groups of settings, such as "large" or "compute medium." Memorizing these names is usually pretty useless, so instead focus on the resources they provide. Some cloud providers let you create your own sizes based on a list of the resources you want. Almost always there are four axes that you will need to think about for your VM—number of CPU cores, amount of memory, amount of physical storage, and network capacity. You might want four cores, 16 GB of memory and 100 GB of storage. Every cloud service has a different way of defining network capacity. Some let you specify how big of a connection (1 GB, 10 GB, and so on), some give you weird text identifiers (medium, large, full, and so on) and others won't let you define anything. Experiment with different settings and figure out what cost versus size is best for your VM.

After you define the image and size of a VM, you will need to define networking. Most cloud providers let you specify an internal network which your VMs will be a part of. You can define what range of IPs those VMs will get by default (usually something inside of `192.0.0.0/8` or `10.0.0.0/8`). Then you can define if connections from outside of the network will be allowed.

If so, the provider will give your machine an external IP address as well. This IP will be public, so make sure your security on your machine is good. All public machines are constantly scanned.

If you're looking for a fun project, you can build a honeypot. A honeypot is a system that looks inviting to attackers, implying that it may have vulnerabilities they can exploit. Instead, though, you log the actions taken by attackers to understand the sort of attacks you might see on the rest of the machines you maintain. There are lots of both commercial and free honeypots, and you can also write your own. Just be careful not to deploy a honeypot that then acts as an actual vulnerability to your system. Put it on a separate network and fully isolate it from things that are important.

Finally, there is extra metadata. Some clouds let you put an SSH public key so that the VM boots configured to allow you to connect by default. Usually, this metadata is specified as a key-value store. So, you could put in keys with names like COST_GROUP, ENV, NAME, or anything else you want to pass in to your VM. Most clouds provide a local metadata service where you can get these values.

On AWS and Google's cloud, this metadata is provided through an HTTP server on a local IP. It is only accessible to the local VM. You can use it to also specify scripts the VM should run when it boots or to pass updated configuration to all of your VMs. Some clouds even let you get temporary access keys through these metadata servers, so you can perform authenticated API requests without needing to distribute credentials to your instances.

Containers

Containers were popularized by Docker and were originally a part of Linux with cgroups and namespaces. Now there are many different systems. The general idea of containers is running many lightweight operating systems on top of one another.

You gain isolation, while still sharing the same kernel between separate containers. This means that containers are faster to create and need less resources per isolated item than VMs do. You do not need a hypervisor, just features that are built into most modern kernels.

Figure 4: A container ship coming into the San Francisco Bay. Containers are often shown in reference to a container ship, where each box is a container and the ship is the VM or server they are all running on top of

If you run containers on top of a VM, you're likely running many layers of virtualization. VMs almost always have a hypervisor, so you end up being a few interfaces away from the actual hardware. Depending on your needs, this might cause performance problems but might make it easier to deploy lots of applications faster. This performance versus convenience factor does require weighing, but for many people, the convenience outweighs the performance losses.

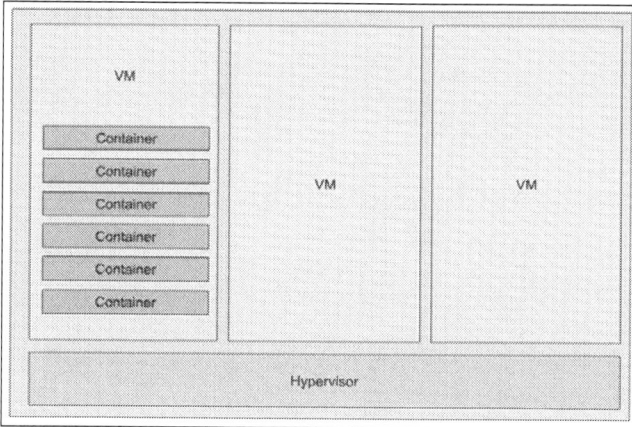

Figure 5: Here we have a host with three VMs and one VM running six containers. Most physical hosts require a hypervisor to manage VMs on the host.

One benefit of containers is the ability to have many identical servers and then use a container orchestration framework to schedule and organize containers across all of the servers. This allows for easy autoscaling of resources and removes the need to have customized servers for every application. For instance, when you create a new application, you define how it runs in a container (using something like a Dockerfile), and then you tell your orchestration framework you want three replicas of the application running at all times. The framework then makes sure there are always three identical containers running. These frameworks often require some sort of service discovery, though, because you will often not know what container is running where, which makes it hard to load balance traffic to. If you can't find your container, how are network packets supposed to?

These days, Kubernetes is quickly taking over as the most popular container orchestration framework, but there are many on the market. Some other popular frameworks include Docker Swarm and Apache Mesos.

Load balancing

Load balancing is the act of having an ingress point that will attempt to spread incoming connections evenly across many targets. For example, in our container scenario, we had three identical replicas of an application. An LB lets us distribute one target, in this case let's say `example.com`. Every request that comes in we can spread across the three applications.

This is very useful because most LBs let you add and remove targets at will. So, if you are deploying a new version of your application, you can add it to the LB and when the new application tasks are healthy, you can start to remove the old tasks.

Most cloud providers offer a LB as a service. Some just provide a layer 4 LB, which can only do packet-level inspection. Others provide a layer 7 LB, which lets it make decisions based on the HTTP request. If your cloud provider does not offer an LB, you can always build your own, with nginx, or HAProxy. That being said, usually LBs provided as a service are more reliable than your own nginx running on a box. If you did want to build your own solution, you could use DNS to load balance between multiple instances of your LB. The downside with this is possible record caching, but if you put multiple A records on a single host, they will come back in a semi-random order.

There are a bunch of ways LBs send traffic across backends. The most common is round-robin, which is just like iterating over an array to decide on who gets the next request. Some other common algorithms include the following:

- Least-popular (also known as least-connected), which sends traffic to the backend that has the least active connections (or using some other metric to determine the least-loaded backend)

- Client hashing, which hashes some aspect about a client available in the incoming request and modulo, with the number of backends to pick which backend to send it to

Autoscaling

Autoscaling is the act of growing or shrinking the number of copies of a resource based on a trigger. This trigger could be monitoring metrics, a time event or really any event. Autoscaling as a service is usually attached to VMs and containers. For web services, often people set autoscaling rules around incoming packet rates, CPU usage, or memory consumption. As they reach a certain level, a new container or instance will be created. Then a timer starts until the autoscaling service should check again to see if another scaling action should be performed.

This timer is often called a cool down. This cool down exists so you do not end up churning your tasks too often. If you make your autoscaler ignore all events until a new resource is healthy, you prevent overgrowing and having to tear down things you spin up. On the other hand, using a cool down will be a lot slower because you have to wait a fixed amount of time between each scaling action. If you're more comfortable with over-provisioning, you can have a shorter cool down.

Storage

There are usually three types of storage offered by cloud providers:

♦ Blob storage

♦ Hard drives as a service

♦ Databases as a service

Blob storage is a key value store for storing large blobs of content. For example, at key `my-file.txt` is a 1 GB text file. Usually there are access permissions to determine if someone can access or modify a file. Some cloud providers provide different durability classes for blob storage. In this case, lower durability objects are stored in some sort of system that is cheaper to keep data in but more expensive or slower to get data out of.

A hard drive service is for VMs. It lets you attach hard drives to VMs and to snapshot them whenever you want to. These are usually faster but more expensive than blob storage.

Database services usually offer a managed version of some databases. They are typically much more expensive than running the database yourself, but provide tools such as automated backups, automated storage management, or automatic performance and security audits.

Queues and Pub/Sub

One of the last common pieces of cloud infrastructure is some form of queue. A queue is a data structure where the first data in is the first data out. This is often referred to as FIFO. Many queues that are for working with multiple servers (instead of between processes on the same machine) use a paradigm called Publish and Subscribe, also known as Pub/Sub. This paradigm says that a publisher writes messages to a queue and then subscribers can subscribe to the queue and get all of the messages in the queue. Some Pub/Sub systems let subscribers define a subset of messages that they would like. Some also let the subscriber get every message that has ever passed through the queue, while others just give the subscriber messages since they subscribed. Many queues do not have Pub/Sub support, though, and instead require you to retrieve messages from the queue, instead of getting them sent to your queue.

Some Pub/Sub queues also let you provide a broker identifier, so that you can spread out work. For example, if I have three identical pieces of client software, and they all subscribe to the queue with the same broker ID, only one will get each message. On the other hand, if they each have different broker IDs, they will all get every message.

In cloud infrastructure, each cloud's queue system is slightly different. Most have a few common semantics though:

♦ They usually deliver messages at least once. This means they can get messages multiple times and the clients will have to deal with deduplication.

Other off-the-shelf systems deliver messages at most once, which means that you might lose some messages. Most systems don't have this yet, but some messaging systems (such as Apache's Kafka) are starting to have exactly one delivery.

♦ Some queues don't support Pub/Sub. For example, AWS has a **Simple Notification Service** (**SNS**) and a **Simple Queue Service** (**SQS**). SNS uses Pub/Sub and sends messages to subscribers when they enter the queue. SQS, on the other hand, requires clients to query the queue to get the latest messages.

♦ If a queue is polling-based, there is often a max time messages can stay in the queue. This is usually a longish time (a few days), but if your client software breaks and does not poll the queue, messages can be lost.

Queues are very useful because they allow for systems to be decoupled and separate the reliability requirements of different pieces of software. For example—writing a message to a queue is usually faster than writing to a database, so if you need to update a database row, you can write a message to a queue, and have something not in the request path actually modify the database. Picking the right system for message passing requires you to think about the semantics of how software is going to work together. You might need to code your client to make sure it hasn't seen a message before or be okay with some messages being lost if you have a very high volume of messages and can't read messages fast enough.

Units of scale

One last thing to consider when thinking about Linux and the cloud is the scale of things. Jeff Dean, a prominent computer scientist at Google, gave a talk in 2002 about latency numbers every engineer should know based on research from Peter Norvig (https://norvig.com/21-days.html#answers), another very prominent computer scientist at Google.

These numbers have been updated and represented by many since then. The most recent numbers I could find are from Colin Scott (`https://colin-scott.github.io/blog/2012/12/24/latency-trends/`), a software engineer at Google, who has been guessing how the numbers change based on historical trends in computer hardware. I got the following numbers from Jonas Bonér, the creator of akka and the CTO of Lightbend, and modified the table (`https://gist.github.com/jboner/2841832`).

Action	Nanoseconds	Microseconds	Milliseconds
L1 cache reference	0.5 ns		
L2 cache reference	7 ns		
Mutex lock/unlock	25 ns		
Main memory reference	100 ns		
Compress 1K bytes	3,000 ns	3 us	
Send 1K bytes over 1 Gbps network	10,000 ns	10 us	
Read 4K randomly from SSD	150,000 ns	150 us	
Read 1 MB sequentially from memory	250,000 ns	250 us	
Round-trip packet within same datacenter	500,000 ns	500 us	
Read 1 MB sequentially from SSD	1,000,000 ns	1,000 us	1 ms
Disk seek	10,000,000 ns	10,000 us	10 ms
Read 1 MB sequentially from disk	20,000,000 ns	20,000 us	20 ms
Send packet California to Netherlands round-trip	150,000,000 ns	150,000 us	150 ms

This table is interesting, but at some point will definitely be out of date. The important point to keep in mind is the magnitude of these operations. Sending a packet around the world will always be slower than reading from disk, which will always be slower than reading from memory, which will always be slower than your local CPU caches.

As an SRE, you will often have to evaluate ideas in meetings or hallway discussions, so being able to use a table like this to benchmark the speed of a decision is something that can help you. It will never be the perfect answer, but as a quick benchmark can be very helpful.

Backblaze, a storage company, has been putting out statistics on hard drives for years (`https://www.backblaze.com/b2/hard-drive-test-data.html`). It states that hard drives have an Annualized Failure Rate between 0.5% and 3%, depending on brand and disk size. Also, as of now, you can get 10 TB drives for reasonable prices (~$300), and that is constantly dropping. We've talked about this a few times, but it's important not to just know how performant something is, but also how reliable and how expensive it is. Many of the larger companies that run datacenters don't publish this data regularly, so we often have to figure out the answers to these questions ourselves.

Example architecture interview

A common interview question is to ask interviewees to design a scalable piece of infrastructure on a whiteboard. This usually has an interviewer describing a business or piece of software, and then the interviewee needs to ask questions to clarify, and then draw out an architecture diagram.

To approach an interview like this, I suggest starting as general as you can and then refining on parts that the interviewer is curious about and wants more clarification on. Three very common questions are as follows:

♦ Design a distributed cron system

♦ Design a scalable URL shortener

♦ Design a large-scale CMS

For building distributed cron, I suggest you take a look at *Chapter 24, Distributed Periodic Scheduling with Cron,* of Google's *SRE Book*, where you can walk through one possible design in detail (`https://landing.google.com/sre/book/chapters/distributed-periodic-scheduling.html`).

For building a CMS, *Chapter 6, Capacity Planning*, in this book has a few example designs you could think about. So, because those two are already covered in decent detail, let us walk through building a URL shortener.

The requirements of a URL shortener (such as `bit.ly`) is that it must store shortened versions of long URLs. For example, if you visited `http://bit.ly/2olDB2E`, you would be redirected to `https://example.com/a/really/long/url?with=params`. What makes this interesting, though, is that you need to store analytics of every visit to the shortened URL so you can charge customers (the creators of the link) for the data.

When designing this, the first thing to think about is the two different user stories you have. The first is someone visiting a shortened a URL, their visit being recorded to analytics, and then being redirected to the long URL. The second is the user who comes in, creates new short URLs, and also views the analytics of previously created URLs. If you can imagine, most of the traffic will likely come from the first use case.

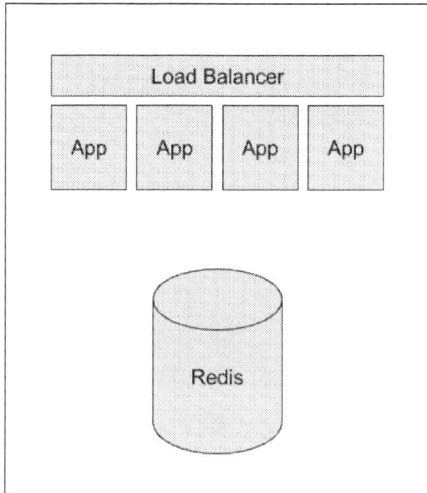

Figure 6: Above is our starting design: an arbitrary number of identical application servers, behind a LB. The servers all talk to a Redis cluster.

We start with a simple design. We have a bunch of application servers sitting behind a LB. Each of these servers know how to deal with all short links. It knows this by talking to a Redis (a key/value database) cluster which stores all short links as key/value pairs (the key being the path of the shortlink and the value being the long URL). I am going to assume that shortlinks can't change, so each app server will also keep a local in memory cache. This cache will be an LRU cache. **LRU** (short for, **Last Recently Used**) means that if space is needed, the oldest thing in the cache is evicted.

The reasoning for this design (it's not the only design that could work, just one solution), is that reads need to be fast but not complicated. This lets us use Redis, which works almost identically to a hash table. The reason for the LRU cache is because accessing memory will usually be faster than any network request (see the preceding table), so if we have a really popular link, it will be performant, and we don't have to overload our network with identical requests. Next, we need to think about analytics.

The reason I chose to use application servers, instead of something like a static file in a CDN, is because I want each server to keep track of requests it sees. We could do this by processing log files after the fact, but instead I'm going with a message queue.

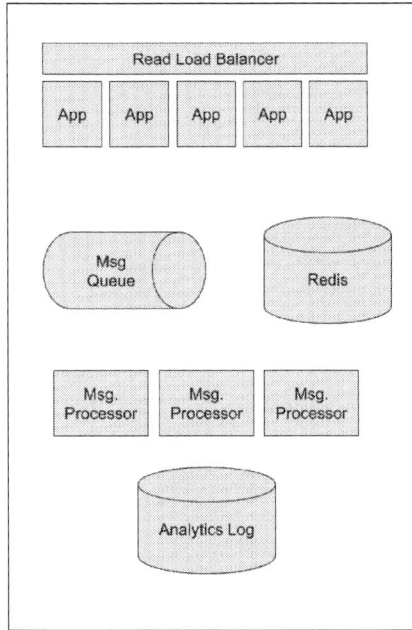

Figure 7: Our previous design updated with a message queue, an array of message processors, and a database where visit logs are stored

Here, we've grown the diagram. I'm not drawing lines to keep it easier to read, but as requests are received, asynchronous messages are sent to a queue. An array of message processors (which could scale up based on the number of messages in the queue) takes messages off the queue and writes them to an append-only database; the thinking being that if it's an append-only database, we can optimize it for that specific case.

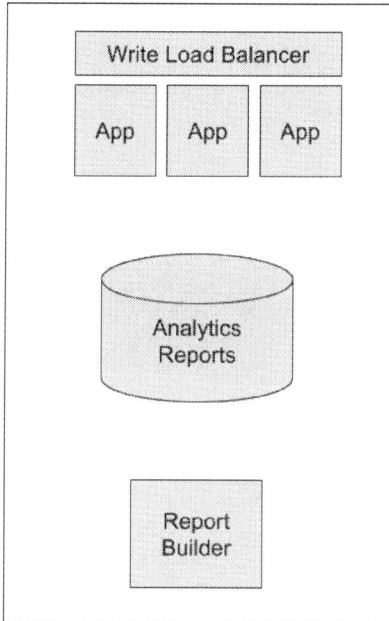

Figure 8: Sitting adjacent to our read stack is our write stack. It contains a smaller array of application servers behind a LB. They talk to the analytics reports database, a traditional relational database. Report builder is a cron job, which reads the analytics log and creates reports and summaries of the data and writes it to the analytics reports database.

Finally, we have our other use case. In this case, users need to be authenticated to do anything. They can create new links, which get inserted into the Redis cluster. They can also view analytics of their links, which are stored in aggregate in the analytics reports database. This database is filled by a cron job that cleans up the analytics log and reads data out of it, and stores data like referrer, geolocation, and visit data. It summarizes data for a variety of periods. We also use this database for billing users for their usage every month.

If you were giving this interview, you could have someone draw up a possible schema for the reports database or have them explain how to scale the report builder. You could also ask them how they might change this design if they wanted real-time analytics instead of summaries.

Another point to think about is how might you change this if your queue doesn't deliver messages exactly once but instead delivers messages at least once. If Justin Bieber tweets out one of your short links, how will your system handle the traffic? What are the failure modes?

This project is also something fun to walk through Dickerson's Hierarchy with. How would you monitor this application? What would be good metrics to alert on? What are automations you could add once the base system is running? What are possible SLIs and SLOs? How might you capacity plan for linear growth and also spikes? Where might you change about the service to make the user experience better? Where are there possible security vulnerabilities?

Summary

In this chapter, we talked about the basics of the core parts of the Linux operating system and common features of cloud infrastructure as a service product. We covered a few basic Linux commands, what the Linux kernel is, and what system calls are. Next, we discussed devices and how everything in Linux is a file. Finally, we talked about common features of cloud IaaS and how to use these services together to design a URL shortening service during an interview.

References

1. *Abraham Silberschatz, Peter Baer Galvin,* and *Greg Gagne, Operating System Concepts (8th ed.), Wiley Publishing, 2008*

2. *Doug McIlroy, E. N. Pinson, B. A. Tague* (8 July 1978). *Unix Time-Sharing System: Foreword* (PDF), *The Bell System Technical Journal, Bell Laboratories.* pp. 1902–1903

3. *The Bell System Technical Journal, Bell Laboratories, M. D. McIlroy, E. N. Pinson,* and *B. A. Tague. Unix Time-Sharing System Forward.* 1978. 57 (6, part 2). p. 1902. and `http://www.catb.org/~esr/writings/taoup/html/ch01s06.html`

OTHER BOOKS YOU MAY ENJOY

If you enjoyed this book, you may be interested in these other books by Packt:

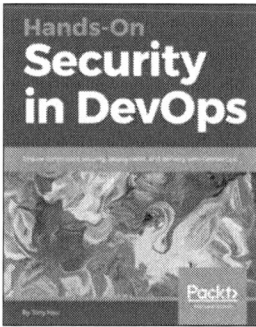

Hands-On Security in DevOps

Tony Hsu

ISBN: 978-1-78899-550-4

- ◆ Understand DevSecOps culture and organization
- ◆ Learn security requirements, management, and metrics
- ◆ Secure your architecture design by looking at threat modeling, coding tools and practices
- ◆ Handle most common security issues and explore black and white-box testing tools and practices
- ◆ Work with security monitoring toolkits and online fraud detection rules
- ◆ Explore GDPR and PII handling case studies to understand the DevSecOps lifecycle

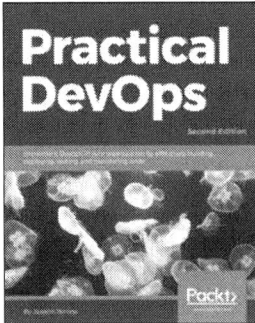

Practical DevOps - Second Edition

Joakim Verona

ISBN: 978-1-78839-257-0

- Understand how all deployment systems fit together to form a larger system

- Set up and familiarize yourself with all the tools you need to be efficient with DevOps

- Design an application suitable for continuous deployment systems with DevOps in mind

- Store and manage your code effectively using Git, Gerrit, Gitlab, and more

- Configure a job to build a sample CRUD application

- Test your code using automated regression testing with Jenkins Selenium

- Deploy your code using tools such as Puppet, Ansible, Palletops, Chef, and Vagrant

Leave a review - let other readers know what you think

Please share your thoughts on this book with others by leaving a review on the site that you bought it from. If you purchased the book from Amazon, please leave us an honest review on this book's Amazon page. This is vital so that other potential readers can see and use your unbiased opinion to make purchasing decisions, we can understand what our customers think about our products, and our authors can see your feedback on the title that they have worked with Packt to create. It will only take a few minutes of your time, but is valuable to other potential customers, our authors, and Packt. Thank you!

Index

Transport Layer Security
    (TLS) 265
Twelve Factor App 173
two device identifiers 279

U

units of scale 305, 307
USDS (United States Digital
    Service) 195
User Datagram Protocol
    (UDP) 259
user-generated content (UGC) 175
user interface (UI) 221
user testing
  about 227
  experience, picking 228, 229
  people, finding to test 230
  test, designing 229
UTF-8 264
UX 221, 223

V

vegeta
  reference 137
Vertica 165
virtual machines (VMs) 297, 298

W

wget 266-270
Wheel of Misfortune (WoM) 140

Made in the USA
Las Vegas, NV
10 November 2021